D1526786

CONTENTS

Dedicated to the Corinth High School Class of 1969

"But why had he always felt so strongly the magnetic pull of home, why had he thought so much about it and remembered it with such blazing accuracy, if it did not matter, and if this little town, and the immortal hills around it, was not the only home he had on earth? He did not know. All that he knew was that the years flow by like water, and that one day men come home again."

Thomas Wolfe, *You Can't Go Home Again* (1940)

PREFACE

The Beater Room Boys is a collection of personal stories about growing up in Corinth, New York, during the 1960s. Located on the Hudson River on the southern boundary of the Adirondack Park, Corinth was then a small industrial community whose social and economic life had been shaped by pulp and paper manufacturing for one hundred years. The Hudson River Pulp Company, which first built a wood pulp mill at Palmer Falls in 1869, was among the companies that led the paper industry's transformation from using cotton rags to wood fiber. Soon after, they became the first to manufacture pulp and paper at the same location, renaming the company the Hudson River Pulp and Paper Company (HRPP) in 1880. By 1895, the mill at Palmer Falls was considered the largest in the United States. The success of HRPP caused Corinth's population to double in 30 years, transforming a sleepy farming community into a thriving mill town.

In 1898, HRPP became the flagship mill of the newly organized International Paper Company (IP). By the mid-1960s, when I was a teenager, IP provided Corinth with nearly 1500 manufacturing jobs. Almost every family in town had a member who worked at the mill or the Cluett-Peabody Shirt Factory. The rest of the community derived their livelihoods from the local economy that both had created. The combined $10 million payrolls of both firms ($87 million in 2024 dollars) and the substantial portion of local taxes paid by IP helped Corinth maintain a progressive civic agenda. Corinth's economy supported a thriving downtown and a secondary commercial area in Palmer, the part of Corinth village adjacent to the Hudson River Mill that was considered a distinct and separate part of the community. When I grew up in the 1960s, Corinth was at the peak of its prosperity.

Some years ago, I set out to create an account of the five summers I worked at the Hudson River Mill between 1969 and 1975. I began the project because, as far as I knew, no one had previously published a memoir of their work at the Mill or their life in Corinth. I came to believe an account was needed to contribute to a better understanding of the history of the local pulp and paper industry, which has only been lightly treated in the Town's several histories. While I lacked the perspective of someone who had spent their entire work life in the Mill, as a child of Corinth's paper industry, a former paper worker, and a historian, I believed I was uniquely positioned to write what I knew and experienced. I made a start on a memoir, but the project was stalled by the sort of life events that often get in the way of creative endeavors.

When I finally resumed work on the project, the Hudson River Mill had been shuttered for 20 years. After 133 years of continuous operation, the Mill was closed by IP in 2002 and demolished in 2011. It had suffered a protracted and painful death, a process that had begun in the late 1960s. When I started to write again in 2022, I had just ended two decades of researching the Mill's history while trying to advance the idea that IP's former administration building on Pine Street in Corinth, commonly referred to as the Time Office, should house a museum of the pulp and paper industry.

The memoir has been both narrowed and expanded from my initial conception. I ultimately decided to describe only my initial summer working at the Mill in 1969, the year I graduated from high school, and exclude the summers between 1970 and 1975. I then added some accounts of growing up in Corinth during the 1950s and 1960s, experiences that were unique to me but might be recognizable to other Corinthians who came of age during those decades. My writing evolved into a historical memoir, with discussions of local and national developments that served as the context for many of us who grew up in Corinth after World War II. The memoir also describes the advent of coated paper manufacturing in Corinth, which was the catalyst for the town's post-war prosperity and the developments that marked the initial phase of the Mill's decline. Parts of the book also venture beyond the 1960s, yet each diversion is about Corinth.

I was one of many Corinth kids who became a third, fourth, or fifth-generation paper worker. My grandfather John Cernek arrived in Corinth from New York City in 1918 to work in the Mill's wood yard. My Father followed him into the Mill in 1937. Together, they spent 87 years working for IP. My Mother's father, Benedetto Rea, who arrived in the United States from Italy via England, worked for IP at the nearby Ft. Edward mill before 1915. Several uncles on both sides of my family also worked for IP for most of their adult lives. Like me, the kids I grew up with in Corinth were in families intertwined with IP and the pulp and paper industry. While I spent only five summers working at the Hudson River Mill in my college years, I felt that it was sufficient to write persuasively about the paper manufacturing process and what it was like to work there.

I was fortunate to have worked at the Hudson River Mill. I had at least ten distinct jobs during my five summers there, although my total work time was less than a year, about 50 weeks. Yet I experienced the same workplace as men who had labored there for their entire lives. I learned about the paper manufacturing process and experienced the rhythm of industrial work, becoming familiar with shift work's often debilitating physiological and psychological effects. I felt the Mill's thick humidity and encountered the intense heat in the "alley" between the No. 3 and No. 4 paper machines in mid-August. I experienced the stew of odors from the many chemicals used in paper manufacturing. I saw first-hand the costs of working at the Hudson River Mill for the men who had been there for 30 or 40 years or more, their faces and bodies prematurely aged by decades of industrial labor, shift work, and exposure to toxic chemical fumes.

Work at the Hudson River Mill offered me invaluable personal experience and direct exposure to the paper manufacturing process. I developed a visceral connection to the men in my family who had worked for IP and the several generations of paper workers from my hometown who preceded me. My varied jobs gave me a familiarity with the mill, a knowledge of how it was laid out and how things worked. This would prove invaluable over 30 years later when I began to collect and identify artifacts that reflected the Mill's history. When I worked at the Mill as a young man, I did not fully understand the degree to which the pulp and paper industry had powered Corinth's economy for much of the 20th century or how much the Hudson River Mill had shaped Corinth's social order. That insight would come later.

I was 18 years old in the summer of 1969 when I first went to work in the Beater Room at the Hudson River Mill. As one of a crew of five young men called "beater helpers," our prime responsibility was moving and processing rejected, discarded, or returned paper called "broke." It was a job that was not vital to the paper manufacturing process. Ours was simply a clean-up operation that recycled manufactured paper. Yet my summer in the Beater Room was the most valuable of my work experiences.

In the summer of 1969, I began to consider IP's role in the lives of those who lived in Corinth. More importantly, I observed the Mill's work culture for the first time, gaining an appreciation for the many years my grandfather and Father had worked. It was then that I realized I was going away to college, in part so I would have the option to become something other than a paper worker. I also knew working for IP was a means to make a reasonably good living for many boys in Corinth of my generation who did not have the luxury of pursuing a college education.

Once I resumed work on the memoir in 2022, my historian's sensibilities, completed research on the Mill's history, and my experience working on the museum idea led me to think and write more broadly than I originally intended. When I realized my final years at Corinth High School coincided with the initial decline of the Hudson River Mill, I placed the late 1960s into a historical context by describing concurrent national and community events.

Ultimately, *The Beater Room Boys* represents only my personal experiences and observations about the community where I grew up. Thousands of kids came of age in Corinth during the 1950s and 1960s. Many had broader and more profound experiences, providing them with more meaningful insights about their hometown than those I offer. Perhaps someday soon, they will share their stories.

I

— • —

STRADDLING THE BLUE LINE

S everal years ago, I drove to Blue Mountain Lake, New York, to research the Adirondack Experience archives, formerly the Adirondack
Museum. I brought along a film made by the International Paper Company at the Hudson River Mill in Corinth in 1919 that I had recently
converted into digital format. Called *The Manufacture of Paper*, the short
film documents the entire paper manufacturing process, from the arrival
of pulp wood to the mill by rail to the shipment of a finished roll of paper.
When I offered to donate a copy of the film to the archives, I was promptly
told that Corinth was not in the Adirondacks. I pointed to a nearby map
to show that Corinth was, in fact, inside the Park, at least some of it was.

While the phrase *"Growing Up In An Adirondack Mill Town"* serves
as the subtitle of this memoir, Corinth is not commonly considered an
Adirondack town. So, my use of "Adirondack" begs for an explanation.
When the Adirondack Park was created in 1892, Corinth was outside the
initial Park boundary created by New York State. Only in 1931, when the
boundary was moved to the east to include the Sacandaga Reservoir and
Lake George, did Corinth fall inside the Blue Line. But then, only part
of it did. The enlarged Park boundary was drawn to bisect the Town of
Corinth and the incorporated Village of Corinth inside it. Most of the

Village of Corinth is now within the Blue Line, while the larger Town is cut along a diagonal, a third of it outside the Park's boundary. However, the community's Adirondack location has done little to shape its identity.

The Park's southern boundary that slices through the Town of Corinth parallels the south side of Eggleston Street in the Village by a few hundred feet as it moves to the east. It moves along a line that places most of the Village inside the Park. But as the boundary moves east, it takes a sharp, northerly turn at 5th Street to cross the Hudson River into Warren County. An Adirondack Park Agency website map shows the Palmer Falls dam within the Blue Line and the former Hudson Mill outside. Once across the River, the Park boundary looks like a line created by an electrocardiogram. It zigs and zigs without adherence to any natural features until you realize that contorting the boundary was necessary to place the Sacandaga and Lake George inside the Park and the City of Glens Falls outside. Politics had to be at work in its creation.

This book has little to offer about the Adirondacks as the region is commonly regarded. It does not provide tales of hiking, hunting, fishing, or any activity that might be construed as a quintessential Adirondack experience. And nowhere do I describe how I plied the waters of Adirondack lakes with my canoe. Like earlier generations of Corinth sportsmen who went north to hunt and fish, I would drive into the Adirondacks in my 20s to fish the Ausable and its tributaries. Yet, I did not consider that I lived in the region because no one told me that I did. Given how the 1931 Park boundary carved Corinth into two parts, Corinth teenagers might have grown up with some Dissociative Identity Disorder. Some could have been confused by whether their emerging sense of self should feature characteristics of an Adirondack personality. When a kid walked down Palmer Avenue east towards the Community Building, he was in the Adirondack Park before he crossed 5th Street, but once on the other side, he was not.

Adirondack Life magazine, which has long served as the purveyor of the region's history and culture, did not begin publication until 1969. So, it was not available at Holmes Newsroom on Main Street as we grew up to help us gauge Corinth's culture against the magazine's depiction of the way of life in communities to our north. Many adults around us were avid hunters and fishermen whose adventures took them inside the Blue Line. These men started the Fish and Game Club of Corinth in 1906, changing the conservation organization's name to the Adirondack Fish and Game Club in 1920. Communities throughout northern New York State were using the name, so Corinth sportsmen considered their local organization an unofficial chapter of a much larger group. Yet the community's business and civic leadership of the 1950s and 1960s did not seek to emulate the Adirondack's rustic character. An Adirondack identity was unappealing, for it clashed with the desire for Corinth to be recognized as a modern, progressive Saratoga County community. This determination represented a purposeful effort to counter the fact that Corinth was simply a working-class paper mill town, no matter what civic boosters tried to do.

Corinth's old farming families, the community's religious leaders, and Jessup's Landing businessmen were troubled by their town's turn toward industry in the decades after the Civil War. They were concerned about how the emergent pulp and paper industry and the industrial workers it attracted altered the community's character. They relished the economic opportunities that industry brought but disliked the community culture that went with it. So, for much of its history, Corinthians have simultaneously resisted being branded a mill town and have discouraged the development of an Adirondack identity. If Corinth was not a mill town and not an Adirondack town, then what was it?

That Corinth did not develop an Adirondack identity may be historical in origin. Since the mid-19th century, Corinth was sometimes viewed as a provincial mountain town by the city newspapers of Albany, Schenectady, and Troy, which often published articles on the curious goings-on in the community. Their characterizations were neither picturesque nor celebratory. Even local papers like the *Saratogian* and Glens Falls *Post-Star* ran accounts of civil disorder in the village. They described gruesome paper mill injuries and deaths, finding their sensationalist nature too tempting to ignore. It was understandable if such representations fostered a desire within Corinth to counter this portrayal by aspiring to be a modern community.

Pulp and paper mill expansion at Palmer Falls may have discouraged Corinthians from identifying with the Adirondacks. The unspoiled Hudson River landscape that had once brought artists and photographers to Corinth to render the River and Palmer Falls gradually disappeared. The Hudson River Pulp and Paper Company increased its control of the River, and its industrial structures altered the landscape. The upriver development by the Curtis family, who built what became known as the Curtis Dam to power its pulp mill, whose product was sold to IP, further diminished the aesthetic appeal of the Hudson. By the early 20th century, Corinth's once admired riverscape had been compromised by industry. By then, the IP mill and the Village were actively polluting the Hudson River with daily solid waste discharges. Civic leaders had accepted that the community's economic well-being and modern sanitation offered by the Village necessitated the Hudson River to serve as Corinth's sewer. Given Corinth's use of the River, embracing the Adirondack ideal would have been challenging.

Seneca Ray Stoddard may have played some role in how the Corinthians viewed themselves. The ubiquitous photographer of the Adirondack region took numerous photographs of Palmer Falls around 1870 and made stereographs of many, which he actively sold. Yet, he carefully edited his images to obscure the nearby pulp mill and the adjacent Palmer Falls Woolen Company. Stoddard purposely included errant logs from river drives in his Palmer Falls images, which tied the site to the Adirondacks where they originated. In one stereograph, he depicted a single male figure sitting on a log at the base of the Falls, posed as a "contemplative observer," a trope common in 19th-century painting. While Stoddard usually identified Palmer Falls in the titles given to his stereographs, he was unwilling to acknowledge it was located in Corinth. Three Stoddard images in my personal stereograph collection identify Palmer Falls but cite its location as either "Near Luzerne" or "At Hadley, NY." It seems improbable that someone born in the adjacent Town of Wilton and who lived most of his adult life in nearby Glens Falls would not know where Palmer Falls was. Stoddard probably misattributed the location of Palmer Falls because his popular Adirondack guidebook featured Lake Luzerne and its hotels just across the Hudson from Hadley, wherein the Falls was suggested as a side trip.

Stoddard also omitted descriptions of Jessup's Landing or Palmer Falls in his 250-page guidebook, *Adirondacks Illustrated* (1880). Yet both locations are briefly mentioned in a five-page chapter dedicated to Lake Luzerne, five miles north on the Hudson, where he suggests the road south to the Landing offers a lovely drive. Lake Luzerne, like Corinth, had industry operating in the village when Stoddard's book was published. The Adirondack Park existed only in the imagination in 1880, so why did Stoddard include Lake Luzerne in the region and exclude Corinth?

Corinth did appear on a large, detailed map of the Adirondack region that Stoddard created for the New York State Forest Commission in 1881, published with the title "Map of the Adirondack Wilderness." Yet in his 1880 book, Jessup's Landing and Palmer Falls were excluded from a similar map and a separate map detailing the road from Saratoga Springs to Lake

Luzerne. A map of the region's railroads shows the route of the Adirondack Railway from Saratoga to North Creek. While the Hadley station, which would have been the stop for visitors headed to Lake Luzerne, is designated, neither the South Corinth nor Corinth stations are marked. The extent to which Stoddard's work contributed to what people thought of the Adirondacks and where they should visit, or how Corinthians thought of themselves relative to the region whose identity was quickly developing, can only be speculated. Yet it is clear from Stoddard's photographs and publications that long before the creation of the Adirondack Park, he did not consider Corinth as being in the Adirondacks or worthy of a tourist's interest.

Like several other upstate New York communities, Corinth exploited the new park boundary of 1931. It branded itself "the "Gateway to the Adirondacks," hoping tourists would spend money in town. Indeed, before Interstate 87 – the Adirondack Northway - was built, considerable traffic passed through Corinth Village in the summer months on the way to Lake George and points north. The "gateway" tagline marketed Corinth in a way that did not require the community to make visitors think they were actually "in" the Adirondacks. For travelers driving into town from the south on Route 9N, there was nothing in the Village other than the "Gateway" sign near the Corinth Rural Cemetery to signal they had arrived in the Adirondack Park.

Corinth lacked any notable Adirondack signifiers. For instance, the town had no log structures in the 1960s, which might have been an indicator of the rustic culture long associated with the Adirondack region. The lone exception might have been the Tradin' Post on West Mountain Road near Hunt, Jenny, and Efner Lakes. Otherwise, you had to drive five miles north to Lake Luzerne, where a traveler who passed the Hitching Post, Rustic Inn, and Potash Inn, each occupying a rustic log building, was given the first clear indication they were in the Adirondacks. It was Corinth's historic disassociation with an Adirondack culture that found many people scratching their heads when the community was named the Snowshoe Capital of the United States in 1978 and, some years later, when the building at the corner of Maple and Mallery Streets, formerly Kingsley's Grocery, was clad in rustic Adirondack siding.

In 1975, Corinth Town officials took a stand against the Adirondack Park Agency. Joining with the Town of Hadley, the Corinth Planning Board actively opposed the State's designation of a section of the Hudson River that runs through the town as "wild and scenic" under the State's Wild, Scenic, and Recreational Rivers System created in 1972. The Town argued the section of the Hudson in question did not meet the criteria for "recreational classification." The Board issued a statement that said the classification of the River as wild and scenic would "cripple industry" in the northern part of the Saratoga County. The chairman of the Town Planning Board affirmed the Hudson as a "working river," and the proposed designation would negatively impact International Paper Company operations. According to the *Post-Star*, the Board's Chairman claimed the Hudson River "represented the bread and butter" of the Town of Corinth. Corinth's civic leaders persuaded the Adirondack Park Agency that the status proposed for the River threatened the local economy, so the Agency relented and withdrew the designation.

Given recent events at the time, the Town of Corinth's decision to oppose the "wild and scenic" designation of the Hudson River within its boundaries was understandable. The Hudson River Mill's workforce had just taken another hit with the loss of almost 100 workers. Employment was now less than 870, down 600 workers from a decade earlier. In March 1975, the Mill was shut down for 16 days due to poor business conditions in the paper industry. It was also in 1975 that the lawsuit brought against the Town and Village by IP for two years seeking property tax reductions was settled. Initially assessed at $1,262,000, the Mill property tax was reduced by $583,000 by the Village and $483,00 by the Town for 1973-1975. While IP declined the $257,000 refund it was due, the reduced valuations created future hardships for both municipalities. Corinth taxpayers were essentially asked to pay higher taxes to keep the Mill running.

Regardless of Corinth's historical indifference to an Adirondack identity and its view of the Adirondack Park Agency, the community is nonetheless a product of the region. The Hudson River, which begins at an elevation of 4322 feet in the heart of the Adirondacks, powered several different mills in Corinth decades before the advent of the pulp and paper industry in 1869. The Corinth Electric Light plant at the Curtis Dam gave Corinthians their first electricity. The Hudson's 87-foot drop at Palmer Falls provided the tens of thousands of horsepower necessary to drive the mill's pulp wood grinders. It did so for almost 100 years until the conversion to electricity in the late 1960s.

Corinth had also been dependent on Adirondack-harvested timber and pulp wood. During the Spring of most years, from the early 1800s into the 20th century, the Hudson above Palmer Falls was clogged with logs destined for downriver sawmills. In some years, the drives would be backed up for a mile or more upriver. The commercial area that became the hamlet of Jessup's Landing grew from early logging and log driving. Since the pulp and paper industry began in Corinth, wood was transported from the Adirondacks to the Hudson River Mill in log drives on the Hudson, rail cars, and logging trucks. Older readers will recall the trucks loaded with pulp wood that passed through the village to the Mill. The community where I grew up was the product of the fusion of Adirondack wood and water. Regardless of what civic leaders and many residents thought of their town or wished to believe about it, Corinth was once very much an Adirondack mill town.

2

— · —

MY PENNY LANE

My parents moved to Center Street in April 1951. The neighborhood, often called "Upper" Center Street, was in the highest part of the village. Like upper Oak, Walnut, and Ash Streets, all of Beech and Eggleston Streets, Center Street sat on top of a terminal moraine, the boulders, rocks, and soil that were left behind when New York's last glacier melted 20,000 years ago and retreated north. The elevation of upper Center Street afforded good views of the Kayaderosseras Range to the west and Luzerne Mountain to the north. Both could be seen from the sidewalk in front of my house.

Upper Center Street was one of Corinth's newer neighborhoods, having not been created until the early decades of the 20th century. Lucien Burleigh's birds-eye view of Corinth in 1888 shows that Center Street had not yet been laid out above the railroad tracks built through the village that year. The street ran only a short distance from Mechanic Street north to Maple Street. In 1888, Upper Center Street consisted of open fields.

In the 1950s and 1960s, Upper Center Street was a mixed neighborhood of paper mill workers, professionals, and tradespeople. The men in the Cancro, Cudney, Mills, Baldwin, Schyberg, Rivette, Wendell, Long, LaFountain, Beattie, and Cernek families worked at the Hudson River

Mill. Harley Clothier, across the street, owned a plumbing and heating business. Howard Swears, who headed the Village's Department of Public Works, lived two doors south. Two lots to the north, in a house set back from the street, was George Senecal, who ran a small grocery and meat market on Hamilton Avenue. Next door to him was Ron Folts, our school's supervising principal. Lew Rose, who lived a bit further south on Center's west side, was an engineer at the Mill. Harry Waring, to the south at the corner of Center and Walnut Street, four doors up the street, operated a downtown pharmacy and was mayor of the Village in the mid-1960s. The differing occupations of the adult men in each family on upper Center Street made for a typical Corinth neighborhood in that era, for there were no elite sections of the town where a middle-class professional might live to signify their social status. The women of Upper Center Street were either homemakers or worked part-time. Like my Mother, a few held full-time jobs. They were typically employed by IP, Cluett's Shirt Factory, or in the school cafeteria. My Mother, who commuted daily to Glens Falls, may have been the only one who worked out of town.

In the 1950s, Center Street was on the western frontier of Corinth village. Main Street paralleled upper-Center on the east, but only some fields and forests were on the west. Past the forest was Sturdevant Creek, and beyond that, Route 9N. Upper Center used to have large red and silver maple trees along its sidewalks, but most are now gone. Many of the trees were cut down over the years because the Village DPW crew didn't like cleaning up the leaves they shed in the fall, and in some instances, their roots cracked village sidewalks. A few maples located in the side or backyards of houses on the street survived the purge. Not long after the Baldwin family across the street from us sold their home in the 1980s, its new owners immediately cut down an enormous silver maple next to the driveway because they feared it would fall onto their house.

I remember when a huge silver maple, perhaps four feet in diameter, was cut down in a backyard on the east side of Center Street. An itinerant character, probably alleging to be a tree surgeon, convinced one of our neighbors that his hundred-foot-tall maple was diseased and should be cut down. The tree was flush with leaves, with no dead limbs in sight. Our neighbor paid for the maple to be cut down without getting a second opinion. It was heartbreaking for my family who lived next door because the maple was so large that it put our entire backyard in the shade for a large part of a summer day. It had also created a buffer between our backyard and the houses on adjacent Main Street. After the tree was cut down, it took our neighbor two years to split the pieces left and clean up the mess.

There were several very tall Blue Spruce trees on Upper Center Street. One of them on the north side of the house at No. 334 Center was still there the last time I was in town in 2022. In the late 1950s, when its lower branches went all the way to the ground, I hid under them early one evening after I overheard my Mother on the phone with Dr. Giordano, arranging for him to come to our house from Lake Luzerne. Afraid he was coming to give me a shot, I bolted out the back door and ran down the street to find a hiding spot to escape the feared needle. I came to the spruce, hid under it, and looked through its thick needles to watch my exasperated parents going up and down the street searching for me, calling out my name as they went. They finally found me and hauled me back home to a notably perturbed Dr. Giordono.

Hundreds of maple trees planted along village streets in the 1890s were cut down when I was a kid. The virtual defoliation of Main and Maple Streets, Palmer and Sherman Avenues, in particular, begs the question of how earlier generations of Corinthians, the ones who actively planted the trees throughout the village for the civility they brought their neighborhoods, and the shade they offered their homes in the summer, managed the fear of being struck down by a falling tree. Or how an earlier generation of public works employees, who lacked modern street-clearing technology, reconciled themselves to the manual clean-up of fallen leaves each Fall.

It can be heartbreaking to view post-cards of early 20th century Corinth and see that village streets were once lined on both sides with maple trees and the occasional elm. Maybe it was easier for modern Corinthians to cut down their trees because, with air conditioners easily accessible, the shade they provided was no longer required to keep a house cool in summer. The differences may have run deeper. Corinthians of the late Victorian era held a higher regard for the aesthetic beauty of tree-lined streets than their mid-20th century counterparts. The cutting down of Corinth's maples was purposeful, the result of the thinking of mid-century civic leaders and residents. Other than a limited attempt in the early 1990s to replant trees along village streets, no subsequent effort has been made to re-foliate the community.

A friendly homogeneity existed on Center Street except for the occasional squabble about property boundaries. My Father had a boundary dispute with the family who bought the home at No. 339 in the early 1960s, prompting him to erect a six-foot-tall wooden fence that visually separated the two yards. I don't think our families ever spoke again after the wall went up. Even though most families got along, I cannot recall any neighborhood picnics, dinners, or parties growing up. Perhaps it was because there was so much social activity elsewhere in town at the time that Corinthians weren't compelled to socialize with their neighbors.

My parents were particularly friendly with the Cancros who lived next door, and Ida Cancro was an excellent friend to my Mother. I would sometimes wander next door to say hello to Ida, who invariably invited me into the kitchen for a Pepsi. I considered it a real treat because my parents never bought soda. Betty Schyberg, who lived on the other side of us in the 1950s, was nice enough to care for me when I started school at age 5. I went to her house in the mornings after my parents went to work and remained with Betty until I left for the Main Street School. Her daughter, Karen, and I were in the same class, so we walked to kindergarten and first grade together. People on Center Street tended to be friends with their immediate next-door neighbors, but social networks did not exist among the families on Upper Center.

There was only one Center Street resident who, I can recall, was ever disagreeable. But then only once. We often used the backyard at 327 Center as a shortcut to the Main Street School, passing through a space that separated two outbuildings at the rear of the lot, which put us right in the driveway at 330 Main Street, across the street from the school. That would have been in 1956 and 1957. Besides serving as a shortcut, I liked using the passthrough to see into the back porch of the Center Street house. On its interior wall was a life-size, black-and-white photograph of a man holding an enormous Northern Pike. I loved that photo. I stopped to look at it every time I passed by. I could not imagine catching a fish that big. But one day, when we were coming home from school, the owner of 327 came out of nowhere to admonish us for passing through his yard. It was probably a bad day for him because we had been going through his property for quite a while, and he never said a word to us. But his appearance that day ended our use of the shortcut.

Many years later, I learned some interesting things about Gil Swears, the man pictured with the pike who chased us from his yard. He was the father of my neighbor two doors to the south, Howard Swears. Howard's wife, Grace, managed the school cafeteria in the late 1960s. Gil had also been a skilled paper maker, a back tender, to be precise. While records are incomplete, rather than return to work during the 1921 Paper Strike and become a scab, he purchased the Corinth Ice Company, which was started in 1896 by Alonzo Herndon, Clarence Grippen, and Julius Burnham, who delivered ice to homes and businesses. Gil harvested ice from the Sturdevant Mill Pond and expanded his operations to the Hudson River. By the late 1920s, he sold the company to Leon Ralph and returned to the Hudson River Mill. Like many 1921 strikers who returned to the Mill after the strike ended in 1926, Swears was forced to work as a common laborer rather than as the well-paid papermaker he had been in 1921. It was not until the late 1930s that he could return to the paper machines and earn higher wages.

Gil Swears had been an active outdoorsman in the Corinth area since the early 1900s. He was considered a local authority on both hunting and fishing. Gil's largest catch as a fisherman was the northern pike, whose picture was displayed on his back porch. Gil's pike, which he caught from the Sacandaga Reservoir while ice-fishing with Walter Graham in 1954, measured 45 inches and weighed more than 25 pounds. Later the same month, the photograph of Gil and his pike was displayed at a sportsman's show held at Corinth Legion Hall. The show was heavily attended due to the appearance of Verde Gaddis, known professionally as "Gadabout Gaddis," who hosted a televised fishing show in the 1950s and 1960s. Gil Swears retired from IP in 1947 and died at his Center Street home in 1973 at 92.

The boys in our Upper Center Street neighborhood often played baseball and football in my backyard. Whenever a sizable number showed up, we moved our games to the empty lot at 335 Center, next door to our neighbor Ron Folts, the school's supervising principal. We were playing football there in the early evening of November 9th, 1965, when the infamous Northeast Blackout hit that cut electricity to 30 million people in the United States and Canada. It was about a half-hour after sunset, so it was easy to notice the lights in the neighborhood had gone out. Someone wondered aloud if the neighborhood went dark because the Soviet Union attacked the United States. That question would seem improbable today, but in 1965, amid the Cold War, the fears of a nuclear attack were genuine. After all, our *Weekly Reader* told us the Soviets were the bad guys, and we had been practicing air raid drills at school. We were literally and figuratively left in the dark for some time, hanging out on our football field long after we could see the ball, wondering what had happened and if the Soviets had bombed us. Finally, after someone in the neighborhood used a transistor radio to pick up a station, one of the kids returned to our field to explain that we had not been attacked. That night may have been the only time we ever felt threatened in our Upper Center Street world.

3

Our House

I grew up in a small, two-bedroom house on Center Street in Corinth that my parents purchased the month before I was born. They met in Corinth at a Community Building dance on a Saturday night in the Fall of 1946. My Mother had traveled to Corinth from Ft. Edward for the weekend to visit her married sister, Rose Sandora. Rose and her husband, Charlie, lived in a bungalow at the corner of West Maple and Paris Avenue. Their house had come to serve as a getaway destination for my Mother and her unmarried sisters. My parents were engaged in 1947 and were married in 1948.

After their New York City honeymoon, my parents moved into the White Apartments on Hamilton Avenue, upstairs over Arthur White and Sons, Corinth's local building supply store. Their apartment, one of two in the building, was accessed by a steep set of stairs. They never spoke to me about what it was like living there other than relating the story of the day my Mother fell down those stairs, getting badly banged up and breaking her shoulder blade. I am sure I heard that story a dozen times. She must have taken the fall before the summer of 1950, for I probably would not be writing this paragraph today if she had been pregnant with me at the time she fell.

I never thought much about my parents' Hamilton Avenue home until one weekend in 2015. It was the same week the old White's store and its upstairs apartments were being demolished. A new hardware store had been built on the other side of Hamilton Avenue, on the corner where the Commercial Hotel once stood. The construction became controversial because the historic Anna Lincoln home, which had served initially as a Methodist Church, was demolished to make room for a parking lot. The Lincoln House, built before the Civil War in the Greek Revival style unique in Corinth, had been honored with a historic during Corinth's Bicentennial activities in 1976. You would think a house so honored would be spared a visit from the wrecking ball. But not in Corinth. A citizen effort was made to save the Lincoln House, but the hardware store's owners could not be deterred. A Corinthian who still lives in town told me they had never seen a car parked in the lot located within the house's former footprint.

When I went down to White's that weekend to buy paint for my Mother's house, I couldn't help but notice the demolition underway. I walked across the street to look more closely at what was happening. I used my cell phone to photograph the backhoe and attached shovel parked next to the half-demolished building. The south side of White's had already been torn down, leaving a cut-a-way view of its interior. I got closer and took more photographs of the building's now exposed hallway and the interior doors that opened to the building's apartments. Still on the ground and looking up into the open rooms on the second floor, I wondered which were from my parents' apartment. It never occurred until that moment that I was likely conceived in one of those rooms and lived there for my first year. With my widowed Mother's passing a few months earlier in 2015, I started to regret never asking about the years my parents lived there or the life they shared before I was born.

Most houses on upper Center Street were simple frame construction representing basic versions of several architectural styles common to residential construction between 1890 and 1950. Our house was one of several one-and-half-story homes built in the 1930s and early 1940s. Like most bungalows of that era, a gable end with a front door faced the street. Our house was initially clad with white-painted wood clapboards, but eventually, my parents covered them with green asbestos shingles. A siding company had come through Corinth selling door-to-door, pitching a medium green shingle about 12 inches wide and 30 inches long. The shingle was unique because it had a two-inch wide, dark green stripe along the top edge to simulate a shadow. It was supposed to make you think the sun was shining even on cloudy days. I am sure my Mother thought the shingles were "modern," so they were installed around 1960. Perhaps thirty years later, my parents put plastic clapboard siding over the green shingles, an effort that was a trend among the owners of village houses at the time. The garage got the same treatment.

The rooms of our house had solid plaster walls and oak floors, standard interior construction for the 1930s. Its two bedrooms and single bath were relatively small. The upstairs, what we called the attic, was unfinished and was used only for storage until I converted half of it into my bedroom during my sophomore year in high school. During my February school vacation in 1967, my Father and I installed cheap wood paneling on the room's pitched ceiling, bought a rug remnant in deep red for the floor, and installed a cheap, hollow core door between the attic's two rooms. It is probably the only project we ever did together. I recall how excited I was to move in, especially when my grandmother offered to pay the five-dollar monthly fee to have a phone extension in my room. I placed my desk at the gable end under the front window to easily see activity in the street below. There was no heat in the room during the winter, only that which a portable electric heater could provide. In summer, the room was like an oven, but my parents bought an air conditioner for me years before they bought one for themselves. My upstairs room became the best place to escape whenever my parents argued during my final two high school years.

My parents built additions to our house and renovated the interior a few times in the 1960s. Each project resulted from my Mother's interest in having the newest or most modern house she could afford. The living room renovation was perhaps the best representation of the ideas she got from the several "home" magazines. The front half of our house had initially consisted of a living room and a small bedroom, but she had the wall in between the two torn out to create one large living room that spanned the entire width of the house. On the south end of the new living room, a non-functioning fireplace was built out of glossy white bricks, with a grey stone mantel and hearth. A wall switch turned on an electric element in the fireplace's opening that simulated a fire that we used only at Christmas. At the other end of the living room were several pieces of mid-century modern furniture that would have been at home in the first season of *Mad Men*: a rose-red armchair, a sleek light blue sofa with a backless section at one end that curved around one corner of the room, and thin walnut coffee and end tables with plate glass tops. On the end tables were three-foot tall modern lamps, one in frosted glass and the other a beige ceramic. Three bronze pieces of Asian-inspired wall art were placed on the dark wood paneled wall above the fireplace mantel. The room was finished with gold wall-to-wall carpeting and white curtains with gold trim. And, of course, there were sheer curtains behind the drapes that were permanently closed. My mother's living room might have been the chicest in all of Corinth in the early 1960s.

My parents' original bedroom at the front of the house was sacrificed to construct the new living room. So, my Mother planned a simultaneous addition to the rear of the house that included a new bedroom with a half-bath and a second room that she called a "den." It was not a den, at least not the sort that Hugh Cleaver used in the TV show "Leave It to Beaver," which would have been my reference point. Mr. Cleaver's den held a stately desk and shelves full of books. No, our den was just a room used to watch TV. For a brief period until the novelty wore off, we watched the news during dinner using the once essential "TV tray," although we never ate a "TV dinner," Swanson's or otherwise. My Mother had too much pride to resort to that. Unlike the Cleaver den, ours hadn't a book in sight.

The few books we owned were in the living room. We had a set of *Funk and Wagnall's Encyclopedias* that my Mother purchased at the Grand Union, a volume each week, along with an *Illustrated History of World War II* that was offered the same way. Both were shelved in a narrow bookcase constructed in the doorway of the old bedroom closet. We also had the first one or two books in other series offered at the Grand Union, but the purchases were not continued for one reason or another. I still have the encyclopedia and World War II sets in storage and an enormous dictionary whose sections were also sold at the Grand Union in installments.

With a cover that was about 9x12 inches, the dictionary was nearly eight inches thick. Once, when I brought the book to elementary school for a "show-and-tell" day, the teacher asked if she could keep it in the classroom and place it on the corner of her desk. From that day forward, whenever anyone in my 4th-grade class had a question about the meaning or spelling of a word, my dictionary served as the authority. That our home's only books were purchased in installments at the Grand Union reflected that my parents, neither of whom had graduated from high school, never developed an interest in reading, except for the daily newspaper and home decor magazines. Yet their presence in our house suggests that my Mother, who did all the shopping, understood that I should have easy access to the knowledge they offered.

The den that was part of the rear addition to our house was small, with large windows that consumed the top half of its south and east walls. It was an odd choice because my Mother had to install thick curtains to keep the room cool in summer. If the windows on the south side were ever left open, the room would become unbearably hot. Where the west end of the den passed to the kitchen, a substantial sliding glass door in polished brass was installed, clearly something my Mother had seen in *House Beautiful* or *Home and Garden*. The door was only five feet wide, leaving less than a 30-inch opening when one side was open. One night, my Father was sitting in the den watching TV, eating two of his favorite foods in a sandwich: horseradish and sardines. He started coughing wildly, his face quickly turning beet-red. Then, it seemed he was choking. He got up from his chair, his body nearly convulsing, and headed towards the kitchen sink to get some water. As he tried to pass through the sliding glass door's narrow opening, he stumbled, hit the door with his left arm, and then crashed to the kitchen floor. He passed out. I can't recall what my Mother and I did to help him, but he was revived after a minute. I never saw my Father eat horseradish and sardines again.

My Mother decided to panel the den wall without any windows or doors. She didn't choose the three-quarter-inch tongue-and-grove or shiplap wood that was most commonly used, but modern, one-quarter-inch thick sheets of 4x8 plywood whose top layer was the wood of choice. A natural walnut veneer panel that had to be shipped from Florida was selected. I remember the day a truck delivered the paneling. Two men off-loaded several large packages wrapped in heavy brown paper. The packs, each holding four panels, were placed in the garage. I was there when the carpenter working on our house opened the first package. An enormous spider crawled out as he peeled the paper back at one corner. It was a *giant* spider, perhaps three inches in diameter. I had never seen anything like it! I was about ten years old at the time and came close to peeing my pants at the sight of it. Maybe I did. The spider quickly crawled down the side of the package and went off towards a dark corner of the garage. It was some before I went into the garage without carrying my baseball bat.

The rear addition to our house that contained the den and new bedroom also included a narrow back porch made of concrete with a black cast iron railing around the edges. My Father loved sitting there to read the paper and drink beer. We could look out from the porch to our small backyard, enclosed by a chain link fence. If you stood at the center of the porch, you could see through Luther Wallace's yard behind our house on Main Street and clear up Oak Street to the school. Our backyard fence was attached to the rear of our garage on one side, and on the other, it met up with the white picket fence at the back of the Cancro yard next door. There was a small opening between the two through which I could squeeze. The narrow space gave me access to the backyards on adjacent Main Street, providing a shortcut to the Oak Street school I attended from the 2nd grade.

The addition took a big chunk of our backyard, where the neighborhood boys and I used to toss the football and play baseball. At the rear of our yard was a huge rock protruding about two feet above the lawn. We always had to watch out for the rock when catching a pass or going after a grounder. Our yard also had twin white birch trees along the stone wall on the south side and a large sugar maple at the right rear corner that turned brilliant orange each fall. My mother told me the maple was planted a few years before I was born, so I always considered us about the same age, almost like the sibling I often wished I had. A red picnic table was under the twin birches where we sometimes had picnics.

A small garage was situated at the end of the driveway. It rarely housed the family car. My Father used it to store ladders, tools, folding lawn chairs, and paint cans. He also used it to hide beer on nights when he thought it best that my Mother did not know he was drinking. He would walk back and forth from the porch to the garage every 30 minutes, picking up a new bottle and disposing of the empty one. My father sometimes went into the garage between beers and pee in the back corner. A missing cement block in the foundation exposed some bare ground, which was the target. The discolored blocks on either side of the target ground suggested that my Father's aim was off the mark the more he drank. I tried peeing there a few times and found that a reasonably accurate aim was required to hit the mark.

The front gable end of the garage held a basketball goal and plywood backboard. The rim was only nine feet and a few inches higher than the driveway, so I could dunk when I got older and taller. But only if I used a kickball whose circumference was smaller than a standard basketball. Mine was the only basketball goal in the neighborhood, so it got lots of play, even in the winter. The cotton nets didn't last very long in the cold, so I became adept at making them out of burlap.

My Mother lived at 341 Center Street for sixty-four years until shortly before she died in 2015 at 97. Cleaning out the house and preparing it for sale might have been easier for me if I had had a sibling to share the job with, but I had to do it by myself, driving from my New Hampshire home to Corinth nearly every weekend for over a year. All the furniture in the house was sold during the estate sale, so I purchased an inflatable bed to sleep on and placed it in the bedroom I had used as a child. I slept there on the weekends when I worked on the house. There was something profoundly sad about the experience. Making the house saleable in a modern real estate market required renovations that erased much of the house I had known as a child. That made selling it a bit easier.

Yet I did leave some of myself behind. On the basement's street-facing wall was the black-painted outline of a ski area I made up and drew one winter day when I was perhaps 12 years old. The light bulb in my bedroom closet, which I left turned on at night with the door slightly ajar to ease my childhood fears, was still just a single bulb hanging by a plastic wire from the ceiling. When I opened the door in my attic bedroom that led to a crawl space under the eves of the house, I found a single plastic bullet from the Mattel Fanner-50 six-gun that I used to play with as a boy. I hoped I might also discover the two shoeboxes of baseball cards I had collected in the 1950s and early 1960s, but I knew my Mother had thrown them away years ago. Still, I left the house knowing that some things I valued as a child had been inadvertently left behind. Would a future house owner find them and wonder about the child who once lived there?

On my last day at the house, just before the closing, I sat on the stone wall that ran from the backyard along the southern edge of our property to the sidewalk. I realized I was leaving behind a home that had been part of me for 65 years. This was not an insignificant event. It was the dinner hour on a late summer evening, and an unusual stillness had set in. I looked up and down the street, and neither a person nor a car could be seen. I began to think about how lively the street had been in the 1950s and 1960s when I was a kid, and all the families who used to live there, the mothers and fathers now dead, and the boys and girls I played with all grown up and long gone. I sat there for a while, closed my eyes, and tried to see them and hear their voices one last time.

4

STAND BY ME

U pper Center Street was owned by the kids who lived there. Children in my neighborhood, like many in Corinth in the 1950s and 1960s, met on the sidewalk or in the street, where we played whatever the group assembled decided to do that day. Wiffle-ball, hide n' seek, red light-green light, and bike riding were the childhood activities played on Upper Center Street, often by both boys and girls. Sometimes, there was hopscotch and rolling skating on the sidewalks. Childhood in the 1950s and 1960s - before texting, email, and social media - would be unrecognizable to kids living in Corinth today. Many kids who grew up before helicopter parents and cell phones developed strong organizational and people skills from our years organizing pick-up baseball, tag football games, or just getting a bunch of people in the neighborhood together to play.

The light on the utility pole across the street from my house, which was ground zero for neighborhood play, illuminated our after-dark games. Although the streetlight was quite dim by modern standards, you could always look up and see moths and winged bugs of all kinds circling it. When we played in the street after dark, as many as twenty kids might hang out together. While there might have been arguments, I don't recall any fighting, verbal or physical. As the evening wore on, one by one, each of us would fade into the night as parents called out it was time to come home. When only two or three of us remained, we would sometimes sit on the stone wall that ran along the side yard of my house. With the streetlamp providing barely enough light to see each other, we would talk about whatever 10 and 11-year-olds spoke about in 1961. Sometimes, looking up or down the street, you might see the beam from a flashlight in the distance where a father and son searched for night crawlers for the next day's fishing trip.

My childhood on Center Street was probably similar to what most kids in Corinth experienced in the 1950s and 1960s. Play was self-initiated with no parental supervision. No one had to arrange a playdate for us or organize our activities for the day. We did it ourselves. The exception was when we participated in community-wide activities with the Corinth Youth Commissions, EMBA (Employees Mutual Benefit Association), or at the Community Building. When I left the house to play, I was told to be home for lunch, dinner, or by dark. The mother of one of my friends would turn on the porch light when it was time for him to come home.

The boys in the neighborhood all played baseball, basketball, and football. We played in our backyards, driveways, or the street. But only a few of the kids played golf. Those who played created a course on Center Street one summer. The number of holes we laid out was limited by the number of neighborhood yards we could use for tees, fairways, and greens. Whiffle golf balls, most commonly used for backyard golf practice at the time, were inadequate for our Center Street course because they could not be hit across the asphalt street, which we considered a water hazard. Instead, we used hollow plastic golf balls that traveled sixty feet or more if well hit. Unlike the golf course on Eggleston Street, which I would help build, we did not have to cut the grass on the Center Street course because our fathers did that for us when they mowed their lawns each week. And because we were using our parents' and neighbors' yards, we could not dig holes in the lawn to use as cups for putting.

We stuck ski poles into the ground to serve as the flag for each hole. My favorite hole was a par five that began behind my house. It took at least two strokes to get the ball from the tee box placed next to the large rock in our backyard, through the narrow lawn on the south side of our house, and then to the broader front yard. From there, it was a long golf shot to get past the sidewalk and across the street. Since we considered the street as water, any player who hit their ball there was assessed a one-stroke penalty. A good golf shot would carry the street and land on the empty lot at 344 Center. From there, you could hit the ball to the elevated green on the lawn next door at 346. Steve LaFountain, one of the boys who played the course, lived downstairs. The next hole, a par 3, began on the lawn at 346 and went back across the street to my house's front yard at 341, which served as the green for that hole. A solid hit was required to get the ball from 346 to the green at 341. We played our course a few times that summer and the next until we got old enough to play at Brookhaven in South Corinth after it opened in 1963.

The older kids on Upper Center strongly influenced the younger ones. Of some thirty boys and girls who lived above the street's railroad tracks, about a dozen of them were ahead of me in school. The older ones, particularly the girls, were likelier to play street games with the younger boys and girls, at least before they reached high school, when they tended to spend time only with their peers. The older boys taught the younger ones how to play baseball and football. Pat Cummings, a few years older than me and living down the street on the west side, got me interested in stamp collecting. After seeing his collection, I started my own.

Warren Baldwin, who lived across the street from me at 342 Center, was one of the older boys in the neighborhood who would often spend time with the younger kids. Warren showed us how to attach playing cards to our bicycle spokes to create a motor-like sound when we rode. His family lived directly across the street from me in a white, two-story, four-bedroom house with majestic silver maple trees, one along its driveway and one along the front sidewalk. Five kids were in the family, although only three lived in the house by the time I started school. Warren was the youngest, five or six years older than me. Through Warren, we got to know his parents, Raymond and Pauline, who were always very friendly to the other kids who lived on the street. The Baldwins had a cocker spaniel named "Flicka," who had a litter of puppies from time to time. Whenever she had a litter, Pauline would call out to us if we were around and invite us to come and see the puppies in the birthing area that had been made for Flicka in their garage.

Warren's father, Ray, went by the nickname "Fuzzy." Fuzzy, who had gone to trade school and had been an Eagle Scout, spent a lot of time in his workshop, which was attached to the garage at the end of his driveway. Whenever his workshop door was open, we would wander over and find him working on some project. Every once in a while, Fuzzy would do something that we knew had to be a trick. He would remove an old metal can from a shelf, lift off its lid, and then use a stick to remove a glob of grease. Fuzzy would then eat the grease with a big smile on his face. We stood there with our mouths wide open in amazement, unable to figure out how he didn't get sick. Fuzzy's grease-eating became yet another one of childhood's unsolved mysteries.

One of the more exciting things about Fuzzy's workshop was the two old wooden toboggans that were stored overhead. The biggest could seat three to four adult riders, five or six kids. One had two sets of steel-edged, wooden runners, with the front one moveable for steering. I cannot recall if it was steered with a wheel, rope pulls, or wooden handles like those on the Flexible Flyers that most of the kids in the neighborhood had. The largest of the two might have been a variation of the bobsleds with a steering wheel made by Fleetwing in the early 1900s. Every time we visited Fuzzy and saw the sleds, I imagined what it might be like to ride the big one.

Then, one winter day, Warren took the big sled down and invited a few of the younger kids to go sledding with him. We pulled the sled a few houses down Center Street to where it intersects with a street now called Park Drive. At the time, Park was simply an unnamed village road paved with loose cinders that sloped down and intersected with another road that passed through the wooden railroad trestle that used to cross Sturdevant Creek next to the old Corinth Firehouse. Lemont Avenue had yet to be laid out, so the road rarely saw any traffic.

In winter, the unnamed road was plowed only to a depth that did not loosen its cinder surface, so the street always remained snow-covered. With Warren at the wheel, a bunch of us kids piled on the back of the sled, riding it as far as Sturdevant Creek, which was a reasonably long distance. We laughed and shouted as Warren, our captain, remained calm and focused. With several kids pulling, returning the sled to Center Street was easy, so we took several rides that day. That day was the only time I ever got on the toboggan stored in Fuzzy's workshop. During those years when a kid's sled or flying saucer was their constant winter companion, the rides I took with Warren remain the most memorable of my childhood.

Three girls who lived in Upper Center, around Warren's age, were members of the class of 1964. I observed them in the neighborhood as active teenagers when I was in the 5th and 6th grades. Roseann Cancro, one of the three, lived next door and occasionally invited some friends to her house to play lawn games in the backyard. Our houses were very close, so I could see what they were doing and often hear their teenage conversations. When Roseann went away to Cortland State to attend college, she brought home a red Cortland sweatshirt for me. I felt so grown up wearing it that I don't think I took it off for weeks. Observing Roseann and her friends gathered in her backyard gave me my first close-up look at teenage life.

For most Corinthians, Upper Center Street began at its intersection with Mechanic Street. Yet those of us who lived on its uppermost reaches enforced a more exclusive boundary. Our boundary began several houses above the railroad tracks where Center Street levels out to a flat plain. The kids who lived on Upper Center rarely ventured down the street to the point where it began to slope toward the tracks. Yet when we did, it was always to see the two attractions at Nos. 320 and 322.

Behind the house at No. 320, where the Rose family lived, was a small, artificial pond made of field stone, maybe five feet to six feet in diameter. The pond had lily pads growing and held several giant goldfish. We would sometimes go to the Rose house, sneak through their side yard, and down to the pond. We would stand over its dark water, looking at the bright-colored goldfish as they slowly moved around and under the lily pads. We went to the pond because we considered it an exotic scene for Corinth. In those days, Corinth had an aquarium on Paris Avenue that sold pet fish, but the pond behind the Rose house was authentic. At least, we thought so. Every time we returned to the pond, we were surprised that the fish were still there and had not been netted or caught by someone. On our way back up Center Street from the pond, we would always be on the lookout for Mr. Wait, who lived at No. 322.

Earl Wait, who had been Corinth's fire chief in the late 1930s, worked with my father in the mill's Time Office. He was always very friendly to my friends and me. The appeal of finding Earl at home was watching him feed a chipmunk who lived in his yard. The chipmunk, whom he named "Charlie," had become so acclimated to human contact that he would climb up on Earl's arm or leg to be fed peanuts. Seeing a wild animal behave this way was quite a sight for an eight or nine-year-old boy. We always watched in amazement at how friendly Charlie was. So, at the far northern extreme of our upper Center Street kingdom was a tamed chipmunk and some goldfish, two spectacles that gave us good reason to venture down the street despite the likelihood that we would encounter Center Street's most peculiar and frightening resident.

At the crest of the Center Street hill, across the street from No. 320, lived a young man who suffered from some developmental disorder. Whatever the nature of his condition, his parents managed it well, for he graduated from Corinth High School in 1960. The years when we encountered him in the street, he was in his late teens. Tall and slender and with wire-rimmed glasses, he often wore a dark blue Dickies coverall like his father, a tradesman. If any of us ever went near his house, even to walk on the sidewalk on the other side of the street where Charlie the chipmunk and the goldfish lived, the young man would invariably come out of his house or garage and approach us and say some extraordinary things. Stuff that made no sense whatever. It was not what he said that made him so creepy; it was his very high-pitched, whiny voice. We probably had nothing to fear, but he scared the crap out of us for years. While some very odd characters lived in Corinth in the 1950s and 1960s, our Center Street neighbor was one of the few we saw up close.

More than fifty years later, in 2015, my mother became a resident at a Granville nursing home at age 96. Sitting at my Mother's bedside one day, I heard that creepy Center Street voice again. It was so distinctive and unforgettable that I had to ask one of the aides whose it was. Sure enough, the voice belonged to the same young man who had lived on Center Street when I was a boy and frightened every kid who crossed his path. But he was now 73 years old and lived only a few doors down the hall from my mother. Hearing his voice that day, which brought back memories of the times my friends and I ran into him, was both disturbing and profoundly sad. It made me wonder what his life had been like and what had become of others who, like him, had existed at the margins of the Corinth community life in the 1950s and 1960s, people we thought were odd, most for reasons beyond their control. I learned only when writing this chapter that Peter Carpenter died at the Granville nursing home in 2016 at the age of 73, not long after my Mother, having survived his parents and both of his siblings.

Like most Corinth kids, I began to drift away from my neighborhood friends as a teenager. My social life became centered within the cliques and groups that formed in school. Junior varsity sports and pick-up games at the Main Street athletic field and tennis courts with kids from across the village gradually replaced backyard football and driveway basketball. I saw neighborhood kids in school and was even a basketball teammate with one of them, yet we never socialized. After I got my driver's license and could take the family car, my bicycle was retired to the garage. My parents continued to reside at 341 Center Street after I left Corinth, my mother for another 50 years, so the house remained a constant in my life. Yet, each year, a return home would reveal a neighbor had retired, moved away, or died. With a strange family now living in their house, the children – those I played with as a kid – never came back. I became the last of my childhood friends in 2017 to leave their Center Street home behind.

5

STRAWBERRY FIELDS

Upper Center Street and the yards nearest my home were my primary playground when I was young. Gradually, I ventured to the fields and woods west of Center Street, where LeMont Avenue is now. The land was developed in 1963 into a residential area called West View Park by Norm Leclerc and "Chubber" Montello. The pair began constructing new homes on the open fields amid its random pine and maple trees. The boys living on Center Street, whose ages varied, would often play together in those fields. Sometimes, if there were an older boy or two, they would pull a prank on a younger kid. I cannot recall if the hole existed or was freshly dug, but one day, one of the older boys thought it would be funny if they put me, the youngest among them, into the hole. This is precisely what they did. Once I was in the hole, it was filled with dirt up to my shoulders. Then they left. I was maybe five years old at the time. I couldn't get out of the dirt-filled hole. I have no idea how my parents found me, but I was rescued just before dark. They were pretty disappointed that I let myself get into such a situation.

The older kids sometimes served as surrogate parents. One summer, a large group of boys got permission to camp out one night in the woods that used to be west of Center Street near Sturdevant Creek, right about where the Village DPW garages are located today. My parents let me go with the group that night, although I was relatively young, maybe seven or eight years old. We headed for a grove of large white pines that would provide a thick blanket of pine needles to set up camp. Tents were pitched, and a fire was built. However, we didn't use it to cook dinner; we brought sandwiches, snacks, and drinks from home. Once it got dark, I became scared, and the other boys thought it best that I be brought home. One of them, probably in his early teens, grabbed a flashlight and led me through the woods back to my house. While the other boys might have made fun of me, the boy who brought me home took care of me as a parent would.

We played "Cowboys and Indians" and "War" in the fields west of Center Street. While I owned a much-valued Mattel Fanner-50 six-shooter and holster and drew my gun quite fast, I enjoyed playing war more, especially after a few of us saw the movie "Pork Chop Hill" together at Corinth's Starr Theatre in 1959. I don't think it mattered that the film was based on a Korean War battle rather than one from World War II, where most of our fathers had served. We got to use our military gear regardless of which war we fought. Some of us carried military items into the battle that our fathers had brought home from the Pacific or European theatres, while others used gear they had purchased at the Army-Navy surplus store in Glens Falls. I sometimes wore the decorations that had been pinned to my Father's uniform and a U.S. Army surplus belt and canteen my parents bought for me. I also took along my coveted Marx 50-caliber flashing machine gun, which was so large it came with a tripod. Not only did the battery-powered gun make a distinctive RAT-A-TAT sound, but a flashing light was encased in red plastic at its center, and the red end of its barrel moved in and out when you pulled the trigger. What boy wouldn't want to go to war with such a weapon?

Before long, our battlefields were gradually torn up by the development of West View Park. There were still forested areas where we could play, further west towards Sturdevant Creek and to the east towards Eggleston Street, but our beloved playing fields were fast disappearing. First, Lemont Avenue was laid out. Then, more of our playground went when house lots were marked and cellar holes dug. Then, the concrete foundations were built. I suppose we could have played in and around the excavations, pretending we were moving through the remains of a bombed-out Italian village as they did on the TV series "Combat" of the early 1960s. I was soon a teenager and too old to play war, so the loss of our fields didn't seem to matter all that much.

One day, a kid in the neighborhood said he heard his parents say that one of the houses being built on Lemont Avenue had a bomb shelter. We had heard about them in school, so we were naturally curious about the one being built nearby. One spring evening, after Norm, Chubber, and their crew had left their job site, we went down to the house where the shelter was supposed to be. The door to the house was unlocked. The house's exterior was completed, and its roof shingles were installed, but the interior was still unfinished. We found the cellar stairs and went down. But what we found in the basement was underwhelming. In the middle of the basement was a small room, maybe ten feet square, made of simple concrete blocks. No doors, windows, beds, storage shelves, or toilets had yet been installed. While the bomb shelter was unfinished, we wondered how a family could live in such a small space even if they had survived a nuclear blast. That the shelter was never used for its intended purpose in the 60 years since it was built offers some insight into the public preoccupation with the atomic bomb in the 1960s. Do the house's present owners know the original purpose of that odd room in their basement?

Upper Center Street kids typically left the neighborhood in winter to sled at the Main Street athletic field. There, I got to play with classmates from school who lived on Oak, Walnut, and Main Streets. We used the slope that descends to the south side of the field from Oak Street, between the former elementary school and the entrance to the field that used to be located at 11 Oak. The stone walkway that led to the entrance is still there, but the door in the fence has long been closed off. The sledding run was so well-used the snow often turned to ice. When that happened, kids turned to their flying saucers. While it was short, the icy run was so fast that you had to hold tightly to the saucer's fabric handles to prevent being catapulted across the field when you hit a bump. In some winters, when it rained before it snowed and then got very cold, ice would turn the entire athletic field into a giant skating rink, permitting you to skate from end zone to end zone. Skating on the field lasted briefly; a snowstorm would invariably blow in to cover the ice.

When I was around 12 or 13, I could skate at the EMBA ice rink. IP employees built it in 1956 adjacent to the softball diamond on River Street. Created by IP in 1924, the EMBA that paper workers managed was a tangible benefit of living in an IP mill town. Built with a warming hut on its north side, the rink was eventually lighted for night skating, and a record player was installed to blast pop songs through loudspeakers. The rink was a terrific place to go after dinner on winter nights. On some weekend after-noons, as many as 200 children would be skating there. The rink was just one of the many activities provided by the EMBA intended expressly for Corinth's children. I suspect a book consisting solely of peoples' memories of the Corinth organization could be written.

I have but one clear memory of all the nights I spent at the EMBA rink coasting around on a pair of used hockey skates. It was the spectacle of a kid about my age whose skating was inspired by the sport of barrel jumping that was shown on ABC-TV's "Wide World of Sports" beginning in 1962. Barrel jumping, which started in the Netherlands in 1920, features a skater racing across the ice and jumping over 16-inch wide wood barrels, set out straight with their rounded sides touching. Competitions would begin with a modest number of barrels, perhaps six or eight, and then a barrel would be added for those competitors who had made it over the previous set. When the sport was broadcast on TV in the 1960s, the world record jump was 14 barrels.

Gerry Bovee was a good-looking Corinth kid, short with a medium build and unusually long hair for the early 1960s. He would often sweep it to one side of his head with the deft stroke of his right hand. Gerry was unique because one of his legs was slightly shorter than the other. But this affliction did not slow him down. While his gait in street shoes was affected by his condition, it was not all that noticeable when he wore his skates. Whether he was simply a daredevil or trying to impress the girls who skated there, Gerry created a modified version of then-popular barrel jumping those nights he was at the EMBA rink.

He would start at one end of the rink and tear off as fast as he could towards the far end. Tall wooden planks had been placed along the edges where the ice ended to create a border. Just beyond the plank border was an enormous pile of snow cleared from the rink by an IP plow. The pile's height could sometimes reach ten feet. Gerry would zoom towards the snow bank at full speed, and just before reaching the planks, he would launch himself up and over the snow pile, quickly disappearing into the darkness beyond. We would watch him in awe as he performed this feat and then stand there, mouths agape, waiting for him to reappear from the other side. Eventually, we would see Gerry's head emerge from behind the snow. He would then pull himself to the top of the bank in the semi-darkness, casually sweeping away the hair that had fallen over his face. He would stand there momentarily before climbing to the bottom to bask in the quiet adulation of those who had watched him. Gerry might make three of four such jumps in an evening.

I also considered Hunt Lake one of my childhood playgrounds away from Center Street. When I was about eight years old, my Father started bringing me to Hunt Lake in the summer to fish at the camp his friend, Walt Ramsey, owned. It was an old camp with a fieldstone fireplace that smelled of creosote and pine. It was a place well-lived in and well-loved. A bookcase in the living room was stuffed with books and board games. Walt and my Father would sit on the camp's screened porch that faced the lake, and I would follow a narrow path through thick ferns to reach a short pier, maybe 100 feet away. I always caught sunfish and the occasional small bass, but little else.

When Walt learned I had never caught a trout, he promptly took me to the stream adjacent to the camp that ran through the forest and emptied into the lake. The stream was tiny, about eight feet across and maybe one foot deep. He told me to bait my hook with a small worm and toss it so it would land right over a flat rock under the water's surface. As soon as I did, a flash of black came from under the stream's bank, grabbed my bait, and darted quickly back. I tugged my line to set the hook, and a minute later, I reeled in an eight-inch brook trout. I left Hunt Lake that day thinking Walt was some fishing god. Of all the trout I have caught in my life, even those I have taken in Montana as an adult, none can eclipse the memory of my first trout.

6

— • —

24 Oak Street

C orinth kids were most likely to get their first job the summer they turned 16, between sophomore and junior years. A few of my friends found summer work in town, while others got a job at one of Lake George's amusement areas, like Storytown, Gaslight Village, or Animal Land. While there were more jobs available in Lake George than in Corinth, the problem with working near the Lake was you had to have transportation. Since only a few kids had a driver's license by the summer of 1967, and none of us had a car, parents or older siblings had to be enlisted to provide a ride back and forth. Even though transportation was an obstacle, many kids perceived a job in Lake George more appealing than working in town, probably because it was *not* Corinth.

Some kids had jobs before they turned 16 years old. Besides earning money from mowing lawns, boys could deliver newspapers, either the morning Glens Falls *Post-Star* or the afternoon *Saratogian*. I wanted to be a paperboy, but the O'Connell family, who lived below the tracks on Center Street, "owned" the local *Post-Star* route that included our house, passing it down to three of their boys in the 1950s and 1960s. The *Saratogian*, the other option, had an office on Main Street in Corinth, but I never applied for a carrier job there since we did not subscribe to the paper, only the *Post-Star*. I figured a *Saratogian* route would be given only to boys whose families had the paper delivered to their homes. I got a job as an "alternate" paperboy for the *Grit*, the third newspaper delivered in town. But its primary carrier, a friend and classmate, Gary Mallery, was always on the job, so I never delivered a single copy. Many girls worked as babysitters, and one female classmate had a job at the Corinth Aquarium on West Maple Street. I suspect other kids had jobs before they turned 16 that I didn't know about.

My parents never told me I should get part-time work while I was in school. But Corinth was a working-class town, so the desire to have a job and earn my own money was a characteristic I acquired early in life. As it turns out, I worked throughout my high school years. I got my first job a few years before most of my friends did, at Lanfear's Store, opposite the Corinth High School. It wasn't a real job since I bartered my services. But I worked, I was paid.

Ruth Lanfear operated the small neighborhood store at 24 Oak Street for decades. She stocked some grocery staples, yet the store was dominated by a large oak, glass-front cabinet, maybe eight feet wide, with three shelves of penny candy. There, you could find red and black licorice, red-hot dollars, peach stones, malted milk balls, and much more. Ruth would wait patiently as you peered through the glass to make your selections, placing the candy you chose into a tiny paper bag taken from a stack on the counter. You could enter the store with only ten cents in your pocket and leave with a bag half full of candy. Ruth also carried lots of candy bars, including Mallo Cups and Skybars. My favorite was the Mallo Cup because of the collectible paper "coins" that came with the candy. The coins came in denominations from five cents to fifty cents. When you saved $10 worth of coins and mailed them in, you received back a package of ten Mallo Cups. I did that once.

Ruth also cooked hot dogs and sold them at lunchtime on weekdays. With a parent's permission, a kid could leave school during the lunch break and eat at Lanfear's instead of the school's cafeteria. Many kids who went to Ruth's never actually ate lunch but instead just hung out, enjoying a temporary escape from school. Some parents did not permit their 7th and 8th-grade children to go Lanfear's out of concern that they would be negatively influenced by the bad habits of the upper-class students who lunched there. Some Corinth mothers, like mine, said the kids at Lanfear's were the "wrong crowd" to associate with.

During most lunch hours on nice days, kids could be seen congregating on the sidewalk and in the street in front of Ruth's, listening to music on their transistor radios and smoking cigarettes. Although nearly half of all Americans smoked cigarettes in the mid-1960s, including many Corinth parents, some adults believed that smoking would put teenagers on a path to degeneration. So many parents refused to let their children take their lunch at Ruth's for this reason. Corinth had plenty of kids in those days who were just one stupid act away from juvenile delinquency, so the parental concern was probably justified.

Lanfear's was a Corinth institution, sometimes called "the school store." Kids hung out at Lanfear's before school, during lunch breaks, after school, and on weekends. Inside, Ruth had a few benches where kids could sit, and by the mid-1960s, she had installed two Gottlieb pinball machines where boys like me could find cheap entertainment. One of the machines, "Sing Along," was a unique pinball with four kick-out holes cut into its surface where your ball could fall for extra points. Once the machine registered the points, it shot the ball out of the hole toward the gobble hole at the bottom of the playfield that you guarded using two red buttons on either side of the machine. The buttons controlled two "flippers" on the bottom of the playing field to bat the steel ball away from the gobble hole. You worked the buttons aggressively with your fingertips.

Some boys used their index fingers to control the flippers, while others preferred their middle fingers. It was a matter of personal preference. Playing pinball required real finesse with the flipper buttons and superb timing to register a good score. Ruth's machines kept a record of its scores, so she gave a prize of store credit to the kid who got the highest one each week. Mike Wilkins, who was in the Class of 1968 and whose family lived two doors down on Oak Street, might have been the most accomplished of Ruth's pinball players. One afternoon, when we were at Ruth's together, one of the machines got stuck in its "play" mode and did not require you to insert a dime to play the next game. So Mike and I took turns playing free games until our "flipper" fingers got tired. We then told Ruth there was a problem with the machine. It never occurred to me that we denied Ruth income by playing games for free; we just thought it was cool to get something for nothing.

Ruth placed wooden benches outside her store for the kids. One bench was situated along the store's front wall, and the other at a right angle to the store under a large maple tree. During busy times, when school was in session or on the night of home football games, the benches could be full of kids with others standing on an adjacent paved area that had once been a lawn. The benches made Lanfear's a good place to meet up with friends. A large red Coke machine was outside next to the front door, where 12-ounce glass bottles were dispensed for 10 cents. The top of the machine consisted of lighted white plastic. After dark, it served as a beacon, drawing kids who passed up or down Oak Street. It was not unusual for kids to meet up at Lanfear's after dark, where they could sit out front, their conversations illuminated by the glow of the Ruth's COKE machine.

Lanfear's was one of eight or nine mom-and-pop neighborhood stores in Corinth during the 1950s and 1960s. Corinth had several supermarkets then – Oneida, Empire (later Grand Union), Kingsley's, and Lent's. Most grocery shopping was still local then, as the large box stores in Glens Falls and Saratoga Springs were decades into the future. Neighborhood stores like Lanfear's sold grocery items like bread, milk, eggs, and often some canned goods and boxed foods. Most mom-and-pop stores sold beer and soft drinks as well. Ruth's was best known for its counter-full of penny candy, while Wheaton's, located on West Maple Street in "the hollow," sold nearly everything. Wheaton's also sold bait for fishing, various curiosities, and bottles of Double-Cola, a hard-to-find soft drink that came in 16-ounce bottles. At 10 cents a bottle, it was the same price as Coke, but you got 33% more soda. What a deal!

Wheaton's was a long way from our house, so I only went there when my Father took me to Hunt Lake for fishing. We would stop to buy a dozen night crawlers for me and a six-pack of beer for him. Wheaton's was unique. Its walls were covered with novelty items displayed on merchandising platforms, like pocket combs, rabbit's feet, and nail files. Some even hung from the store's low ceiling. You don't see these types of random products anymore. Wheaton's was also where I bought my first cigarette. Not a real one, but one made of plastic. You put flour into an opening at one end and then blew into a small hole at the filter end to simulate real smoke. That a neighborhood store would sell such a toy and that a young boy would want to pretend that he was smoking suggests how ubiquitous cigarettes were in the 1960s.

My house on Center Street was only five minutes from Lanfear's, so I often hung out there on weekday evenings after dinner and on weekends. I could see up Oak Street from our back porch, and at night, I could detect the light coming from the Coke machine at Lanfear's. While kids often gathered at Ruth's to hang out, it was also a place where boys would meet up on the weekends to organize basketball or touch football games. Basketball was played on the tennis courts, where a two-goal court was set up on the south end. Football was played almost every Sunday afternoon in the Fall on the broad lawn between the former Oak Street Elementary School and the fence bordering the Main Street athletic field. We used the exterior classroom doors of the elementary school as the goal lines for our imaginary gridiron. While our dads were likely to be home watching an NFL game, we preferred to be playing football. We had a great time with as many as eight to ten boys playing at once. We would go to Lanfear's for a Coke when we were finished. The elementary school lawn, the site of countless touch football games in the 1960s, is now a parking lot.

Ruth Lanfear would also open her store for home football games on Friday nights. A raucous crowd often gathered there, particularly after a home team victory. I remember an altercation across the street in the school parking lot following one game. I might have been in the 7th grade at the time. We left Ruth's and walked across Oak Street in time to see one of the two arguing men jump into his car to drive off. Before he could put his car into gear, the other guy - yelling at the driver - punched his fist through the car windows, first the driver's window and then the rear window. Shouting the whole time, he went behind the car and broke the two windows on the passenger side. I don't know if the man injured his hand by smashing the car windows, but I was overwhelmed by the rage and violence I witnessed that night. I had never seen anything like it, not even on TV.

One day, while I was hanging out with some friends on the outdoor benches, Ruth came out and asked if I would help her with something. I might have been 12 or 13 years old at the time. When I went into the store with her, she asked if I would help her fill the Coke machine. I said I would. We went out of the store's back door, past the house trailer that was her home, and to the garage, whose large front door faced the Oak Street Alley. When she opened the garage, wooden cases of soda, nearly all Coke, sat stacked neatly on one side. She showed me the hand cart that I was to use. I stacked maybe five or six yellow-painted wooden cases of Coke on the cart, each containing 24 bottles.

I wheeled the Coke-loaded cart along the paved path on one side of the store out to the front. Ruth showed me how to open up and lock the machine, leaving me to fill it independently. Inside the device was a large, square metal container where all the change fell after being put into the machine. Ruth must have trusted me because the coin box was half-full. When I finished loading the machine, I closed it up, locked it, returned the hand cart to the garage, and then went back to the store to tell Ruth I was done. She gave me $1.00 in store credit for my work. That doesn't sound like much, but in 1963, when I was 12 years old, the federal minimum wage was $1.25. So I received $1.00 for about a half-hour of work. I was probably already spending more than that amount in the store each week anyway. Whenever I was at the store after that, and Ruth needed to fill the Coke machine, she would ask me to do it for her.

Lanfear's store at 24 Oak Street was torn down in 2011. At the time, a heavily trafficked Corinth Facebook page asked visitors what they remembered about Ruth and her store. Nearly fifty posts offered fond personal memories of Ruth, with several people writing that they loved her. The names of those who commented and the situations they described suggest that generations of Corinth students held Ruth in warm regard. While the garage she used still stands on Oak Street Alley, the store's footprint and the former site of her residential trailer are now part of someone's lawn. Yet, as this chapter is written, someone is seeking permission from the Village to construct a modular home where Lanfear's stood.

Ruth Lanfear operated her store at 24 Oak for nearly 50 years. Like many structures that played a meaningful role in Corinth's history and the lives of people in the community, Lanfear's survives only in the memory of those of us who made the store part of our daily lives. Kids who pass by 24 Oak Street today could never imagine that the store once located there served as the center of social activity for two generations of Corinth youth. Teenagers lived at 24 Oak Street before, during, and after school and on weekends. For many of us, it was our second home.

Ruth worked as a telephone operator after graduating from Corinth High School in 1920. In 1931, she married William Colvin. Ruth had a child, Richard, the following year. After she and her husband divorced, Ruth and Richard lived with her parents through the 1930s and 1940s. Richard, who worked at the IP mill after high school, was killed in an automobile accident in April 1954 at age 21. Ruth lost her mother, Nellie, two weeks later. Ruth operated her small store independently until 1968, when she married Phil Winchell, who helped her in the store and provided Corinth kids with another friendly face.

Ruth Lanfear was a soft-spoken, unassuming woman of small stature with a big heart. She offered an inviting and welcoming environment for Corinth teenagers from the 1930s through the 1970s. Her Oak Street store was a venerable Corinth social institution for five decades, yet it has been little recognized for its contribution to the community. If any place in Corinth deserves historical recognition, it is 24 Oak Street. Ruth Lanfear and her husband Phil both died in 1980.

7

_._

GOD ONLY KNOWS

A merican youth made adults anxious in the 1960s. Drugs, rock music, pre-marital sex, and anti-Vietnam War protests increasingly dominated popular culture, activities that convinced parents, teachers, and civic leaders that many young people had contempt for adult authority. While television and the press generally depicted American youth as rebellious and sharply critical of "the establishment," most Corinth kids were remarkably docile and compliant. Being raised in a God-fearing community with six churches that provided religious education for its children might have contributed to the conservative bent of Corinth's teenagers. There were exceptions, but most local kids were generally respectful to their parents and teachers in the 1960s, unlike the teenagers our parents saw in magazines and on the evening news.

Methodists and Baptists were the most prominent among Corinth's Protestant churches. The Catholic church was likely the largest congregation, with two priests required to conduct four masses on Sunday to manage parishioner demand. Most of my best friends from the Classes of 1969 and 1970 were raised Catholic and attended catechism from elementary through high school, twice weekly at first. Saturday morning classes at the Immaculate Conception ended by the time we got to the 9th grade, but after-school classes continued during the week until we were in high school. It was my junior year when I took my last class, yet what I experienced in Catholic catechism class had a life-long effect. And only sometimes to my benefit.

The work of the Immaculate Conception Church in Corinth was all-inclusive. Boys could become altar boys when they were eight or nine years old. Several of my best friends served, but I never did because I mistakenly thought you had to be invited into the fold by one of the parish priests. While a priest might have asked a few boys to enlist, I suspect parents encouraged their sons to serve the church as altar boys. After watching friends stumble half-asleep across the altar during the 8 AM mass I regularly attended with my Mother, I was glad she didn't push me to become one of them. She probably figured that she prayed enough that she didn't need me to become an altar boy to bring more of God's grace into our home. Like all my catechism classmates, I received the Eucharist (First Communion) for the first time at age six or seven and Confirmation when I was five years older. We knew First Communion and Confirmation were big deals because the Bishop of Albany came to town to officiate. So, along with Baptism, I had three of the Church's seven sacraments covered by the time I was 13 years old, well on my way to becoming a good Catholic.

The Bishop came to our parish on another occasion, not in person, but in a movie. One Sunday during mass, a small screen was set up at the front of the church, and a film projector was rolled in on a cart from the vestibule. This was sometime around 1958 or 1959, for I was pretty young. The projector was turned on by a member of the Knights of Columbus, and the Bishop appeared on the screen. He asked that all parishioners take a pledge to adhere to the tenets of the Catholic Legion of Decency, promising that we would not view motion pictures that "offend decency and Christian morality." Everyone at mass that day recited in unison the pledge that appeared on the screen, including kids who had no idea what was going on. That children were required to take the pledge was strange since the closest we ever got to immoral, objectionable behavior was watching the anthropomorphized yet pant-less Daffy Duck, Bugs Bunny, and Porky Pig in our Saturday morning cartoons. In retrospect, I probably first violated my pledge to the League when, in 1964, I began watching the sexually suggestive TV series *Peyton Place* after my parents went to bed. I was among the thousands of teenage boys who developed a crush on Barbara Parkins while watching the show.

Catholic girls had a different option than boys. They could become members of the church's Junior Atonement Club, whose motto was "Sanctity Through Unity." An excellent photograph of the Club at our church was taken by George Holland in 1963. It features 16 girls, mainly from the Classes of 1967 and 1968, nicely dressed and flanked by Father Polumbus, the Assistant Priest at the time, and an unnamed parish nun. Another photo, taken the previous year, shows 28 Club members and Sister Joseph Adele. The Club was pretty popular among Catholic teenage girls.

The doctrine of atonement refers generally to Christ's sacrifice on the cross to redeem the human race. In practice, the Catholic Church's Junior Atonement Club sought to connect young adults with Jesus Christ and the Church. There is no surviving written account of what Corinth chapter members did in the spirit of atonement. Yet, similar clubs in other Catholic parishes had a social function, like a sister organization in Troy. That club once held a Halloween party that Atonement Club members were expected to attend dressed as their favorite saints. That the nuns who administered the Clubs in the 1960s expected Catholic girls to have a favorite saint, at a time when teenagers were crying and screaming for the

Beatles, spoke either to a veiled teenage piety or the degree to which the Catholic Church was out of touch with the times.

The most devout among men in the parish who enjoyed socialization could join the Corinth chapter of the Knights of Columbus, Rev. John E. Dignon Council 3271. They could also join the Holy Name Society, a confraternity dedicated to spiritual works whose community activities included an Annual Corporate Communion Breakfast, an event that no doubt was intended to infuse IP management and local business owners with a dose of Catholic values. As one of the many religious and secular fraternal organizations in Corinth, the Knights were involved in activities that benefitted both the community and individuals, particularly Roman Catholics. From time to time, the Knights could be seen marching from their meeting hall at 10 Heath Street to the Immaculate Conception on Palmer Avenue, its visiting leadership dressed in full organizational regalia, wearing black suits with white sashes, black flowing capes, and hats with white plumage, and swords. I never understood what the swords were for, but I supposed that if you called yourself a knight, you had to carry one. The Knights regularly hosted Sunday morning breakfasts for its members and special guests. As a soon-to-be graduating Catholic senior, I recall attending a breakfast at the Knight's Hall.

The Corinth chapter of the Catholic Daughters of America (CDA), Court Father Joseph Hickey, was the most influential of the organizations in our parish. Led by its Grand Regent, the CDA organized social and educational events for members and raised funds to support other local organizations. Working under its "Unity-Charity" motto; the CDA might have been best known in the community for the yearly Christmas bazaars it sponsored and for its fund-raising minstrels that were staged in the high school auditorium, beginning in 1953. With forty or more performers on stage, CDA minstrels had become so popular by the 1970s that four shows had to be offered to accommodate all who wanted to attend.

Some of the CDA's earliest shows, from the 1950s to the early 1960s, maintained the historic tradition of American minstrels, a form of racist theatre. For these shows, some CDA members performed in blackface. The 1957 minstrel, for example, featured a two-act comedy set in the plantation garden of a Louisville, Kentucky colonel. George Holland, the editor of the *EMBA News*, took several cringe-worthy photographs of the CDA's minstrel's blackface performance in 1956, the same year that a young Martin Luther King, Jr. led the Montgomery Bus Boycott after Rosa Parks's arrest for her refusal to move from a "white" seat on the bus to the back. Corinth's CDA chapter was not the only mainstream American organization in the 1950s and 1960s, religious or secular, that denigrated African Americans by staging minstrels in blackface. That the CDA of Corinth promoted such racist stereotypes to raise money for the Catholic Church is an overlooked yet inescapable fact of the community's history.

As a teenage communicant at the Immaculate Conception, I witnessed the Second Vatican Council upend hundreds of years of church faith and practice in the 1960s. The "modernizing" of the Church promoted by Pope John XXIII resulted in Mass being said in English instead of Latin and the reversal of the altar so that the priest faced his parishioners rather than keeping his back toward them. Other changes prompted by the Second Vatican Council made a Catholic Mass more like a Protestant service. These universal changes made my church and our Sunday mass unrecognizable. During a decade of rapidly changing cultural values, the Second Vatican Council swept away centuries of tradition to make the Church seem relevant.

Perhaps the most dramatic change was the transformation of the Immaculate Conception itself, alterations that made it look more like a

Methodist or Baptist church. Except for the Stations of the Cross that remained positioned on the interior side walls of the church, all of the original ornamentation of the Immaculate Conception's interior, particularly the statues that had long been considered symbols of idolatry by critics of Catholicism, was removed. The church's blue, white, and gold patterned ceiling and walls were painted white, and dark brown imitation wood beams were attached to the sloped interior to make the building appear rustic. And all of the statues of saints, perhaps as many as ten, that used to be on the altar at the front of the church and in the vestibule were banished to the church's basement.

Once, when Father Walsh asked me to go into the church basement to retrieve something for him, I saw all the statues standing together in a corner. While I never understood what each figure represented, when I saw them cloistered in the semi-darkness, I realized that I missed them, their presence during a Mass having offered a measure of serenity. While I was troubled by the transformation imposed by the Vatican Council, my Mother, who had been raised in a traditional Italian Catholic household, had an essential part of her life turned upside down and inside out. She was devout and unquestioning, so she conformed to the Church's new practices and attended Mass each Sunday until the early 2000s.

Just about the same time the Second Vatican Council brought dramatic change to our church, many of my closest friends and I stopped attending Mass with our parents. Instead, we began to meet as a group for the 10:30 AM service. Rather than sit in pews, we convened in the choir loft at the rear, which was usually empty. Sitting close to the church's vestibule still allowed us to say that we went to Mass, but our distance from the altar gave us the feeling that we were not part of it. We whispered and giggled throughout most of each service, making attending Sunday mass just another social occasion. While separating ourselves from the pews where we ordinarily sat with our parents may have been a normative expression of adolescent rebellion, I am persuaded that it was also a visceral protest to the changes we saw around us.

Some of us realized by then that much of what we had been taught in catechism all those years, from second grade on, did not make much sense anymore. Empirical thinking had inevitably devoured our faith. Yet we kept going to Mass out of habit and blind obedience. By the time I was a senior, I had stopped attending church. I would leave our house on Center Street for the 10:30 Mass, but instead of going to church, I would drive to my grandparents' house on Upper Heath Street. Since they were Lutheran and loved it whenever I visited them, I knew they would never tell my Mother I had gone to their house instead of attending Mass. They might tell my Father, but he wouldn't have cared. So, until I left for college in September 1969, going to my grandparents every Sunday morning at 10:30 for a late breakfast became a practice that replaced the ritual of attending Mass. In all the years since I left Corinth in 1969, I have returned to the Immaculate Conception only for weddings and funerals.

The building that was the Church of the Immaculate Conception still stands. Yet, if there is one measure that can be used to understand how much Corinth has changed since the 1960s, one need only look at its Catholic Church. After a compulsory consolidation with the Lake Luzerne parish after its own Church of the Holy Infancy was closed, the combined congregation is now called Holy Mother and Child Parish. Mass, once held four times every Sunday at the Palmer Avenue church in the 1960s, is now offered only once. And the 8:30 AM Sunday Mass is also live-streamed on YouTube. The Corinth parish, which used to have two full-time priests and three Franciscan nuns, now shares but a single priest with Lake Luzerne's communicants. The nuns left decades ago. The former rectory, convent, parish hall, and brick two-car garage next to the church, once part of the former Immaculate Conception campus, were either burned down or torn down. A parish center that was constructed on the footprint of the former parish hall and garage is sheathed in grey-painted, T-111 plywood siding, a cheap exterior surface material that is incongruous with the red Glens Falls bricks and Indiana limestone used for the church when it was built in 1905. The Immaculate Conception church of our youth now exists only in memory.

8

— : —

MERRY CHRISTMAS, NOW BEND OVER

Corinth's school system joined parents and the community's churches in establishing the guardrails for acceptable youth behavior in the 1950s and 1960s. One of its best-honed tools for discouraging misconduct was corporal punishment, a child-rearing technique sanctioned in the *Bible* that became common in most Western societies. While the primary purpose of the practice is to punish a transgressor by inflicting pain or discomfort, it is also supposed to serve as a deterrent to future inappropriate behavior. Corporal punishment was never administered to me in the Corinth schools. Yet, I observed it as early as kindergarten at Corinth's Main Street School, which housed about half of Corinth's kindergarten and first graders who lived in the Village in the mid-1950s.

There was one boy in my kindergarten class who always got into trouble for using foul language. I don't recall hearing his words, but whenever he offended our teacher, she would wash his mouth with soap. The boy would be made to stand on a stool in front of the sink in our classroom, where the teacher forced him to put a small piece of wet soap into his mouth. Eating soap in this manner caused him to gag and vomit into the sink. While some people suffer from the compulsion to eat soap, a behavior called sapophagia, the ingestion of soap is known to cause inflammation and liver damage. Soap eating as a form of punishment, intended to represent the symbolic cleansing of a youth's foul mouth, did not appear to change my five-year-old classmate's behavior. The mouthwashing and the humiliation of the boy continued throughout the year. Soap-eating was used in New York State public schools as punishment in 1956 when I started school, yet it is shocking to think a Corinth kindergarten teacher would punish a small child that way.

A few years later, another Corinth elementary school teacher used a variation of the soap method of punishment. This time, it was in my 6th-grade art class. I don't recall what the boy did that required discipline, but our art teacher made him come to the front of the classroom and sit on a stool to face the class. She then gave him a large tub of art paste and a spoon and told him to start eating the paste. Most art paste today, called "wheat paste," is made of flour and water paste and is not toxic. Some kids are known to like to eat it. However, the paste used in our 1962 art class was not made of flour because the kid did not enjoy eating it.

With our teacher standing over him and the whole class looking on, the boy spooned the paste out of the tub and into his mouth. When he looked like he was about to explode, the teacher let him leave the room and go down the hallway to the bathroom to puke. She at least had the good sense to save the boy from the embarrassment of being seen barfing his lunch in front of twenty-five classmates. Soap and paste eating, legal corporal punishment in New York State until the mid-1980s was violent and humiliating. It would not be surprising to learn that victims of corporal punishment in the Corinth schools later had post-traumatic stress disorder.

Paddling was a more common form of corporal punishment in Corinth schools in those years. It was performed mainly by male teachers. Our elementary school principal, in fact, once bragged to someone that he used a paddle with holes in it, which, by offering less resistance, resulted in a faster stroke and presumably more pain. While I observed occasional paddling in every primary school grade, one event from my 5th-grade class remains very vivid, mainly because it was a group event, something like a mass execution.

The event remains clear because the paddling was administered by a beloved teacher, one of the few male teachers in the elementary school. He was progressive, played semi-pro baseball, coached boys' sports teams, and had a wonderful sense of humor. Boys like me loved him because we could relate more easily to him than our female teachers. Yet something about him suggested that as an elementary school teacher, he was working well below his capacity, that he possessed both the intelligence and the personality to do so much more.

Our 5th-grade teacher constantly challenged us academically. The most memorable way was when he required that we learn vocabulary words well beyond our grade level. We were given a new vocabulary list each week to study and were then quizzed on what we had learned. Before long, some of us were spelling at an 11th or 12th-grade level. We were so proud of ourselves. He also sought to expand our vocabularies in other ways.

One day, when groups of students were engaged in various activities around the room, he called a few of the boys up to his desk. He was thumbing through the pages of a black-and-orange paperback copy of *Roget's Thesaurus*. It was the first time I had ever seen one. He turned to the page with the word "fool" and rapidly read its many synonyms, inflecting words he thought were odd or amusing. We all laughed at all the words that could mean "fool." I remember that my eyes watered from laughing so hard. I am unsure if he was trying to have some fun with us or trying to get us to think about the meaning of words. Soon after, I persuaded my parents to buy me a copy of *Roget's* so that I could explore the humorous synonyms of other words. I still have the *Roget's Thesaurus* in my office bookcase, and I think of my 5th-grade teacher whenever I see it.

One day, he became unrecognizable. It was the day before our Christmas vacation was to begin in 1961. He told us he realized he had failed to deal with some inappropriate behavior during the Fall term but that he would now address it. He then stood at his desk with a wooden paddle, slapping it gently against his palm, and pledged to paddle every kid in the class who deserved it. He began with the first kid in the row nearest the window, reviewing their behavior during the previous few months for all to hear and concluding whether they deserved belated punishment. Our teacher went down each row in this fashion, across the entire classroom, calling out boys and girls alike as he went. When a kid's name was called, they went to the front of the room. Punishment varied widely, from what seemed like a single gentle "swat" to several fairly hard "whacks!"

Our teacher paddled girls that day, too; it was the only time I saw or heard of girls getting paddled in our school. The mass execution of corporal punishment that day remains vivid after all these years, probably because I was the only boy in my class to escape punishment. At that age, I was a good kid, always polite and respectful, but our teacher could have made something up to justify giving me a whack or two. I never understood why he didn't.

9

— · —

CRIME AND PUNISHMENT

C orporal punishment reached new levels of creativity and severity
at Corinth High School. Problem students were often sent to the
main office for discipline, where our principal, a World War II veteran and
former English teacher, a man some kids thought possessed the demeanor
of an executioner, administered punishment. The principal's office appeared to receive lots of traffic. His services were used primarily by the
school's female teachers, who were less likely than their male colleagues
to employ corporal punishment on a student. Some kids believed that
because our principal's services were used so often, he utilized an "electric
paddle" to keep up with demand.

Employing mechanized paddling made perfect sense. Smacking kids
regularly could result in "paddler's elbow," an affliction known to have a
high incidence rate among high school principals in those days. A paddling
machine would compensate for this, reducing wear and tear on one's paddling arm. We thought the electric paddle rumor to be especially credible,
for our principal, who the kids called "Stiff," had a very rigid posture that
was believed to have resulted from a war wound. It was widely speculated
he carried a surgically implanted steel plate as a result that restricted his
upper body movement. No one knew for sure, but we suspected his range

of motion was limited. Besides the practical benefits of using an electric paddle, corporal punishment meted out by a machine would not be considered "personal." It would be just business.

It was never confirmed that an electric paddle existed, so it had to be imagined. We used to think that after the kid to be punished arrived at the principal's office, he would be positioned in the "machine," for which only a few construction details ever became part of our collective vision. We realized that it had to have intensity control to determine the force of each blow and a counter of some sort to set the precise number of hits to be administered. The total paddle count from the machine for a week or month, illustrated on a line chart or bar graph posted in the teacher's lounge, might have served as a great conversation starter. "Hey, I see your paddle count was up again last week. Great work!" We also thought the electric paddle should include a built-in microphone so paddling sounds could be piped into the school's P.A. system and broadcast through a speaker in the lobby. Once the controls on the paddle were set, the principal would turn it on, returning to his desk to continue necessary paperwork or even pour himself a cup of coffee while the machine wailed away at the kid bent over in front of him. The machine's paddle arm would generate the "whack, whack, whack" sound audible in the hall. No one we knew ever admitted to being subjected to the electric paddle, yet the belief that the machine existed in the principal's office remained a part of the school's 1960s folklore.

Our high school principal was the go-to guy if a teacher needed some paddling done, yet some male teachers were do-it-yourselfers. One of the most notorious was a young science teacher who taught us 10th-grade biology in 7th grade as part of an experiment funded by the IP Foundation. We called him "the Missing link" because he had a muscular build, balding head, and dark, thick body hair that showed through his white shirt. His black eyebrows were as wide as hedgerows, and he walked with a kind of jungle strut, toes pointing inward, with a slight bounce in his step. One-on-one, our biology teacher was soft-spoken and thoughtful. He was very likable. But when he entered "the punitive zone," he was fully transformed into someone else, a veritable King Kong. Instead of holding an airplane atop the Empire State Building, he held up a wooden paddle at the front of the classroom.

When the Missing Link decided to punish a kid, he had his victim come to the front of the room and bend over his desk. He seemed so comfortable with a paddle in hand, so adept at taking big swings, that you could almost imagine him offering after-school paddling clinics for new teachers. He would remove his sports coat and lift a two-foot-long paddle from a hook next to the blackboard. I recall the paddle was inscribed with three Greek letters, presumably those of his college fraternity. Standing behind his victim and planting his feet on the floor like he was standing in a batter's box, he would cock the paddle as though he was preparing to launch a fastball into left field at Yankee Stadium. When he stepped up to the imaginary plate behind a kid, we would almost expect him to take a practice swing or two. Holding the paddle with both hands, he would pull it back slowly and then quickly smack his target with such force that his victim's backside would be lifted several inches. Even the toughest boys would return to their seats humbled after being subject to such brutality.

I clearly remember the biology class on the first warm day in the Spring of 1964. All the large windows in our second-floor, Oak Street-facing classroom had been lifted wide open. One of my best friends who sat next to me in class was caught by the Missing Link throwing a penny out of one of the windows. Our teacher stopped the class, called my friend to the front of the room, and ordered him to bend over the edge of his desk. The Link stepped up to him, took several forceful swings, and paddled my friend until he cried. Our biology teacher, whose punitive measures were well within the law in New York State in 1964, taught in the Corinth schools for another 25 years.

We had a 10th-grade math teacher who was a pacifist compared to the Missing Link. Yet when he resorted to punishment, it was only after his efforts to intimidate us psychologically had failed. He had just graduated from college in June and was only 23 when he arrived in Corinth. He was relatively short, yet he talked tough, trying to make himself appear more of a threat than his body size suggested. Once, when he was sitting in his desk chair, about six of the guys in the class encircled it, towering over him. He responded to our perceived intimidation by telling us that when he played football in high school, he learned how to tackle an opponent so that one of his legs would be broken. He even had a name for the move.

This teacher used creative punishments rather than corporal methods when anyone got out of line. While he soon learned he had every reason to use the paddle in the classroom or send his most problematic students to the principal for an encounter with the electric paddle, he never did. This could have been because he was only a first-year teacher, or he had been subject to corporal punishment himself while in school, or perhaps because, as a short kid, he got beaten up a lot. No matter the reason, the use of corporal punishment for the first time in your career, on which kid and for which kind of offense, must have posed quite a dilemma for any new teacher. Instead, our 10th-grade math teacher resorted to punishments that mainly relied on humiliation while inflicting only moderate physical discomfort.

There were a lot of bright kids in our geometry class that year, but it also had a few disruptive characters. Our teacher punished one kid who misbehaved early during one class period by having him "duck-walk" up and down the aisles of the classroom for the entire period. The "duck walk" is performed by squatting nearly to the floor, with your back upright and knees forward. Then, you move forward slowly, one bent leg at a time. Moving around this way, which is both awkward and uncomfortable, would quickly lead a kid to regret whatever they did to elicit the punishment. Yet the disruption to the class that resulted from the "duck walk" was more significant than the offense committed. Our attention was directed at our classmates' movements and crude hand gestures instead of our teachers' lessons.

Another classroom incident with the same kid resulted in another form of punishment that was also a classroom distraction. This time, our classmate was forced to sit beside the teacher's desk inside a tall, green steel trash barrel. I can't recall precisely how he negotiated his entry into the can, but after he did, his legs were folded at the knees over one side of the barrel while his back was inside up to his shoulders, leaving both arms hanging to the sides. The kid's head was entirely above the barrel's rim. Besides looking pretty silly, the position must have been quite uncomfortable, yet our very willful and determined classmate would never let our teacher see that he was in pain. The boy's body was hindered by the barrel, but he continued to make faces at his classmates, ensuring that our attention would be on him rather than our teacher, who was busy writing geometry theorems on the blackboard.

However, the teacher's most notorious punishment was the "military brace." One day, he was compelled to punish my irreverent, duck-walking, barrel-diving classmate for some misbehavior. This day, he made him stand with his head and toes wedged into the front, right-hand corner of the classroom near the door. He then told him to put his hands behind his back and slowly step backward three feet while keeping his head fixed in the corner. Our classmate was forced to stay in that uncomfortable and somewhat painful position, his body at about a 60-degree angle to the corner, until class was over. For the rest of the period, rather than looking at our teacher, who attempted to continue the class, we kept our eyes on our classmate as he made hand gestures behind his back. Our teacher told us that he had learned the "military brace" in the US Army, yet we wondered how he could have squeezed in college attendance *and* military service and still be only 23 years old.

My math classmates did not appreciate our teacher's unconventional punishments, no matter how justified they might have been. So we struck back. The most notorious instance came a few days before the Christmas break 1966. We had just finished a holiday classroom party that featured all sorts of goodies baked for the occasion by our moms. With a few of us still nibbling at chocolate brownies and sugar cookies, our teacher resumed the class and started writing a theorem on the blackboard. A few of us quietly tore up the aluminum foil that had covered the treats we had just enjoyed and passed pieces around the room so every kid had enough foil to roll up into a golf ball-size projectile. When our teacher turned to face the board, on cue, we each hurled our foil balls toward him. Some hit the blackboard, but many bounced off his back, shoulders, and head. After the last aluminum ball had fallen to the floor, our teacher turned toward us without saying a word; his shoulders slumped, and his face flushed with defeat.

Sadly, none of the punishments meted out to address misbehavior succeeded in controlling our class. As a result, most of the class failed the New York State Regents exam in June of that year, requiring that we retake the course after school the following fall with another math teacher and then retake the exam in January. We got another chance at geometry, but our teacher didn't. He was fired at year's end. Not long ago, when I came upon his obituary, I was happy to read that he had moved on from Corinth High School to have an active and meaningful life and a large family. He had been involved with his church and volunteer organizations, including serving as a Boy Scout leader. After leaving Corinth, he served in the U.S. Navy before resuming his high school math teacher career at a small school in far northern New York State, about eight miles from the Canadian border. He continued to teach at schools in the Adirondacks until his retirement.

The more I read about his life well-lived, the more guilt I felt for being party to the behavior of my fellow 15-year-olds who had made his first teaching position so miserable. I could only imagine how he must have felt to lose his first job. Yet the Corinth School District was not without fault. Years later, I wondered why a 22-year-old recent college graduate was hired to teach New York State Regents geometry to an accelerated 10th-grade class. The high principal knew the kids in the class and their reputations. What was he thinking?

We had an 11th-grade American history teacher who preferred intim-idation to corporal punishment. He was just under six feet tall, stocky, and wore a crew cut. We called him "Bulldog." He also coached football, often wearing classic coach footwear in the classroom, black sneaker-like shoes with thick rippled soles shaped like waves. All the high school coaches wore them in those days. He would often walk around in front of our history classroom, barking out a question for us to answer or spelling out the instructions for completing an upcoming assignment. Once, when we were asked to read something outside of class and write about it, he warned us not to "make things up" in our paper because, as he said in his most threatening voice, "Guess who remembers what he reads?"

This teacher's intimidating warnings were always issued in the cockiest of ways. He even had a favorite posture when he gave commands. He would stand at the front of the room, feet wide apart and hands on his waist, which made him appear larger and more imposing than he was. Sometimes, he would rock back and forth on his heels in this position.

He used that same stance with me one day in track practice, where he occasionally helped out the head coach. I was a shot putter. One day, he approached the shot pit and told me I needed to get the shot higher into the air to get more distance. So he walked into the grassy area between the cement pad from where I threw the shot and the cinder pit where it would land, taking his famous wide stance about ten feet in front of me. He stood there stoically, even defiantly, the look on his face saying, "Hit me with that shot and see what happens." To put the challenge into perspective, the shot I was about to throw was a 12-pound steel ball. Well, it worked. I tossed the shot over his head into the pit behind him, getting more distance than usual.

While our history teacher's threatening demeanor could be effective in the classroom and on the athletic field, students didn't like him very much. While we often found ways to get back at teachers who offended us, it wasn't easy to do so with him. But we did get to laugh at his expense on one occasion, from something of his own doing. He was sitting at his chair one day, tilting it back as though he was going to put his feet on the desk. While he delivered one of his contentious orders, he suddenly fell backward, disappearing quickly from view. The sounds of crashing wood and metal and the "thump" of our teacher hitting the floor reverberated around the room. None of us got up to see if he was OK. We just sat there, stunned. Eventually, he gathered himself up, more embarrassed than hurt, trying to preserve a measure of dignity while resuming where he had left off. It was difficult not to giggle or smirk for the remainder of the class.

Our history teacher left Corinth High School shortly after the Class of 1969 graduated to become a school administrator in another part of the State. In 1979, he was invited by the Corinth Alumni Association to speak at its banquet at the Hidden Valley Dude Ranch. It was the year of my class's 10th reunion. I remember being anxious to attend the dinner. I had just received a Ph.D. in American history the previous year and was teaching at a college in New Hampshire. I thought my former teacher would be interested in what became of me and would be pleased by my accomplishment after being, at best, a mediocre student in high school. But when I approached him to say "hello," he was rather indifferent, almost as though he didn't even remember who I was. I told him what I had done, yet he didn't say anything to show that he was interested or pleased. His indifference shook me.

Here was a teacher who had become an iconic, if not a notorious, figure in the classroom and on the athletic field. He had either forgotten me after ten years or didn't care what I had done with my life since leaving Corinth. It was that night in 1979 that I first began to realize that perhaps some of the teachers who had been at the center of my life for so many years, some whom my friends and I idolized and even considered friends, maybe didn't care much about us. They were our teachers, but teaching was just a job. I was so demoralized by my experience at my high school reunion, so terribly disappointed by my former teacher's response to what I had shared; all I could think about as I walked away was that day in 11th-grade history when he fell on his ass in front of the entire class.

10

— · —

TOWN WITHOUT PITY

The 1960s, perhaps more than any other decade in the 20th century, was characterized by a discernible "generation gap." The pervasive youth culture that emerged in those years widened the traditional divisions between teenagers and adult authority. While most of the Corinth kids I knew were apolitical, the Vietnam War and Civil Rights Movement provided evidence that the dominant culture our parent's generation represented was deeply flawed. Teenage angst was an inevitable consequence.

Corinth teenagers in the 1960s, while living in a rural Saratoga County backwater community, nonetheless grew up in an era of rapid social and cultural change. Our parent's world was quickly receding, but anybody's guess was where the road ahead would lead. We lived in a small industrial town that adhered to and was bound by traditional American values, shaped by Christian principles, a conservative political ideology, and a working-class culture. Like the generations of Corinth kids who preceded us, what we weren't taught at home or school, we learned at Sunday school or catechism class. Yet it was in the street, in the locker room, from an older sibling, or in the back seat of a parked car that teenagers learned the behaviors that most concerned adults.

Corinth's community institutions sought to discourage teenage rebellion by providing organized activities to keep us busy and engaged. The Employee Mutual Benefit Association (EMBA) kept many Corinth boys busy with organized basketball, softball, bowling, and boxing at the Community Building. At the same time, the Corinth School system fielded several boys' junior varsity and varsity sports teams that harnessed and redirected adolescent testosterone.

Girls who came of age in the 1960s had fewer options than boys. The only organized teams for girls in my Class of 1969 were the cheerleading squad and the high school girls' bowling team. It is a curious fact of Corinth's history that Corinth High School fielded girls' basketball teams in the 1920s and 1930s. Corinth girls won three consecutive Adirondack School League titles from 1928 to 1930, yet by the late 1930s, the high school team was eliminated. Corinth girls who wanted to play basketball had to join a town team that included the Cluett-Peabody Arrows, organized in 1941. Not until the adoption of Title IX in 1972 did Corinth high school girls, like others across the county, begin to have athletic opportunities comparable to boys.

Our parents and neighbors – nearly all working class – were hard-working, God-fearing, and generous people who grew up during the Great Depression and served in World War II. Difficult times, to be sure. Yet I never recall hearing my parents or any other adult of their generation complain about how difficult it was to live through the 1930s or how frightened the men were to find themselves fighting in Europe or the Pacific when many were still teenagers.

I recall going to an air show in the 1990s to see a B-24 bomber, the aircraft my Father flew in as a radio operator with the 43rd Bomb Group in the Pacific during World War II. I was permitted to enter the plane and walk to the middle section of the fuselage that held the radio equipment my Father would have operated. The aircraft was just a metal shell, a long, narrow can with no finished interior. I tried to imagine what it might have been like for a 22-year-old like my Father, who came from a small rural town 10,000 miles away, to serve in such a plane for three years, flying nighttime bombing missions over the Pacific with enemy guns trying to shoot the aircraft down. He never talked about the War and never complained about his ordeal. Like most of the Corinth men who served in World War II, he did what he had to do.

Our parents wanted the best for us, yet many sought to recreate the world they had known as kids. But that world was long gone. We lived in the Nuclear Age, the threat of destruction increasing dramatically after 1949 when the Soviet Union detonated its first atomic bomb. We had also entered the age of television, which, even by the 1960s, had become a cultural wasteland. Literature, music, and art were all experiencing a radical change in the 1950s, much of it influenced by Modernism, the Cold War, and the Bomb. And those cultural changes only intensified in the 1960s.

Those of us who came of age in that decade increasingly found that our parents' values and aspirations were at odds with our own, making us susceptible to influences outside our community, particularly irreverent ones. And those influences were all around us. The world beyond Corinth inevitably seeped in, regardless of how much our parents and other adults tried to shield us from its influences. While Corinth teenagers were prevented from careening out of control by numerous community guardrails, some nonetheless did.

Many forces were in play in the 1960s to shape a teenager's emerging worldview, even in Corinth. Radio, TV, and the popular magazines on display at the Corinth Newsroom on Main Street, all easily accessible in the 1960s, contained messages that encouraged us to question authority and to doubt the legitimacy of the way things were. Rock music represented the primary conduit. All a kid needed was a small transistor radio to hear the often-coded messages embedded in many songs' lyrics.

It was the arrival of the Beatles that tore a gaping hole in normative youth culture in 1962. I recall a day in the 6th grade when two female classmates, cousins, came running up to me in the hallway, wild with excitement, pleading that I tell them who I thought was the cutest Beatle, John or Paul? While some of the girls in our class became hysterical over the Beatles, a few of the boys emulated them, learning to play the guitar and even starting a rock band.

Many boys who wanted to look like the Beatles started to grow out their hair so that they, too, had bangs. Hair was increasingly considered a symbol of rebellion in the 1960s, particularly for boys. The longer it was, the further outside normative culture you would appear. Corinth's high school yearbooks from the 1960s suggest that teenage boys in Corinth were not yet engaged in cultural rebellion, at least not outwardly. Judging solely by appearance, especially hairstyles, there are several boys from my Class of 1969 whose senior portraits could have put them comfortably in a 1950s yearbook.

Each generation reacts and responds to the growing pains of adolescence, often challenging the status quo that parents and teachers represent. Youth is, to some degree, irreverent by nature. Yet those of us born in the decade after World War II came of age during a time when powerfully disruptive forces were assailing American society and culture. Most of us were too young in the 1950s to understand the impacts of the hardening Cold War and its future implications, but we found the dour mood of the adults around us palpable.

In the 1960s, Civil Rights protests, urban violence, and the growing anti-war movement increased the sense that our parents' world was coming apart. Somehow, we learned how to cope with our angst despite the tragic loss of JFK, his brother Robert, and Martin Luther King Jr., each of whom had come to represent hope for a better future. Some of us were guided forward and inspired by other figures, characters whom many emulated. We had heroes, but not the ones our parents wanted for us.

The organization of the Corinth School District contributed to the challenges of adolescence. There was no middle school in Corinth in the 1960s, so 7th graders went to school in the same building as 12th graders, six grades altogether. People I met later in life were often astounded whenever I explained this fact. As 7th and 8th graders, being around so many big, older kids was uncomfortable, but we thought this was how all schools were organized. How could we know otherwise? It was a retrograde system, for it exposed 7th graders, many of whom were still twelve years old when they began school in the fall, to the adult behavior of seniors at least five years older. Some seniors who had been held back a year or two were 19 or 20. And there were plenty of those kids.

Middle schools were common in the United States in the 1960s, although few small upstate New York communities had one. Corinth's conservative fiscal practices would have made constructing a middle school problematic even though International Paper was footing about 60% of the local tax bill. The School District had already spent much of its political capital building a new elementary school in 1956, so constructing a middle school never even entered the civic conversation in the 1960s. It would be another 30 years, in 1998 to be exact, before Corinth offered its children a real middle school.

Corinth provided an educational system that placed kids who were still children in the same environment as adult teenagers. The setting could be particularly difficult for girls. Upperclassmen generally disregarded the 7th graders among them, but not the more physically mature girls who became objects of male attention. So, it was not unusual for a teenage girl to get pregnant at age 13 or 14 while attending Corinth High School. It was thought that three girls in my class who disappeared from our 7th-grade homerooms left school after becoming pregnant. At the time, we didn't know what happened to them. No one told us, and no one asked. Girls whose pregnancy resulted from sex with a steady boyfriend, a casual sexual encounter with a high school boy, or an incestuous Uncle Larry often gave up their newborns for adoption. It was possible to obtain an abortion in the days before the Roe v. Wade decision, yet getting one in the 1960s was both illegal and medically problematic.

Getting pregnant as an unmarried teenage girl was not considered a form of adolescent rebellion, but the sex that preceded it indeed was. The birth control pill became available in 1960, but it was difficult for a teenage girl to obtain a prescription without parental permission. As a result, high school dating couples who were expecting a child and did not seek an illegal abortion or opt for adoption got married and kept their baby. Corinth families whose parental marriages began this way were well-known. Many girls of my generation, including several in my class, came to maturity before they could benefit either from birth control or the Roe v. Wade decision, changes in the broader social order that made it easier for girls who grew up just ten years later.

Boys in the 1960s did not have to face as severe consequences for a failure of self-restraint as did girls. Some Corinth boys escaped responsibility for their complicity when their child was given up for adoption. Still, there were Corinth boys known to have married their girlfriends while still in school due to pregnancy. Of course, boys could get ahead of a potential problem by using a condom. While our community's three pharmacies in the 1960s might have stocked them, boys generally purchased condoms from dispensers in men's bathrooms at restaurants, bars, and gas stations.

Most of the boys in my class, like me, were quite naïve about sex in the 7th grade. My first exposure to the subject was indirect, from a 6th-grade classmate the previous year. Rusty had been held back two years, so he was a teenager in elementary school. Several boys were on a bathroom break one day when, without provocation, Rusty opened up his wallet to show us the condom he kept inside. The fact that this 6th grader carried a wallet suggested he was far more worldly than the rest of us. I had no idea what Rusty's condom was or what it was for, but he sure thought it was cool to have one. Nor did I understand why Rusty got so excited when he held the condom up and started bragging about being with some girl.

The other thing that set Rusty apart was the tattoo on his inner forearm that spelled out "RUSTY." When I asked where he got it, he said he did it himself. What? I was still reluctant to pull off a band-aid, and Rusty had given himself a tattoo! The only guys I had seen in Corinth with tattoos before then were veterans of the U.S. Navy, like my Uncle Charlie, who had tattoos of a woman on each forearm, one a mermaid and the other dressed in sailor garb. Rusty's tattoo was simple, yet it made him seem more grown up than the rest of us.

But then again, Rusty was way ahead of us in other ways. He was 14 when we finished the 6th grade in the Spring of 1963. Two years later, he quit school and soon joined the U.S. Marines. In 1966, when his former 6th-grade classmates had just entered the 10th grade, Rusty served with the 3rd tank battalion in Vietnam. He was there until 1968, rising to the rank of sergeant. Rusty finished his tour of duty in Vietnam before his former classmates even graduated from high school.

I began to understand why Rusty had become so excited when he talked about girls when I entered the 7th grade the following year. The junior and senior girls I saw in the hallways daily were strikingly different from those in our 7th-grade class. Older girls, indeed, were physically more mature. I recall going early to my first class after lunch as a 7th grader to sit on the hallway floor next to my classroom door. There, I would watch a senior girl go to her nearby locker. I was too naive to understand why I did what I did, but I just knew I had to get to my class early to see her.

The Class of 1969 and several classes ahead and behind us at Corinth High School were shaped by many social and cultural forces, most beyond our control. The traditional divide between adults and teenagers was widened further by the seismic events of the 1960s. Some of us felt more comfortable in the world our parents made, while others sought inspiration elsewhere to assuage our sense of detachment from that world we lived in.

II

— · —

What Me Worry

Kids who grew up in Corinth in the 1950s and 1960s who found the adult world in which they lived unsettling could find solace in the company of several imaginary characters. Many of them, appearing in popular cartoons, embodied the mythological trickster who uses his intellect to play tricks on others to get what he wants in ways that suggest an indifference to societal norms. Cartoon characters who embodied the trickster, viewable when we were young, were highly influential with many post-World War II kids.

Foremost was the Warner Brothers' cartoon character Bugs Bunny. Although Bugs originated in the 1930s, his Warner Brothers creators gave him his carefree, snarky personality much later. He was pitted against various antagonists. Bugs almost always won by using his intellect, while his Brooklyn accent was used to deliver cutting insults. Bugs Bunny was shrewd and irreverent, always outsmarting his adversaries in a typical trickster fashion. Cartoons featuring him were often shown to Corinth kids at the Corinth's Starr Theatre before the main attraction. *The Bugs Bunny Show* eventually became a staple on ABC-TV in 1960, bringing his cartoons into our living rooms every Saturday morning.

Wile E. Coyote was another cartoon character from our youth who used his intelligence to try to outwit the Road Runner, whom he was always in pursuit. The coyote, a mythological figure familiar to America's indigenous peoples, was also a trickster who tested the bounds of the social order. While he never captured the Road Runner, Wile E. Coyote was relentless, using over 260 traps in 40 separate cartoons to try to catch him. He was also indestructible, surviving hundreds of incidents that would have been fatal to any other living creature.

A less obvious but determined trickster on television every day beginning in 1955 was Mr. Bunny Rabbit, a regular character who appeared on the *Captain Kangaroo* show. Mr. Bunny Rabbit was always trying to con the Captain into giving him some carrots. Bugs Bunny, Wile E. Coyote, and Mr. Bunny Rabbit were all fictional characters based on the mythological trickster whose social impertinence was a formative influence on young kids like me who were watching at home.

An influential cartoon series during the years when we were most impressionable was *The Rocky and Bullwinkle Show*, which ran on TV from 1959 to 1964. Set in the improbable location of Frostbite Falls, Minnesota, Rocky, a flying squirrel, was often sarcastic and delivered the show's social satire. Bullwinkle, a moose, was rather dim-witted, yet he offered the cartoon's wry humor. The pair were always trying to escape the clutches of their criminal, scheming adversaries, Boris Badenov and Natasha Fatale, who hailed from the country of Pottsylvania.

The show's Cold War humor presented through the interaction of these four characters was subversive material for its time. Much of the show's irreverent nature, created for adult viewers by *Rocky and Bullwinkle's* jaded Eisenhower-era cartoonists, got through to kids like me. A similarly humorous vision of atomic warfare was inherent in Stanley Kubrick's 1963 film, *Dr. Strangelove, or How I Learned to Stop Working and Love the*

Bomb, often referred to as a black comedy. Watching *Rocky and Bullwinkle* exposed us to the idea that America's anti-communist hysteria was both exaggerated and comedic.

Any consideration of the fictional characters that might have served as role models for irreverent youth in the 1960s must include Eddie Haskell. Played by Ken Osmond on the TV show "Leave it to Beaver" from 1957-1963, Eddie Haskell was the duplicitous friend of Beaver's older brother Wally. Eddie sucked up to adults when they were present, but behind their backs, he would make jokes at their expense. The side of himself that he presented to Wally's parents represented the perfect teenager. Yet, the compliments he paid to Mrs. Cleaver, Wally, and Beaver's mother were so exaggerated that the hyperbole served as a form of social commentary on how far out of touch parents were with teenagers.

Mrs. Cleaver seemed to know that Eddie was being deceitful. That she never revealed her awareness was a subtle affirmation of female insight as her husband, Ward, remained clueless. While Eddie is often described as being a sneak by saying one thing and then doing the opposite, his antics showed kids how to get away with something behind a parent's back. Adults viewing "Leave it to Beaver" saw Eddie making benign cracks about Wally's parents. Yet, kids viewing the show at home could translate his actions into behaviors that could be more threatening, like sneaking out of the house after Mom and Dad went to bed, smoking cigarettes in the basement, or sharing a bottle of Ripple with some friends. By any measure, Eddie Haskell represented one of the many anti-authority characters in our 1960s world.

MAD magazine's iconic mascot, Alfred E. Newman, with the slogan "What Me Worry" on every cover, was the most critical force in shaping my thinking as a teenager. First published in 1952, the monthly relentlessly critiqued America's dominant culture, using political satire to undermine many of the nation's Cold War assumptions. Nothing in American life was off limits to *MAD*. Advertising campaigns, the American family, big business, Democrats, Republicans, and hippies were all in the magazine crosshairs. Tom Hayden, a leading figure in the Anti-War movement of the 1960s and co-author of the 1962 *Port Huron Statement*, a document that set an ideological agenda of the New Left in the post-World War II years, once said that "My own radical journey began with MAD magazine." I recall many Sunday afternoons spent with my classmate Steve Lent, hanging out in his Beech Street basement devouring *MAD* magazines. Spy vs. Spy, the cartoon that spoofed the Cold War, had been my favorite regular feature.

Some consider the Smother's Brother Comedy Hour, which aired on CBS TV from 1967 to 1969, to represent the high-water mark of social and political satire in the 1960s. Yet, network executives repeatedly censored the show out of fear advertisers would desert it. At the same time, the show was opposed by conservative affiliate stations in southern states who disliked the Smother Brothers' ridicule of the nation's dominant culture. *MAD*, which did not have advertisers to contend with, was the far more threatening counter-cultural force despite having a smaller audience. The cumulative effect of my encounters with these fictional characters and the impudent Zeitgeist of the 1960s fostered a perceptible irreverence in me and some of the kids I knew.

The derisive disposition shared by some members of the Class of 1969 became evident in the 7th grade, foreshadowing how some would behave in high school. It was the first warm day in the Spring of 1964. Not long after the homeroom bell rang, the principal's voice came over the P.A. system, sternly instructing homeroom teachers to send to his office every boy who had come to school not wearing socks. That's right; boys had come to school with shoes but no socks!

I was the kid who delivered my homeroom's daily attendance report to the nurse's office, so I got to see who got caught up in the no-socks dragnet when I walked by the main office. When I got to the lobby, the principal had ten boys lined up military-style, their toes against a line on the floor. He was admonishing them for coming to school dressed as they did. When I dropped off the attendance report further down the hallway and returned to go past the lobby again, the boys were leaving the school through the front door, having been sent home to change.

Seven of the ten sockless boys were in the 7th grade with me. Most were my friends. While a few boys coming to school without socks was terrible enough, seven from the same class must have appeared to our principal as evidence of a plot to undermine school authority. The kids who became casualties of "sockgate" that spring were left with a permanent stain on their school record.

Other events distinguished members of the Class of 1969 early on. The following year, in the 8th grade, three boys in my class "broke into" the school by entering one evening through a library window one had unlocked during the school day. The entry had no real purpose, only to prove they could do it. It was pretty simple: being in the building when you weren't supposed to was pure defiance of school authority. After entering the building and wandering around, the three were caught as they left it. They might have escaped, but one of the boys was compelled to return to the school when a custodian yelled his name after recognizing him.

The kids didn't do any damage, but the three were sent to detention. Their punishment included sitting in a classroom for an hour after school and being required to enter every room after everyone had gone home to ensure all of the school's windows were closed and locked. They were supposed to remain in detention for the rest of the semester, but our school's principal ended their punishment after a few weeks, placing them on "parole." This event added to the growing legacy of the Class of 1969, contributing to the low regard held for us by many teachers.

I don't know if my female classmates watched the same cartoons I did or if they read *MAD* magazine, but several were as irreverent as some of the boys. They could be sarcastic and satirical, bitingly so. Most seemed to redirect any hormonal drive they possessed into social relations and school work. With only one notable exception of coupling, the group I hung out with consisted strictly of platonic friendships. The girls I knew best, members of the Classes of 1969 and 1970, were children of pre-feminist America. Their social behavior, and like the career choices open to them at the time, was far more circumscribed than it was for boys. The recent TV series, "Good Girls Revolt," set in a fictional national magazine in 1969, offers a view of the patriarchial world Corinth girls faced when they graduated from Corinth High. Their career options were limited to teaching, nursing, and secretarial work. Still, a few broke through the gender barriers to become successful in other fields despite the limitations imposed by their time.

12

— • —

Everyday People

The Hudson River Mill had a leveling influence on the Corinth community. The Mill was a force that kept Corinthians within a defined social space; their outward appearances and behaviors were self-managed within a narrow range of community acceptance. Class differences were barely perceptible. The Mill's hourly paid paper workers and salaried professionals played in the same golf and bowling leagues and attended the annual EMBA sports banquet together. The Hudson River Mill Quarter Century Club included all retired employees and men with 25 years of service. Paper workers often fraternized with salaried personnel, notably if the latter had risen from an hourly paid employee to a salaried foreman or superintendent. Hourly paid paper workers were known to socialize with Corinth professionals. The parents of one good friend whose father worked on the paper machines often dined with the parents of one of my classmates whose father was a dentist. In Corinth, one's job or class did not necessarily serve as a deterrent to socialization.

There were exceptions, of course. One notable difference was that only the Mill's hourly-paid paper workers belonged to a union. At the time, most were members of either the International Brotherhood of Pulp, Sulphite, and Paper Mill Workers or the United Papermakers and Paperworkers. The latter union's contract with IP provided skilled machine tenders and back tenders with yearly incomes higher than many of the Mill's salaried workers. Some salaried professionals, mostly its engineers and draftsmen, belonged to the Hudson River Mill Technical Association. The *EMBA News* often published photographs of the group enjoying a banquet dinner at a restaurant in the area. While the Mill's hourly paid and salaried employees participated in the same bowling leagues at the EMBA's Community Building, they belonged to teams determined by where they worked: Upper Office, Repairs, Paper Machines, etc. The organization of the EMBA sports team by workplace was one of the few ways Corinth men were segregated by occupation.

An exception to the mingling of paper workers and the Mill's salaried employees was evident in outdoor recreation. The annual sports banquet held at the Community Building beginning in 1950 recognized the winning teams in EMBA sports like basketball, softball, and bowling organized by the workplace. The EMBA gave trophies to local fishermen in several categories, yet the winners were invariably hourly-paid paper workers or their sons. This is not to say the Mill's salaried employees did not fish, but paper workers who entered their catches in the annual contest nearly always won. The children of salaried employees, however, did go home with trophies. I was given on in 1962 for catching a 3-pound largemouth bass at Hunt Lake the year before, at age 10. My Father worked then as a salaried timekeeper.

Men who worked together also hunted together. George Holland, editor of the monthly *EMBA News* from 1942-1975, regularly published photographs of the deer killed and fish caught by IP employees. Before the *EMBA News* era, a local paper noted in 1934 that several men who worked in the Repairs Department ventured together into Siamese Ponds near North Creek and brought back eight deer, one bear, and a red fox as trophies. More than 1500 Corinthians reportedly viewed the kill when it was displayed at the George Johnson home on Pine Street. Paper workers appear to have been more enthusiastic and successful hunters in an earlier era. Over 50 deer were harvested by Corinth hunters during the 1933 season, a record year. Many of the hunters were paper workers. However, there is little evidence of equivalent hunts in the post-World War II years.

Some of the Mill's salaried managers still aspired to the trappings of a middle-class lifestyle. One example is when several took advantage of the opportunity given to them by IP in the early 1960s to purchase surplus property that the Company owned around Hunt Lake. This was land initially owned by Hudson River Pulp and Paper in the 19th century and used as a source of pulp wood. IP assumed ownership when it purchased the Hudson River Pulp and Paper in 1898. Several of the Company's salaried employees, including my Father's boss, Ken Kendall, built summer camps on Hunt Lake on the lots they purchased. The only hourly-paid paper workers I knew who had a camp on Hunt, Jenny, or Efner Lakes in the 1960s were those men whose spouses inherited lake property.

While the Hudson River Mill may have homogenized its employees into a singular workforce, Corinth was hardly a classless society. Some families had significant means, and some lived in poverty. Corinth's profession-al and commercial class - its lawyers, doctors, dentists, pharmacists, and business owners - existed in rarified community space outside the Hudson River Mill. They were the citizens who comprised the 100-plus members of the Corinth Rotary Club and, with some exceptions, usually held village and town elected offices. The men among them were not often part of the social and sporting networks that radiated out from the Mill and the EMBA. Operating outside the Mill's orbit allowed Corinth's professional class to enjoy some latitude in affirming their class status if they chose. More so than the men who worked for IP, the community's professionals could aspire to and express a middle-class lifestyle, although doing so had limitations. I was reminded in 2015 of how humble Corinth business owners used to be when I observed a Corinth business owner park his $70,000 BMW just outside the entry to his store. Such a purposeful display of materiality was less likely to be seen when Corinth was considered a mill town.

Class status was often expressed in Corinth in subtle ways. I had a close friend whose father was a medical professional. His parents always traveled out of town for dinner, to either Greenwich or Saratoga Springs restaurants, but never in town. I became a bit envious whenever I heard him talk about going to one of those places, for my parents and I never went out to eat, except for occasional take-out at the New Way Lunch in Glens Falls. My Mother would have thought dining out was a waste of money since she could cook dinner at home for much less.

The family of a classmate whose father operated a local grocery also owned a camp on Long Lake. Whenever he told me he was going there with his family, I tried to imagine what it was like to have a second home, especially one deep in the Adirondacks. I had spent a few afternoons at an old Hunt Lake Camp owned by a friend of my Father, so I had a sense of what the Long Lake summer home might have been like. Another friend jetted to Brazil in the summer of 1968 to participate in an international exchange program. Other than his trip to South America, I cannot recall when a kid I knew in Corinth in the 1960s traveled by airplane anywhere. There was the occasional trip to Florida by car or the summer weekend at Old Orchard Beach in Maine, but as far I as knew, that was as exotic as it got. While some kids got to do things and go places I never did, I didn't think they were more prosperous than we were or that my family was inferior to theirs.

My parents were not socially adventurous. We never went out to restaurants and rarely went anywhere that required an overnight stay. They were children of immigrant, working-class parents for whom eating out and traveling were considered a luxury. I knew of other kids in town whose parents were the same way. While my parents often took off the same weeks for their summer vacations, as a family of three, the most we ever did was go on day trips. Our most frequent summer destination was Sherman's Amusement Park at Caroga Lake, located west of the Sacandaga Reservoir, about an hour-and-a-half drive from Corinth. Now closed, Sherman's had been around since the early 1920s, so my Father had probably gone there as a kid. The exception to our summer vacation activity was the few times we made three-day trips to Canada to visit my Mother's sister, Edith, and her family. Her husband, John, managed a chemical company in St. Jean, Quebec. We stayed at their house rather than a motel. I didn't consider our trips to Canada as a vacation since all we did was sit around the house and yard all day. Besides, my Uncle John didn't appear to like his wife's family all that much, so our visits often became uncomfortable when he had been drinking.

The furthest afield I ever traveled as a kid was the 1964 New York World's Fair. The Cluett-Peabody shirt factory, where my Mother's sister, Rose, had worked for many years, sponsored a bus trip to the Fair for its employees and guests. So, my Aunt Rose invited my Mother and me to go along. I was excited about going, for my Father told me he went to the 1939 Worlds Fair in New York, where he had seen television for the first time. Our trip to the 1964 Fair was a single-day trip that left very early in the morning. I recall we went to the General Electric and General Motors buildings and had to wait in long, long lines for two hours before entering. There seemed to be more people waiting in those lines than were in the entire town of Corinth. Since my Mother's family were devout Catholics, we made a requisite pilgrimage to the Vatican pavilion to see Michelangelo's *Pieta*. The Fair's many international pavilions offered restaurants that showcased national dishes. One of them was a recreated 18th-century village where I ate a Belgian waffle for the first time. I was overwhelmed by the enormity of the fair, the crowds, and the excitement. I was so excited by what I had seen and done that day I desperately wanted to return in 1965 during the Fair's final years. But no bus trips were offered from Corinth, so I never saw the World's Fair again.

Reliable signifiers of economic status - large homes and luxury automobiles – were uncommon in Corinth. An interesting historical instance of a local citizen using an expensive car to signify his wealth was Theodore Elixman, who purchased a seven-passenger 1915 Pierce Arrow. If the vehicle was insufficient to show how well-off he was, Elixman hired a chauffeur, George Bird, to drive him around town. But in the 1960s, the Cadillac was the most recognized and coveted automobile in working-class Corinth. One was owned by a well-known and respected citizen, the son of a local merchant who immigrated to the United States in 1889 and operated a successful dry goods business in town. He owned a black, 4-door Cadillac Coupe de Ville that was often parked on the street in front of his home. The father of one of my best friends, who operated a local market, also drove a Cadillac, as did the owner of the local lumber yard. I think that was about it: three Cadillacs, maybe four. The Cadillac was a large automobile, even by 1960s standards. Today, it would take up the length of two parking spaces.

Men who could afford Cadillacs had to go to Glens Falls to buy one, but a Corinthian could get a new car in town. In the 1960s, there were three car dealerships in Corinth: Higgin's Chevrolet, Brust's Pontiac, and Rich's Plymouth/Dodge. So, it was easy to trade in and trade up. Many mill workers like my Father bought into Alfred P. Sloan's strategy, which resulted in the creation of five automotive divisions at General Motors that manufactured distinctive models, each with unique attributes that resulted in an ascending order of desirability and cost. Chevrolet represented the entry-level vehicle, Pontiac was the second rung, Buick occupied the third, Oldsmobile the fourth, and Cadillac was the top.

After driving used Buicks and Oldsmobiles for years, my Father's first brand-new car was a 1962 Chevy Impala. He bought another new Chevy in 1964 and another in 1965, a pattern that revealed yet another way to show you were doing well: to buy a new car every year, even if it was the same make and model. This was not an uncommon practice in Corinth. One year, my Father skipped over a rung in the GM status ladder by getting a red 1966 Oldsmobile Jetstar 88, the car I learned to drive with. Then, he slid down a GM level to a Pontiac when he purchased a gold 1968 Catalina four-door. My Father bought his cars from Corinth dealers, except for the Olds. While he ignored Sloan's expectation that car buyers would move up the status hierarchy, he remained a loyal GM man for many years.

It is worth mentioning that my father was not the least pretentious. His car purchases were made not as the result of a status calculation but were always spontaneous. One day after I came home from school, I found a brand new two-door Chevy Impala parked in our driveway. It wasn't an "SS" model with the 396 cubic inch engine; it was just a sporty coupe. My father had taken a vacation day and was sitting on the back porch drinking when he decided to go out and buy a new car. A two-door Impala would have been impractical for us and unappreciated by my Mother. I looked at the car and immediately persuaded him to return it so that I would not have to witness an argument when she got home from work. I was probably 15 at the time. It took some doing, but I finally convinced him to return the car to Higgins's Chevrolet on Pine Street, just across the street from the Mill entrance. My father had been a good customer there, and John

Higgins was a good guy, so returning the new car did not pose a problem. My Mother entered the front door as we pulled into the driveway with our old car. I don't know if she ever learned about the new Chevy we owned for a few hours that day.

One paper worker appeared to use his automobile to signify his economic well-being and eligibility as a bachelor. He was in his mid-30s in the late 1960s and had a well-paying paper mill job. He was somewhat stocky with black curly hair. He was notable in town because he drove a big Buick, a dark green Electra 225 coupe. The Electra, while not a Cadillac, was considered a luxurious car. The interior was well-appointed and powered by a V-8 engine with 340 horsepower. He would drive around town, slightly crouched in his seat, the forefingers of his left hand wrapped around the chrome edge of the side window vent common to cars at the time. With his right hand on the steering wheel, he would appear to pull against the window edge with his left hand and lean into the door as he made turns, turning the wheel with the palm of his right hand as though he was providing leverage necessary to move the two tons of steel beneath him. You would usually see him driving around town wearing a black polo shirt. When I returned to Corinth to visit my parents some years later, I would occasionally see him still driving around town in a big Buick.

While the car a man drove could reflect his economic status, real or imagined, his home could be yet another signifier. But in Corinth, even the well-to-do had modest homes, nothing that screamed "estate." When I graduated in 1969, the Hudson River Mill manager's home at the corner of 3rd Street and Palmer Avenue may have been the community's grandest. By then, the Warren Curtis homestead, an eclectic Victorian house on Palmer Avenue that was the Curtis family's summer home, was on the verge of demolition. The home had been gifted to the Town of Corinth in the

1930s and served as the community hospital for thirty years. It was replaced by the new 50-bed Corinth Hospital, which opened in late 1969.

A few other homes suggested an elevated economic status, like the former Theodore Elixman home at the corner of Main Street and Palmer Avenue. It was a large, rambling house in a lovely setting. It was sold by a local family to Shell Oil in 1965, who promptly demolished the home and built a modern, three-bay service station. There were a few other large homes in town with distinguishing features: the Steadman residence – previously the Shorey home – at the corner of 2nd Street and Palmer Avenue; the former Warren Curtis winter home at the intersection of Main and Mechanic, designed by Saratoga's acclaimed architect, R. Newton Breeze; and a few houses on Palmer Avenue which bore distinctive late Victorian architectural details. But for the most part, Corinth was a community without lavish homes.

The lack of an elite class in Corinth may explain the preponderance of unremarkable homes in the community. Sure, there were doctors, lawyers, and business owners who could afford to build charming dwellings, but no one was so rich that they were compelled to spend their money on a house as a sign of their class status or financial success. Besides, a professional in Corinth had mostly paper workers as customers and clients. Their working-class incomes limited the fees they could be charged. Warren Curtis, the superintendent of the Hudson River Pulp and Paper Company and owner of Curtis Manufacturing, who built two houses in the village, may have been the notable exception. The fact is that most of the wealth that was created in Corinth left the community to build great homes in other towns. HRPP stock was owned by only a handful of people before 1898, and IP's profits were widely disbursed to its stockholders in the 20th century.

None of the men, for instance, who owned HRPP ever resided in Corinth. Albrecht Pagenstecher, the man most associated with the company, used the wealth he generated from Corinth's pulp and paper mill to build an opulent lifestyle elsewhere, first in New York City and then at Cornwall-on-Hudson where in 1905, he and his wife Helene built a 20-room estate called "Upyonda." Albrecht aspired to social status that could not be found in a place like Corinth. His wife and children were listed in New York City's Social Register, and their granddaughter, Dorothy, a New York Junior League member, was a debutante for the 1932 season. The Pagenstechers returned a small portion of their real estate to Corinth in 1919 when the family gifted to the Village the park known for generations as The Cedars, requiring that it be renamed "Pagenstecher Park." In 1937, a second Pagenstecher Park was created in Cornwall, New York, from a gift of land by Albrecht's daughter, Bertha, that had been taken from her parent's estate. In both instances, the gifts to the communities were intended to establish a Pagenstecher legacy.

Many towns in New England and the Northeast, similar in size to Corinth, also once had thriving industries. In some, grand 19th-century homes and commercial buildings made of brick, a far more expensive building material than wood, were built. They were constructed by mill owners who resided in the community and invested in the town where their business was located. Their company's profits remained in the town. Corinth does not look like any of these places because the bulk of the profits generated from Corinth's pulp and paper industry were used to build grand homes in Germany, Herkimer, New York City, Cornwall-on-Hudson, and elsewhere.

The leveling effect of the Hudson River Mill evident within the Corinth community extended to Corinth High School. Sure, there were a few kids who were a bit pretentious, who dressed or acted in a superior way. The more imperious were usually the sons and daughters of college-educated fathers or mothers who had come to Corinth from elsewhere to take a job at the paper mill as an accountant, a manager, or engineer. One kid I knew seemed to learn his subtle arrogance from his parents and older siblings. His father, a World War II officer, habitually wore his dress uniform during Corinth's annual Memorial Day parades. The practice distinguished him from other paper mill workers who were drafted into the military or served as enlisted men and for whom sergeant was most often the highest rank attained. This is one of a few instances when an IP professional could show they were not a paper worker. Yet the effort likely did little to assuage the fact they were building their career and raising their family in a backwater, southern Adirondack mill town. One could rise only so high in such a place.

13

HARD DAY'S NIGHT

M ost kids who came of age in Corinth during the 1960s had parents who were teenagers during the Great Depression, an era when economic times were challenging. Corinth fared better than many small upstate communities since the Hudson River Mill operated three or four days a week. Many parents, however, quit high school before graduating to get a job to help support their families. Our parents' experience as adolescents and young adults during the Depression profoundly impacted their beliefs about work, ideas often conveyed to us, their children.

My Mother, Caroline, was a perfect example. She quit school in the 8th grade to get a job as a needle worker at the Clark Brothers glove factory in Glens Falls. Her school's principal protested, coming to the family's home one day to urge her parents that Caroline remain in school. My mother often told me she dropped out of school because she was tired of wearing her older sisters' hand-me-down clothes. Undeterred by the principal's plea, my Mother took a full-time factory job when she was 14.

Caroline came from a hard-working Italian family, so she and her siblings regarded work as a religion. She worked full-time until she was 65, except for the two years she took off after I was born. My Mother expected me to be industrious, although she never pushed me to find a job as a teenager. Instead, like other kids my age, I got work because I wanted money to spend. There was always a need for cash for the movies, 45s, shakes at Stewarts, or gas for the family car. A job that put money in a teenager's pocket or purse provided personal freedom and a reassuring sign of character to our parents.

I got my first real job at the end of my 9th-grade year. At the time, I didn't count my work for Ruth Lanfear as a real job since cash was never exchanged. It was the early summer of 1966 when Father Walsh hired two friends and me to paint the six-foot tall steel fence at the front of St. Mary's Cemetery on Saratoga Avenue. I cannot recall how or why we were chosen, but one of my friends, Jim, was an altar boy, so he likely had been asked by Father Walsh to paint the fence and to invite some friends to work with him. Jim, Tom, and I were hanging out together then, so I suspect Jim just asked us to join him.

At about that same time, the three of us spent an overnight at Jim's house on Gobel Avenue when his parents were out of town one weekend. We stayed up late into the night, lip-syncing and performing popular songs, even some by the Supremes, including the 1965 hit "Stop! In the Name of Love," high on nothing more than a large tub of chocolate ice cream. We stood side-by-side, singing and dancing, disregarding how silly we might have looked.

Painting the cemetery fence was tedious work, but we enjoyed it because we got to do it together. We first had to scrape the entire fence with wire brushes, removing all the old paint and rust from each of the four sides of the fence's several hundred square vertical posts and horizontal rails. Once that was done, we put large fabric mitts on our right hands and dipped them into a bucket of yellow primer, running the mitts up, down, and across the bars and rails of the fence. Not only was the painting monotonous, but it was also very messy. Yellow paint got splashed all over the grass on both sides of the fence and our clothes. We then used new mitts to apply two coats of dark green glossy paint as a finish coat. It took us three weeks to finish the job, although admittedly, we worked only a few hours each day. While we felt fortunate that Father Walsh gave us the work for which we earned $1.25 per hour, the minimum wage at the time, I suspect that we were much cheaper for him to hire us than getting an adult man or two to do the job.

After we finished the fence, Father Walsh asked me if I would like another job. So, in the summer between my freshman and sophomore years in high school, I became the caretaker of Corinth's Catholic cemetery. I have no idea why Father Walsh asked me, but it was probably because I was the biggest kid of the three of us, and he figured I could handle the work. I cut the entire Catholic cemetery every few weeks for the next two years. At first, I used a conventional power mower that I brought from home in the trunk of my father's car. Mowing the cemetery was tiresome and time-consuming because I had to maneuver the mower around all the headstones. I could not push the mower in a straight line for more than several feet before reaching another stone and taking another 45-degree turn. And then two or three more feet and another turn, and another. Turn after turn after turn.

Mowing the cemetery was all about the corners. I had to get as close to each stone as possible because I didn't have a powered trimmer, just a standard scissor-style hand tool that I borrowed from our garage at home. I always brought the trimmer to work with me but never used it. Whenever I arrived at the cemetery to mow and looked across the ten-acre site and saw several hundred headstones in the distance, the pure enormity of the task of trimming around each one quickly overwhelmed my good intentions. Father Walsh didn't seem to care that most headstones had long grass growing along their sides, for he never complained about my work nor told me to cut closer to the stones.

One day, I was mowing on the cemetery's north side. While most areas of the cemetery had healthy-looking grass and weeds, the soil where I mowed was sandy with large bare spots. As I pushed the mower across one grave, the earth beneath my feet suddenly collapsed, my right leg plunging below the ground's surface. I had fallen into a grave up to my hip! It happened so fast that I didn't have time to think. I quickly launched out of that hole, perhaps the fastest I had ever moved, gaining leverage from something hard below me. Once I extricated myself, I quickly moved away from the grave. I walked back slowly to stare at the hole for a few minutes before stepping carefully toward its edge to peer into the void where my leg had been. But all I could see was a dark space. I stepped back from the hole yet remained shaken for several minutes. The event scared the shit out of me! That was it for me that day. I recall shutting down the mower and moving it to the cemetery's main gate to wait until my Father came to pick me up. I don't think I ever mowed that grave again.

My walk-behind mower was soon replaced by a rideable Gravely tractor. The Gravely had been donated by a well-meaning parishioner, a member of the Knights of Columbus who likely sought to gain favor with Father Walsh or perhaps a reduction of time in Purgatory. The Gravely resembled a piece of farm equipment more than a conventional lawn mower. It was big, heavy, and unwieldy, with oversized tires. It was a riding mower with two sections. The front section consisted of the engine and the cutting deck with long handlebars extending back towards a separate rear section. A swivel hitch connected the two. The rear section of the Gravely consisted of a steel frame with an elevated seat fixed over two wheels. The person mowing sat on the seat and used the handlebars to steer the engine and deck section.

Using the Gravely was more like driving a car than a lawn mower. It was also more trouble than it was worth. Sure, I could quickly cut large stretches of lawn with its 30-inch deck, but wide open grass at the cemetery was limited. After using the Gravely, I still had to use the small power mower to cut in and around the headstones. I am sure Father Walsh thought he was making my work easier when he accepted the Gravely as a donation to the Church, but by doing so, he created a new problem. It had to be stored.

Once the Gravely was at the cemetery, Father Walsh realized the machine could not be left out and exposed to the elements and potential theft. The regular lawn mower was easy enough to get back and forth to the cemetery in the trunk of a car when it needed to be used, but a truck would be required to transport the Gravely. Father Walsh's solution to the problem was to purchase a storage building. So, one day, after he called my house to say that the storage building he ordered had been delivered, I rode my bike to the cemetery to check it out. When I got there, I found an oversized cardboard box about seven feet long, twenty inches wide, and maybe a foot tall. The box contained all the pieces of a metal outbuilding that had to be assembled. To be clear, I had to assemble.

The picture on the box showed that it would be a large building, about ten feet wide and eight feet deep. After letting it sink in that putting the shed together would be my responsibility, I rode my bike back to our Center Street garage to gather the tools the box's instructions said I would need. I returned and got to work. I had some experience building with my Erector Set when I was young, so using a screwdriver was nothing new. Yet it took me a few days to put the building together, with all the time required to screw the separate panels together that made up the walls, roof, and doors, using hundreds of little screws, washers, and plastic lock nuts. Although the process was aggravating, I was proud of myself for erecting the building without assistance. Father Walsh showed up just as I finished the job, pleased that the building was up and that the Gravely could be stored and locked inside.

While Father Walsh's acceptance of the mower from a parishioner made my cemetery work more difficult, he was a great employer. So was Father Meehan, who succeeded him in 1967. Whenever I gave them the number of hours I had worked, the total was never questioned, and a check was promptly written. I never received phone calls complaining the cemetery needed attention, nor was fault ever found with my work. I was given full responsibility for the cemetery's care. I liked to think my work for the Church also gave my mother some sense of solace because I had not become an altar boy. While my mother never expressed her disappointment, she also never got to see me wearing a cassock on the altar during a Sunday mass; I know that she found pleasure in the fact that at least I worked for the church.

I periodically visit Corinth's St. Mary's Cemetery today to tend to my parent's plot. Just last year, in June 2023, I returned to check on the two shrubs I planted the previous fall. They were doing great, but as I picked some weeds from around the headstone, I glanced to the rear of the cemetery and saw two concrete crosses about twenty inches tall sticking out of the weedy shrubs. When I walked over to look more closely, I discovered two more crosses nearby and the remains of the four stone columns that once graced the cemetery's two front entrances. I recalled the columns were still standing in 2022. I suspected one or more of them had been damaged or their stonework had been compromised. I was troubled by the fact the parish chose to demolish the pillars rather than repair them, and their remains were trashed and left in full view.

Seeing the discarded crosses and pillars reminded me of a visit I once made to the Corinth Rural Cemetery, where most of Corinth's Protestants are buried, including my Father's parents, who were Lutheran. One day after visiting my grandparents' grave around 2010, I drove through the rear of the cemetery to look for the graves of Class of 1969 friends Kris Boerner and Gary Mallery. At the cemetery's eastern edge, near its border with Sturdevant Creek, I observed piles of recently deposited soil through which the tops of several decorative stones protruded. I stopped my car and got out to take a closer look. I pulled the soil away from them. Each stone appeared to be about five feet long and six inches square. They had a pyramid-shaped top. The stone might have been granite, but its subtle marbling was unlike any I had ever seen. They were undoubtedly decorative stones from a family plot.

As I left the cemetery, I drove past the cinder block garage close to the railroad track, where I saw a truck parked. Two men were inside, the cemetery's caretakers, I soon learned. I asked what they knew about the stones I had seen. They told me they had grown tired of mowing and trimming around them, so they tore them out and dumped them near the creek. I saw them only because the guys were still burying them. The admission dumbfounded me. The laborers employed by the Corinth Rural Cemetery Association had removed several nicely finished stones that had been used to proudly mark the boundary of a family cemetery plot for perhaps 100 years. So much for the principle of perpetual care, I thought. I found the disrespect shown for the dead and their families to be very troubling. How could the Board of the Cemetery Association permit such a thing?

14

— · —

THE 700 POUND MIDGET

The summer I assembled the storage building at the cemetery, my friend Tom got a job at a summer camp in Maine. We both turned 16 that year. He was the only Corinth kid I knew who left town for the summer to work. We wrote to each other a few times while he was away and, in one letter, he said his father had bought a car for him. It was unclear if he bought the car for Tom as a reward for working all summer or as a "thank-you" for getting out of the house for two months. Regardless, Tom sounded pretty excited about it in his letters. 1967 was the year when most kids in my class could get our driver's license, so Tom would be the first among us to have his own car.

The car parked in his Ash Street driveway when Tom returned to Corinth was different from what he expected. His dad had gotten him a King Midget. Considered a micro-car, the Midget was initially sold as a kit but later came pre-assembled. The first model in 1946 was single-passenger, but Tom's Midget was a two-seat convertible, probably a used late 1950s version. Midgets weighed about 700 pounds, rode on eight-inch wheels, and were powered by 9-12 horsepower engines, somewhat smaller than the engine in the Gravely I used at the cemetery. The car was about eight feet long, from headlights to taillights. Some might have considered the Midget closer to a go-cart than a car.

I went to Tom's house to check out the Midget when he returned to Corinth. His dad, who was at home, showed me all the car's features. We wanted to take the Midget for a drive, although it was neither licensed nor insured. And I don't believe Tom had his driver's license then, either. Corinth police were pretty forgiving of benign juvenile transgressions in those days, so we weren't too worried about getting pulled over by Chief Doherty or Bill Mohl when Tom drove the Midget down his driveway and west onto Ash Street. I can't recall how far we drove or where we went, but I remember our return.

Heading back towards Tom's house on Ash past the school bus garage, we reached the intersection with 1st Street. There, Ash begins to slope down until it dead-ends at 4th Street, a half-mile away. Tom was going maybe 20 miles per hour as he crossed 1st, certainly too fast to make a safe 90-degree turn into his driveway just three doors down. Whether the brakes didn't work or the Midget's steering was less responsive than required, Tom could not negotiate the right-hand turn. The Midget went across the driveway's street opening, onto Tom's front lawn, and over the mailbox post planted in the front yard before rolling to the edge of the property. When the Midget finally stopped on the far side of the yard, we turned around to see the flattened mailbox behind us and Tom's father standing in the driveway, hands on his hips, shaking his head. I don't recall I ever got back into the King Midget after that day, nor do I think Tom ever registered it. But at least Tom had a Midget to drive. I had only a Gravely,

The following year, in 1968, I gave up my cemetery job. In June, I began the first of the two jobs I would have that summer. This was the summer when having my driver's license and access to a car allowed me to get a job outside of Corinth. My first job was at Gaslight Village, an amusement park in Lake George, where two friends and I were hired to work weekends before school was out for the year to help prepare the park for its summer opening. I had purchased a 1962 white Chevy Corvair that spring with $525 saved from working. ($5000 in 2024 dollars). So I drove Bob, Tom, and me the 35 miles back and forth to Lake George daily. Our initial part-time work consisted of clean-up and some painting, earning us full-time jobs when the park opened on the last weekend of June—the hours seemed ideal, with our work day beginning at 2 PM and ending at 10 PM when the park closed. Driving to Lake George and working at Gaslight felt much more grown-up than having a summer job in Corinth.

Tom and I started out running the Antique Car Ride together. We were required to wear white shirts, colorful vests, and "Gay 90s" straw hats. The cars used for the ride were made to resemble a Stanley Runabout two-seater from around 1910, although they were powered by gasoline rather than steam. We helped people get into the cars, gave them some general directions, and let them go on their one-lap trip around a fixed asphalt course bordered by heavy wooden guardrails. We had lots of fun working on the cars and even met some Lake George High School girls who periodically visited the park to enjoy the rides. One girl's parents owned the Palmer Motel on Route 9 across the road from Gaslight Village. The other girl, Russ Ann, who lived outside the village, once invited Tom and me to her home on our day off, where we drank Cokes and played pool with her and her sisters. There was no romantic interest; we thought hanging out with girls from another town was cool.

Maybe Tom and I were having too much fun operating the Antique Cars together, for soon, the park manager separated us and assigned me to another ride. I first went to the Flying Teacups, a ride intended for children. With most teacup-style rides, like those at Disney World, riders sit in large teacups that rotate individually within a large circular horizontal platform that also rotates. As the cups turn, so does the platform. The Gaslight Village version, however, had the cups attached to the ends of long metal arms connected to a motor-driven hub, like spokes on a wheel. As the wheel, arms, and cups rotated counter-clockwise, the spoke housing moved slowly, up and down, which then moved the cups up and down. A teacup, which could hold one adult and a child or three kids, was the tamest ride in the park and the most boring to run. Some nights, I could stand around for half an hour or more just waiting for a rider, especially after dark when most small children had already left the park. And no girls my age ever paid to enter Gaslight Village so that they could ride the Tea Cups. From there, I went to the Round-Up, clearly the scariest of the rides at Gaslight Village. But I had been promoted, so I thought.

The Round-Up consisted of a wheel about forty feet in diameter framed with inch-thick hollow steel. The ride was similar to a bicycle wheel lying on its side. In its resting position, the Round-Up was parallel to the ground and elevated above it by about ten feet. Riders had to climb stairs and proceed along a narrow circular walkway inside the wheel to one of two dozen vertical "seats" where they would belt themselves along the inner rim. Riders remained standing for the duration of the ride. Since the Round-Up was just a round steel frame, you could see through the wheel from my operator's platform and the ground. The spokes of the ride converged at the center of the wheel, where an axle was powered by a large motor that put the Round-Up in motion. The engine was located under the operator's platform where I stood. I would slowly start the ride when I saw everyone was buckled in.

The wheel holding the riders would initially rotate clockwise, increasing speed gradually as I moved the throttle. After the wheel revolved at nearly full speed, I would pull a separate lever to raise the center arm of the wheel so that the passengers were soon spinning at about a 30-degree angle to the ground. Most people laughed or screamed at this point, while a few turned white. On one occasion, a woman vomited at the Round-Up's highest point, her puke projecting out 10-15 feet towards the center of the wheel before centrifugal force pulled it back towards her and every other person who rotated through the vomit field. It took me several minutes to return the wheel to the horizontal position and slow it down. As the ride came to a stop, just about every rider had vomit on them when they walked down the stairway to the ground. Crouching down behind my console when I saw the rider first get sick, I was the only one who escaped unscathed.

While I managed the Round-Up quite well, I always wondered if it was legal in New York State for a minor, someone who had just turned 17, to operate it. I ran the Round-Up for several weeks until early August. Having grown weary of the commute and the nature of my work, I left Gaslight Village for a job in downtown Corinth.

15

THOSE WERE THE DAYS

Many people living in Corinth today would be hard-pressed to imagine the community as it was in the 1960s. The decade arguably represents Corinth's "golden age." When my friends and I were teenagers, Corinth was an economically prosperous southern Adirondack community. Several photographs and postcards from the era reveal how vibrant it was. While alcohol flowed freely in its eight bars, drug use was not evident, people seldom locked their doors, and social media's impact on the community was decades in the future. Corinth was a conservative town by any measure. Yet, the pulp and paper industry, especially International Paper, had been good for the community, giving it an identity and economic stability while contributing to its social ordering. Only after the closure of the Mill in 2002 did the influence IP had on Corinth become apparent.

In the mid-1960s, Corinth's principal employers – the International Paper Company and the Cluett-Peabody Shirt Company – employed over 1600 people. Their combined earnings contributed to a community economy that approached $100,000,000 (in 2024 dollars) and supported two distinct business districts. The largest district - located adjacent to the Hudson River where the original settlement of Jessup's Landing began in the 1770s - radiated from the intersection of Main and Maple Streets. The majority of the community's stores and restaurants were located there. The streetscape of downtown Corinth was still largely intact at the time of the Town's 1968 sesquicentennial, marred only by the parking lots that had been constructed at the corners of Main and Mallery Streets and Main and River Street, spaces left vacant by a fire in one case and building demolition in the other.

The Grand Union created a new supermarket in 1960 at the corner of Main and Mallery Streets, on the lot where Brady's Hotel once stood. Stewart's Ice Cream built a new store across from the Grand Union at the corner of Main and River Streets in 1968. Rather than build their new stores on the sidewalk where the prior buildings had been situated and place parking behind them, the Grand Union and Stewarts disrupted the village's streetscape by placing the stores at the rear of the lots and parking spaces between the buildings and the street. Of course, nothing prevented them from doing this because no zoning ordinances were in place to give civic leaders a say in planning or construction. The placement of Grand Union and Stewart's stores, which represented the initial substantive breaks in Corinth's once unified streetscape, served as a harbinger of things to come.

The other business district in Corinth was located in the Palmer section of the community, along Palmer Avenue between 4th and Heath Streets, near the Hudson River Mill. There were two barber shops, two bars, a restaurant, a pharmacy, a post office, dry cleaners, a florist shop, two gas stations, an elementary school, and a Chevrolet dealership. Angel's Store on Palmer Avenue near 3rd Street and Taylor's Grocery on Lower Pine Street were also part of the area's business district. Corinth Hospital was located there, as was the Community Building, with its bowling alley and public commissary, which were also part of Palmer's commerce. Businesses in Palmer comprised a notable portion of Corinth's 117 Rotary Club members in the mid-1960s.

Civic leaders took pride in the mid-decade recognition given to the community by local, regional, and national newspapers. The Hudson River Mill's No. 11 paper machine was even pictured on the front page of the *New York Times* in 1965. That same year, a full-page article in the local *Saratogian,* whose headline asserted that Corinth "Looks to the Future with Confidence," described the sources of the community's prosperity and ticked off Corinth's many infrastructure and educational achievements. The *Saratogian* described Corinth's municipal and business leaders as "aggressive" in their desire to continue to shape Corinth into an even more progressive community. Corinth's status in the region and the lifestyle its citizens enjoyed in those years was primarily a result of the success of the Hudson River Mill and, to a lesser degree, the Cluett-Peabody shirt factory.

Corinth's political leadership could afford to engage in progressive community thinking in the 1960s, given that IP paid a large proportion of local taxes, something like 60 percent. The Company also contributed financially to the community through IP Foundation grants to the Corinth School District, the construction and operation of Brookhaven Golf Course, maintenance of the Community Building, care given to the EMBA Field, and the operation of the adjacent winter skating rink. The Community Building, in particular, hosted numerous social events attended by adults and children alike. Even though IP did not own the houses where its employees lived, Corinth could indeed have been considered a company town. Yet civic boosters in the 1960s wanted even more from IP.

Manufacturing coated papers in 1940 marked the beginning of the Hudson River Mill's most prosperous era. The growing public demand for magazines that was accelerated during World War II and the desire of companies to buy magazine pages that could print advertisements for their products in color required the development and manufacture of high-quality coated papers. When coated paper production began at the Hudson River Mill, the paper had to be transferred from a paper machine to a Bracewell coater that treated and finished it, referred to as off-machine coating. The process coated just one side of paper used primarily for labels. By 1947, the mill had begun the expensive process of paper machine conversion by installing on-machine coating technology, which added a coating to both sides of the sheet that was necessary for the paper used by magazines. Since coated paper needed to be much whiter than newsprint or specialty papers the mill had produced previously, a bleach plant had to be constructed as a necessary addition to the paper manufacturing process. When the Glens Falls *Post-Star* described the Hudson River Mill as "the largest mill of its type in the world" at the time of International Paper's Company's 50th anniversary in 1948, the Mill produced 360 tons of coated paper daily. At the time, national magazines such as *Country Gentleman, Seventeen, Farm and Ranch, Popular Mechanics,* and the *Farm Journal,* which had an annual circulation of 24,000,000, were printed on Hudson River Mill paper.

The Hudson River Mill manufactured ground wood and sulfite pulp in the two decades following World War II. The sulfite process, which cooked wood chips in large digesters, produced a persistent, pungent odor that spread throughout the Palmer section of town. The mill also operated a Core Plant that manufactured shipping cores made of heavy brown paper with attached steel end caps that facilitated moving the mill's finished rolls. A Binderene plant was also operating, recycling the spent liquor from the sulfite pulping process and selling it as an adhesive. Before the Binderene plant was built in 1916, the spent liquor from the Mill's five sulfite digesters, which included sulfuric acid and the lignin that the process removed from the wood, was discharged into the Hudson River. As early as 1906, the State's Conservation Commission reported that sulfite effluent from the mill contributed to the pollution of the River, which was first observable on the Hudson at Corinth. State regulations that would mitigate pollution of the Hudson were decades away.

The Mill continued to increase its output of coated paper in the 1950s. After three older paper machines were converted to coated paper production, a brand new machine, the No. 11, was designed, built, and installed by the Beloit Corporation in 1958. The No. 11 Machine represented state-of-the-art paper manufacturing technology, designed to produce 2000 feet of paper per minute on a 208-inch wide roll. As a testament to the ingenuity of Hudson River Mill's engineers and paper makers, the No. 11's production speed was increased to 2300 feet per minute, or one mile of paper every two minutes and 20 seconds. After the No. 11 Machine came online, the Hudson River Mill could produce 540 tons of coated paper daily, or 190,000 tons annually. In 1958, the mill employed around 1450 and had an annual payroll of $8,000,000 ($82,000,000 in 2024).

The installation of No. 11 resulted in the loss of much of the original Hudson River Pulp and Paper Company plant. This included the architecturally unique red-brick office building with its distinctive tower built in 1888, a structure featured in a book on IP's history published for its 50th anniversary in 1948. The demolition of the 1888 building that was required to build a machine room that could house the new No. 11 Machine led to the removal or abandonment of machines Nos. 1, 5, 6, 7, 8, and 9, and with it, the jobs needed to run them. Adding No. 11 to the Mill became an abject lesson for how innovative technology used to increase production could result in the net loss of jobs. Nonetheless, by the end of the 1950s, the Hudson River Mill had been wholly transformed into a producer of high-quality coated papers to print the high-resolution color images demanded by the nation's advertising industry.

The number of Hudson River Mill's employees in 1958 was more than double the 700 on the payroll in the early 1930s. Throughout the next decade, the total number of workers varied by only 100 employees in any given year. Besides the 60 percent of local taxes paid by IP, the Mill's payroll was responsible for a vigorous local economy. By the middle 1960s, Corinth Village and Palmer combined boasted at least eight restaurants and bars, three car dealerships, four supermarkets, several neighborhood groceries, two furniture stores, two department stores, three pharmacies, five barber shops, a lumber yard, a bowling alley, a pool hall, a movie theater, and a hospital. The community's civic leaders, who took great pride in Corinth's enviable economic standing within Saratoga County, were busy mid-decade installing a new community water supply and planning for a 50-bed regional hospital. There is little question that the adoption of coated paper production after World War II ushered in a "golden age" for the Town of Corinth.

There was a cost to Corinth's success in the damage inflicted on the environment and its citizens. The pulp and paper industry has long been known as a source of air and water pollution, a producer of solid wastes, and an intensive consumer of fossil fuels. During the 1960s, solid waste could be seen floating on the Hudson below the Mill, to Clothier Hollow and beyond. Aerial photographs of the plant in the 1950s and 1960s show white effluent streaming from the Mill into the River below the Palmer Falls dam. I recall fishing with my Uncle John near Clothier Hollow, a mile downriver from the Mill, and watching brown "islands" of solid waste from the Mill float in the current. We thought this was normal. Following the closure of the Mill in 2002, a former IP employee told me that he was part of a crew in the early 1970s that sprung into action whenever the Mill's manager received notice that a New York State plane was on its way to conduct an aerial survey of the Hudson as part of an effort to enforce new environmental regulations. He said that in these instances, he and other workers would be required to carry buckets of blue dye to the river's edge and dump them into the water to camouflage light-colored effluent that was then discharged from the Mill into the Hudson.

Both industrial liquids and solids were being dumped into the Hudson River from the Mill in the 1960s. Mill waste totaled 16 million gallons daily by the decade's end. Solids included groundwood and kraft paper pulp, clay, starch, and wood particles that escaped wood room screening. Forced to construct a waste treatment plant by the State of New York to manage Hudson River Mill waste, IP had spent $2.8 million on the project when the plant began operating in 1972. The coated papers produced at the Hudson River Mill were manufactured with as many as twenty-five chemical formulas. Besides their impact on the Hudson, the chemicals used at the Mill were felt directly by its workers. In 1958, a pipe carrying liquid chlorine gas used to bleach sulfite pulp broke and poisoned 80 paper workers, sending most to local hospitals. State investigators determined that falling ice from a roof was responsible for the break, but a faulty check valve had failed to shut off the flow of chlorine after the break occurred. The Department of Labor offered five recommendations to the IP to improve worker safety, yet surprisingly, none of the injured workers took legal action against the Company for the accident.

Pulp and paper production also polluted Corinth's air. Sulfite pulping that began at the Mill in the early 1890s initially spilled spent liquor from the Mill's five sulfite digesters directly into the Hudson. The effluent from the digesters contained sulphuric acid and lignin, the naturally occurring polymer in wood that provides the structural support for cellulose fiber. By the early 20th century, it was discovered that the waste liquor from the sulfite process could be recycled and converted into a salable adhesive called "binderene." A dedicated Binderene Plant was built, sharply reducing discharges from the Mill to the Hudson while creating an additional income stream for IP. Yet the sulfurous gases emanating from the mill's five digesters fouled the community's air, particularly in the Palmer section of town.

The Hudson River Mill also spewed fumes from the fuel oil it burned for power. By 1969, 23,000,000 gallons of oil were being burned at the Mill annually. While concerns over carbon emissions and climate change were only beginning to emerge among scientists, the Hudson River Mill released over 560,000,000 pounds of carbon into the atmosphere in 1969 alone. Thoughtful mill employees and community members understood the damage inflicted on the environment by pulp and paper manufacturing at Palmer Falls. Yet, they also understood that Corinth's economy depended on it. Despoiling the environment was the price of Corinth's material and economic progress during the post-World War II era.

I don't believe that within the Corinth community, the Hudson River Mill was ever openly considered the source of ill health for its paper workers. I never heard the suggestion made in all the years I lived and visited there. Yet, numerous studies have linked the pulp and paper industry to high incidences of cancer. A book published in 2020, *Mill Town*, describes the ecological and health consequences of the paper industry in Mexico, Maine. It notes that the Androscoggin River region, where IP built a large mill at Jay in 1965, has been called "Cancer Valley." It is curious, given that at one time, five pulp and paper mills operated on the upper Hudson River, including Corinth, that a study of the health of its paper workers and their communities was never undertaken.

IP was both the driver of the local economy and the force behind much of Corinth's social life in the 1950s and 1960s. The EMBA (Employees

Mutual Benefit Association), whose origins date to 1924, organized numerous social and recreational events in which many local citizens participated. While there were social, fraternal, and religious organizations elsewhere in Corinth, none did more to develop and maintain social relations in Corinth than the EMBA, an organization IP heavily subsidized.The Community Building, where organized EMBA events were held, pulsed with activity through the winter months. Originally built to house strikebreakers during the 1921 Paper Strike, by the mid-1920s, the building hosted dances and banquets. A gymnasium, bowling alley, boxing area, shooting range, and cafeteria were eventually added. The EMBA opened an ice skating rink in 1957, and the Brookhaven golf course began operations in 1963. Before the skating rink and golf course opened, over 1,000 different Corinth adults and children participated in EMBA-sponsored activities yearly.

The IP-produced *EMBA News* was the mirror that reflected the relationship between the Hudson River Mill and the Corinth community. Started in 1942 to inform local men serving in the Armed Forces during World War II of what was happening at the Hudson River Mill and in the local community, the monthly *News* soon became a staple of life in Corinth. George Holland was the force behind the *News* from its inception to his retirement in 1975. Local families eagerly awaited the arrival of the monthly magazine, whose distribution peaked at 3100. Initially, the *News* was paid for with dues contributed by members of the EMBA, but in 1959, International Paper began to fund the publication fully.

All elements of Corinth's social life were regularly reflected in the *EMBA News*. Often containing as many as 16 pages, the *News* was illustrated with dozens of photographs, including articles on Mill developments, promotions and retirements, sporting news, community organizations, and school groups. By 1965, the *NEWS* began to feature a year-end

summary of the Mill's production and payroll. George Holland sometimes wrote editorials that provided an insider's view of the Hudson River
Mill, including his personal opinions on community events. During the
1960s, the *NEWS* contained articles on developments at other IP mills,
and sometimes color inserts that were copies of advertisements for IP products that the Company's public relations office had supplied were included.
While *EMBA News* coverage of the Company widened during the 1960s
as community articles decreased, the monthly still provided a reliable way
for Corinthians to see who they were and what they had accomplished.

Every generation that lived during the town's 200-year history might
profess their time represented the town's "golden age." Still, I think it is
fair to say that the 1960s was Corinth's last period of broad community
prosperity. Yet just as the Mill and the community where it resided had
reached the pinnacle of success, developments were underway in the 1960s
that signaled the beginning of the decline of both. While it was impossible
then to anticipate the long-term impact of these forces, historical perspective provides the insight necessary to understand what happened and why.

While the final years of the 20th century brought a sharp decline in
the operations of the Hudson River Mill that resulted in a corresponding
downturn in the community, most people would agree that Corinth's de-
terioration accelerated rapidly after the Mill's 2002 closure. Today, Corinth
consists of a thoughtful and generous citizenry working hard to reinvent
the community and create the best life for themselves and their families.
Those of us who knew Corinth in better times wish them well and hope
they succeed. Yet many who walked the streets of Corinth as children and
teenagers in the 1950s and 1960s are deeply saddened when we return to
Corinth today to find the hometown of our youth unrecognizable.

16

TEACH YOUR CHILDREN

High school played a determinative role in the lives of most kids who grew up in Corinth during the 1960s. Our earnest and dedicated teachers were the adults many of us admired and respected the most. Their importance in our lives was more significant than they knew. Several of the younger teachers, not long out of college and some newly married, came to Corinth and never left. Those who remained to spend their entire careers in the school system had to resign themselves to the realities of living in a rural and conservative mill town. Corinth's civic leaders wanted our town to be recognized as a progressive upstate New York community, yet many of their ideas were conventional and unimaginative. Other teachers who, by intellect, style, or temperament, found themselves ill-suited for life and work in the southern Adirondacks went elsewhere after only a few years. I have wondered how our high school experience might have been different if some of the bright lights who left Corinth had remained.

Many of us who passed through the hallways of Corinth High School in the 1960s were fortunate to have had some excellent teachers. Yet those of us who became teachers or professors have the experience and perspective to view our education critically rather than sentimentally. Yet it was the guidance office, in my experience, that was the weakest link in the high

school educational system that I encountered. The two guidance counselors who staffed the office during my time in high school, a former coach
and a former teacher, were both too burned out to remain in the classroom
until retirement. I know of at least two teachers I had during high school
who were then completing a Master's degree to qualify for future administrative openings in guidance or as a principal. Administrative positions
were viewed as a logical exit ramp from the classroom and, for some, a road
to more authority, money, or both.

The guidance counselor to whom I was assigned had little professional
training, at least not any that was current or useful to me. I was called into
his office for the first time at the beginning of my senior year, ostensibly
to determine if I had college plans. While I certainly could have benefitted from some academic guidance before my final year of high school, I
don't recall a counselor, teacher, or principal ever offering me any. Corinth
High School did not practice academic intervention in those days. After I
entered the guidance office and sat in front of the counselor's big desk, he
asked me what I was interested in studying in college and what I wanted to
do afterward.

His eyes seemed to glaze over while listening to my response. Looking
straight at me, he casually raised his right behind his head and pointed
toward the college catalogs on the bookshelf behind him. In a graceful,
sweeping motion, he moved his hand from left to right, telling me I might
be interested in one of "these institutions," his index finger indicating a
single shelf of catalogs. The gesture was made with such precision that it
was clear he had used the move to give the same advice to other students. I
suspected he had read transcripts of my grades, for when I squinted to read
the names of the colleges on the spines of the catalogs, I saw that he had
pointed to several New York State colleges: Plattsburgh, Oneonta, Oswego,
etc. That was it. That was the extent of the college guidance I received at

Corinth High School. It was the only academic guidance I received, period. My counselor was either lazy or had determined I was not worth his time. I never returned for a second appointment, conducting college research independently and completing my applications unassisted.

Some of our teachers showed us they were people, too. The younger teachers, often only seven or eight years older than us, seemed slow to conform to community and school norms. One English teacher came to Corinth when she was 25 years old. Her most distinguishing classroom trait, often mimicked by the girls in our class for its runway quality, made it into the "REVENGE" page of the Class of 1969 yearbook, where its editors wrote: "There's a certain kind of walk you walk when you are teaching English." Another entry, the cryptic "The best balloon blower in Rutgers county," reflected the close relationship that some members of our class developed with one of the young and more irreverent teachers who would sometimes host small student groups at his Lake Luzerne apartment.

One of these teachers left only after a few years of teaching, while the other remained in the classroom for a decade or more until teaching at Corinth High School finally became untenable. A few teachers found the prohibition of classroom discussion of current events, such as Civil Rights and the Vietnam War, problematic. When teachers complied with the order, it was likely out of concern for their jobs. Most of us revered our teachers when we were in school and thought little about the personal challenges some faced. Yet, in later years, some of us wondered about those who had found their way to Corinth in their 20s and never left.

The collective character of the Class of 1969, for all of our shortcomings, was the product of factors beyond our control. The same could be said for other Corinth classes in the 1960s because we were all governed by similar community forces. One significant factor for my class and others was the village-country divide. Many kids living in outlying rural areas of the Town of Corinth were bused to school daily. By the mid-1960s, there were at least ten Corinth school buses. Kids who lived in the country, "bus students" as they were sometimes called, were not typically part of the teenage social networks that operated in the village.

All my close friends – village kids - could walk to school and each other's houses. It was easy for village kids to enjoy the friendships and cliques that began in school during the 7th grade and continue them on weekday evenings and weekends. But not so for the kids who had to ride the bus daily. Even if they made friends with village kids in the classroom, they could not easily hang out with them after school at Lanfear's store because they had to catch a bus home, nor could they easily share a pizza at Kayo's on Saturday night unless they could get a ride back and forth into town. I am sure our classmates outside the village were socially engaged on the weekends, but I never knew what they did. Sure, many showed up for school dances and football and basketball games, but as soon as those events were over, they were picked up by a parent or driven home by an older sibling.

The village-country dichotomy that separated many of my classmates, a condition common to Corinth classes of the 1950s and 1960s, was exacerbated by tracking, an alienating practice that was socially divisive. Begun in American high schools in the 1930s, tracking is grounded in the belief that students should be presented with a curriculum and instruction that suits their intellectual ability. IQ and achievement tests typically place students in one of three academic tracks. Tracking has been subjected to intense criticism in recent years, although it remains a fixed method for organizing students into classes in most parts of the country. Most of the national debate over tracking has centered on its impact on student learning and achievement, particularly for those students in the less-achieving track.

The Class of 1969 was not the only Corinth High School class where tracking was used. Yet, in my class, a small group of us - about fourteen in all - were separated from most of our classmates for nearly all of our courses while in high school. While I cannot attest to its academic effect on my classmates, I can only write about my experience and observations. Tracking, whatever its academic merits, was a socially divisive educational practice at Corinth High School.

Tracking resulted in limited to no academic interaction with students in other tracks. The practice also gave those in the accelerated group an underserved sense of privilege. We often regarded ourselves as "the smart class." I recall once, when one of the "smart" classes went on a field trip, we bought a postcard of the location we visited – the Bennington, Vermont battle monument, I believe - and mailed it to a kid not with us who many of us knew, writing something snarky like "wish you were here." This classmate could get under your skin, so some of us probably figured he deserved the missive. Still, I went through my high school years without having a single class with many students in my grade, except for gym class and study hall.

To some degree, participation in sports and school clubs countered the academic segregation that tracking created. Yet, it did little to erase the sense that select groups of kids existed in a rarefied educational space. For instance, I was a member of the varsity track team for four years, yet I never sat in a single classroom with either of my closest teammates, both members of the Class of 1969. Not long ago, a member of my class who was among those in the "smart" track remarked to me about the same thing, complaining that we were never in a classroom with 80 percent of our classmates. Regardless of the academic intent of tracking, its practice had adverse and enduring social consequences.

Some of the "smart" track courses offered at the high school were developed with International Paper Company Foundation support. The Foundation originated in the early 1950s and provided grants to the Corinth school system to work with the Columbia University Teachers' College faculty. Jud Hannigan, manager of the Hudson River Mill in the early 1960s who also served as President of the School Board, was well positioned to advance IP Foundation objectives. Columbia Teachers College was the leading institution of its kind in the United States. Our school administration supported the relationship with the Foundation and Columbia because it made them look innovative and progressive. While teachers involved no doubt believed in the efficacy of the courses developed with Foundation funding, some benefited from cash stipends offered by the Foundation for summer work and from scholarships provided to support the completion of advanced degrees. In 1968, when 13 of my senior classmates and I took a team-taught humanities course, the IP Foundation provided $400,000 ($3.3 million in 2024 dollars) to the schools in the communities of IP's Northern Division mills.

As students, we were never told that a class we took was a product of the school's relationship with the IP Foundation and Columbia University. Our parents were probably not told either. The *EMBA News* often printed photographs and short accounts of Corinth teachers and administrators meeting with IP Foundation board members or leaving on a trip to New York to meet with Columbia University faculty. The articles, which never mentioned precisely what they did at those meetings, seemed satisfied in showing that Foundation grants to the school were another perk of living in an IP mill town.

An exception to the limited information provided in the *EMBA News* about IP Foundation activity was its coverage of the Summer Forest Program. Sponsored by the IP Foundation, the Program offered by

Corinth High School started in 1963 on 50 acres of Company land near Hunt Lake. The program evolved over the years, from tree, insect, and bird identification to offering canoeing and orienteering instruction. Photographs of kids gathered in Corinth forests made for some excellent optics for readers of the *News*, far better than photographs of kids sitting in a classroom solving math equations or conjugating verbs. Most summers, the Foundation paid two or three Corinth teachers to manage the Forest Program. Eventually expanded to include children in grades four through eight, the school system funded the program after the IP Foundation's financial support ceased. The School Forest Program, in which nearly 500 students participated over the years, was discontinued after 1979. The Program served as the most visible evidence of how teachers and administrators who were agents of IP Foundation funding demonstrated they worked in the best interests of Corinth students.

Many kids who took classes at Corinth High School that were a product of Foundation support benefitted academically. Studies have shown that less capable students benefit more from classes taken with their higher-achieving peers than if they are tracked into separate courses. So, the kids in the Class of 1969 who were not in a classroom with their classmates from the"high-achieving track were unlikely to have gained as much academically as they might have had tracking not been used. One legacy of living in an IP mill town is that funding by the Foundation supported tracking in the Corinth schools for two decades or more. It was done ostensibly to promote student achievement, yet it resulted in both academic segregation and the systemic social disengagement of class members from each other.

17

— · —

SOUNDS OF SILENCE

T he community where we lived and the school we attended helped shape the character of the Class of 1969. However, our teachers didn't have much to work with. My classmates and I were good kids, generally polite and respectful, and many were intelligent and aspirational. But most of us were unmotivated underachievers, and we knew it. Many of our teachers disliked us, and they told us so.

The editors of the 1969 *Corinthian* yearbook admitted as much. Suggesting they felt compelled to conduct a "self-appraisal" of our class after thirteen years of school together, they were painfully honest in suggesting the Class of 1969 was generally indifferent to academic success. The editors wrote: "We feel that, although we may not have been outstanding and hard-working, we have tried to make the best of our years at Corinth." This understatement - that translated to "we did the best we could under the circumstances" - might have earned a literary award for its humility and self-awareness. Our class had a few bright stars, yet overall, it was a poorly illuminated constellation. And I count myself among the stars that did not shine bright.

Perhaps the most intense light among us was Hugh Lavery, who always seemed to exist in a rarified intellectual space. He was so damn smart, yet he was so very humble. Hugh rarely said anything in class, but you could always tell from his knowing look he knew the answer to every question and problem posed. Hugh had open heart surgery in the 3rd grade, which made him seem, understandably, a bit precious. Hugh was also an accomplished pianist. He belonged to several clubs in high school and received academic honors that included recognition as a National Merit Scholarship finalist. Hugh shrewdly applied to and was accepted at Tufts University in the 11th grade. So off he went to Boston without going through a senior year. I am sure Hugh couldn't wait to get out of school and out of town. Even though Hugh did not graduate with us, our class's yearbook editors at least had the good sense to dedicate a whole page to him in the 1969 *Corinthian*.

Hugh must have been so bored in Corinth. He was an only child and probably quite lonely at times. Sadly, I don't recall anyone in high school suggesting that Hugh be included in a social gathering. This is one of the oversights that still nags at me. When I arrived at our class's 50th-year reunion at the Holiday Inn in Saratoga Springs in 2019, I thought about Hugh and wondered if he had been invited. I found that he had not been because his name was not listed with the Class of 1969 or with any class, for that matter. Hugh has since been added to the Class of 1969 roster, but will he show up for our 55th in 2024?

I learned that as an undergraduate, Hugh transferred from Tufts to M. I.T., where he obtained his degree in chemical engineering before earning a Ph.D. a few years later. After I discovered him online, retired and living in New Jersey, we emailed for a while, having found some common ground in our shared interest in the Hudson River Mill and the paper industry. Hugh is married with children and, like his father, enjoyed a long and successful career in the paper industry. Had Hugh attended our 50th class reunion, he would have been the most accomplished among us.

Like most adolescents, some members of my class could be brutally cruel. The photographer Diane Arbus, who made images of people outside the margins of normative society during the 1960s, once remarked that the first thing you notice about a person is their flaw. Kids are adept at finding flaws in other kids, becoming experts at calling attention to their defects by teasing or, worse, by making them unforgettable with a nickname. This impulse likely existed within every class who went through the Corinth schools. Yet, I know only the propensity I observed and experienced in high school. Still, having your flaw called out often became an exercise in public humiliation. Skinny, fat, unusual-looking, and nerdy kids got the worst of it.

Editors of the 1969 class yearbook made the flaws of some classmates enduring. They listed everyone in our class by name and then described each in five categories, some shrewdly alluding to our flaws. The yearbook editors who might read this paragraph today will undoubtedly claim it was innocent and done in good fun. The descriptors don't seem all that funny when you are in your 70s. Could the cruelty inflicted on some of their classmates explain why the editors did not include the customary photograph of the yearbook staff in the publication?

The flaws that many of us carried made our class of around 100 kids relatively unremarkable. Yet being overweight, having large ears, or lousy skin does not often diminish one's character. Some individuals in my class were remarkably accomplished, yet our class lacked the chemistry necessary to become notable or memorable. For the Class of 1969, the total was less than the sum of our parts. We eventually came to believe what our teachers told us: we were "irresponsible, immature, and lazy," descriptors used by our yearbook editors, which originated with our 20-something 11th-grade English teacher with the runway walk. Many of my surviving classmates are likely to say there was nothing wrong with us that wasn't also true of every group of kids who ever made their way through Corinth High School. They could be right.

Yet I suspect many kids I went to school with who are now senior citizens often think back and feel they missed something at Corinth High School. I do. When our class had its 50th reunion in 2019, it was heavily attended compared to prior reunions and to the other anniversary classes in attendance at the Saratoga Springs Holiday Inn that night. Many in our class seemed to come to the banquet looking for a high school experience that we had never shared, class connections that had never existed.

Looking across the room at people I had not seen in 50 years was surreal. I am sure others felt the same way. Some former classmates, like me, held a blank stare. What were we all doing there? We barely know each other in high school! The palpable desire for community that was evident that night in June 2019 has recently found expression in the creation of a class Facebook page that currently includes 26 members and counting. It may not be too late.

When I attended our reunion and saw some of my classmates who had lived in the rural parts of our town when we were in school, I recalled the village-country divide that existed then. To a person, the former country kids I spoke with had become interesting and successful adults. It was great to talk with them. I began to feel bad for having been a village kid. I regretted not getting to know more of them in high school and missing the opportunity as a teenager to have counted some of them as my friends.

At the reunion, I realized I knew the fathers of some of my classmates better than I knew them. Cindy was a perfect example. Her home was next door to the clubhouse at the Brookhaven Golf Course in South Corinth. I went to Brookhaven frequently during high school and every summer when I was home from college and not working at the paper mill. The course had become my second home. I was at the course early one August evening, sometime in the mid-1970s. It started to rain, and a dense fog set in, sending golfers into the clubhouse. At the time, the clubhouse had only a tiny snack bar run by Mary Eno. Most players went home, but several adult men, myself, and another young man, Mick Towers, stayed on, sitting at the counter to get something to eat.

One of the men at the bar, Cindy's father, worked as a groundskeeper at the course. He suddenly got up from his stool and left the clubhouse to go to his garden next door. He picked a bushel of corn and carried it back to the snack bar. A few guys shucked the corn while Mary got some water boiling in two large pots. While the corn was cooking, Mary set out a stick of butter and a salt shaker in front of each guy sitting at the counter. Before long, she served ears of corn to each of us. Ear after ear after ear. I ate seven that night. A few of the guys ate even more. It was the most spontaneous and memorable meal I ever had. While I spent many years playing at Brookhaven Golf Course, that night eating fresh corn picked by my classmate Cindy's dad remains my most memorable experience.

In October 2016, I returned to play at Brookhaven. I had just retired from my full-time college teaching position that spring. As I turned off Alpine Meadows Road and approached the clubhouse, I saw Cindy's father tending his garden. He was no longer the spry man who had been a competitive downhill skier, operated the local dairy, and served as Brookhaven's head groundskeeper. I parked my truck at the road's edge near the garden, walked over to him, and introduced myself. I don't think he knew who I was or remembered me. Yet I recounted the night in the clubhouse when we feasted on the corn from his garden. While he didn't recall the event, seeing him again and describing that memorable night was still satisfying. Cindy's dad, Earl "Junior" Towers, died the following March at age 93.

Two years later, during our 2019 reunion, I saw Cindy and told her of my fond memories of her father: the night he harvested corn for hungry golfers and the afternoon when I spoke to him in his garden almost 50 years later. Cindy had been one of the kids who lived far outside the village when we were in school. I never knew her very well, and sharing my stories of her father when we were both 68 years old did little to narrow the social divide that existed between us as teenagers. I had expected that telling her stories of her father would make me feel better, but it didn't.

The divisive factors that characterized the Class of 1969 - some forced, others voluntary – ensured there was little that bound us together. We had our 1951 births in common, but this fact resulted from sheer coincidence, the product of the conception roulette played by our parents. Many of us shared the junior prom, and nearly all, graduation, yet such events do not contribute to one's character, nor do they create a legacy that a group can claim.

Every member of the Class of 1969 carries the scars left by the transformative events of our time: the assassinations of President Kennedy, Martin Luther King, and Robert Kennedy; the indelible images of Black teenagers being blasted by Birmingham fire hoses and chased down by police dogs; the endless procession of boys and young men returning home from Vietnam in flag-draped coffins. I am still unable to watch clips from Abraham Zapruder's film of JFK's assassination whenever they are shown on TV. While some of us were affected more than others, these and other historic events of the 1960s unite us in a peculiar way.

18

— • —

A Wide World of Sports

The preeminence of organized sports in Corinth in the 1950s and 1960s was, in many ways, a product of the town's history. Formal games were played in Corinth as early as 1873 when an intra-community baseball game saw the Landing Boys defeat the Palmer Falls Boys. This event signaled that the advent of pulp and paper manufacturing at Palmer Falls in 1869 had created a distinctive community near the Mill that was considered separate from Jessup's Landing. By the mid-1880s, a town team was organized in Corinth to play against other communities. The earliest of the teams was called the Papermakers. By the mid-1890s, the town team was called the F.A. Smiths after its benefactor, Dr. F.A. Smith, a local physician. Corinth baseball teams became notorious for playing "dirty ball" and their fans for being rough on visiting teams. The correspondent of a Glens Falls newspaper once remarked that visiting teams did not want to return after playing their first away game at Corinth. Under the leadership and coaching of Bus Waldron, Corinth continued to field semi-pro baseball teams well into the 1950s.

Basketball started in Corinth later than baseball, with little evidence of organized play before 1920. The high school team got off to a slow start, once getting thrashed by Hudson Falls, 82-13. But the team improved over the next several years, going undefeated during the 1928-1929 season. Corinth High also organized a girl's team in the 1920s that won consecutive Adirondack League titles in 1928 and 1929. Two town basketball teams in the early 1920s merged to form the Internationals, which played in the Tri-County League well into the 1930s. On at least two occasions, the Internationals played a charity game against the Renaissance Five of New York, a team billed as the "World's colored basketball champions." Coming into the game with an 81-17 record, the New York team defeated the Internationals 47-21 before a crowd of 800, the largest ever seen in the Community Building's original gym

As kids, we knew nothing of our town's sporting history. Yet its traditions were instilled into our fathers, who came of age in the 1920s and 1930s, and were then passed on to us after World War II, primarily in the activities of the EMBA, which was arguably one of the most significant benefits of living in an International Paper mill town. The EMBA began in the 1950s to provide a wide range of sporting activities for the Corinth community, much of it in the form of organized league play for boys and men. Girls and women were limited to using the bowling alley, the EMBA rink winter, and, after 1963, the Brookhaven golf course.

Many of the activities offered by the EMBA were held at the Community Building on Pine Street. It became a hive of frenetic activity, particularly on winter evenings. Dozens of kids would go there to hang out with their friends even if they didn't have a scheduled game. It would be impossible for boys living in Corinth today to grasp what it could be like at the Community Building on a weekday night when basketball games were being played in the gym, bowling teams were competing in the alleys, boxing classes were being held upstairs, and the shooting range was open downstairs. It was mayhem on some nights.

The Community Building was about a mile from my Center Street home, so I went there far less than my classmates who lived in Palmer. Yet I was obsessed with sports by the 3rd or 4th grade. In the 6th grade, I started hanging out at the Main Street athletic field during afternoon high school varsity baseball and football practices. When the football team moved towards the south end of the field to practice, I would go out into the north end, gather a random football and kick it around. It was exciting actually to handle a ball that the big kids used. I was there when I first observed Jimmy Hopkins practice punting, watching the technique that produced his towering spirals. Afterward, I would try to kick as he did.

In the spring, I would hang around the baseball field during varsity practice, often picking up bats, balls, and random pieces of equipment and returning them to the wooden benches that served as the home team's dugout. After doing this for a few weeks, the coach asked me if I wanted to travel with the team to an away game at Glens Falls the following week. I was excited to go, so my parents permitted me. My Mother packed some snacks in a brown paper bag for me to take on the bus to Crandall Park, where the game was played. I enjoyed performing "bat boy" duty for the team that day, but my reverence for the team fell sharply after the team's pitcher stole my food on the way back to Corinth.

In the early 1960s, Corinth boys had to wait until they entered the 7th grade to join a school team. And then only basketball was offered. I was on the 7th and 8th-grade team both years when we might have played five or six games during each season. It's funny; I cannot remember who our coach was, although I can recall games we played in Saratoga and Hudson Falls.

It was in the 9th grade that boys were eligible to join all the sports teams offered in the high school. Our introduction to high school sports teams came with the start of freshman football in August 1965. Every high school boy trying out for football that year converged on the Eggleston Street practice field, where we ran some laps and did calisthenics together. The varsity coach, George Spieldenner, had us gather around him where he gave a welcome, this-is-what-the-season-looks-like speech. Then he told us where the varsity, junior varsity, and freshmen players should convene on the field, except for me. He told me to go with the varsity linemen.

"Varsity Linemen? But I am a freshman," I thought to myself. "What are you talking about? I didn't sign up for football to play on the line!" It did not occur to me until that very moment that my height and weight had predetermined my role in Corinth football. Not only would I be separated from my friends and classmates by practicing with the varsity team because the coaches thought my size offered promise, but I would be expected to block and tackle. Yes, smash into other players and be hit back. I had never done either. I should have felt proud the coaches thought it was a good idea for me to practice with the varsity linemen. Yet, it was not from confidence in my ability they made the decision, but rather from the fact they figured my large body would provide an obstacle for opposing teams. The idea that I try out for the varsity as a freshman was purely based on physics, nothing more.

Playing football in our neighborhood didn't prepare me to block and tackle. Most boys who grew up playing touch football in Corinth did only two things. They threw the ball, and they caught it. Well, they kicked it, too. In the games played with my childhood friends, whether in the neighborhood or on the elementary school lawn, even the center who hiked the ball to the quarterback went out for a pass and could score a touchdown. And so did everyone else on the team. Having only passed the football and caught it as a kind, not once did I consider that on the high school team I would be expected to play a position where I would never touch the football. Because I lacked the enthusiasm and aggression needed to play varsity, I was demoted to the freshman team after a week or so. I was not bothered by the move, for it was great to be back on the team with my friends, although we lost all four games we played that season. The varsity did little better, finishing the season 2-4-1.

None of the junior varsity and varsity sports teams I played in high school had a winning season. Few kids at Corinth were ever "cut," which led to some unskilled players on school teams. While mounting losses were commonly blamed on poor players, some adults considered team failures due to mediocre coaching. Corinth had a basketball coach in the early 1960s who was blessed with a team whose players towered over their opponents, a once-in-century team for a small town like Corinth. Some people believed the team had more height than area college teams. Yet they still lost games.

I remember hearing my Father and his good friend, who also went to Corinth High School, complain about the team's record, saying the varsity basketball team, I believe the 1963-4 version, should have been undefeated. A photograph of one of the early 1960s teams recently made the rounds on social media, where a subtle comment was made that contested the reverence held for Corinth's sports and their 1960s-era coaches. Adult basketball fans in Corinth thought better coaching would have produced more successful teams given the talent team members possessed; high school students, on the other hand, would have been reluctant to attribute a team's record to a coach.

But a win-loss record wasn't the only measure of a good coach. When I played J.V. basketball, the coach seemed to think I lacked the speed to start at center, although I was a good shooter. He preferred to play thin, aggressive kids. I recall with great clarity the week before the season's final game in my second year on the team, which would have been in March of 1966. The starting center missed the last two practices before the game.

I took his place in practice and did so well that I was confident our coach would start me for the final home game against Warrensburg on Friday night.

Not a chance. I sat on the bench for almost the entire game. With our team behind by more than 20 points with less than a minute remaining, our coach got up to see who was sitting on the bench. Looking at me as though he had just remembered he left the stove on at home before leaving for the game, he put me in with 32 seconds left on the clock. It was so humiliating to be put into the game at that point. I would have been less embarrassed if I had remained on the bench. Here it is, some 60 years later, and I remember the event as though it happened yesterday. The coach had absolutely no idea what he had done.

The 1967 varsity football team, my favorite team, lost as many games as it won, yet I considered it a winning team. It was an excellent team that could have won more if we had better coaching. I am convinced of that. One of our coaches behaved like a military drill sergeant; the other was ill-tempered and prone to yelling at his players. I was once on the receiving end of such behavior.

The coach's conduct did not rise to the Bobby Knight level of player abuse, but I was troubled by it. It was during a Friday night home game. I was on one of the special teams; I cannot recall which one. I returned to the sideline after the play was over since I was not a member of the next team to go onto the field. I didn't realize it, but a penalty had been called that allowed the opposing team to run the play over again. The referee yelled to our coach that we had only ten players on the field. The coach turned to face his players, saw me standing there, and realized that I was the missing 11th player just as I did. He yelled something derogatory at me while smacking my helmet hard with his hand as I went onto the field. While I should have been more alert to the situation, the coach's action in front of a grandstand of hometown spectators, including my Father, was humiliating. Yet, if our coach were on top of things, he would never let me leave the field in the first place. I was embarrassed enough by my oversight, but his conduct made the situation far worse. Yet I had seen this type of behavior from him before.

The 1967-68 basketball season began shortly after football ended. I wanted to play, so I tried to put the sideline event behind me. This was necessary because the coach who smacked me on the head was also the basketball coach. On the day that we were to sign up for the varsity team, before I had even made it down to the coach's office to enroll, a friend who had already signed up came to me. He said that when he had gone down to the gym to join the team, the coach told him I would have to lose weight before he would let me play. I was rattled by what my friend reported, yet my personality was not aggressive enough to ask the coach about what he said. I wondered why he would say that to another potential team member. I was 6' 2" then and would have been one of the team's two tallest players. I was also about 215 pounds, lighter than players on earlier teams, 1963 and 1964, so why couldn't I play? Perhaps the coach planned to speak to me about my weight when I signed up, but I thought it was unprofessional and inappropriate that he shared his thoughts with someone else first.

While basketball was my favorite sport, and I was pretty good despite my weight, I decided not to join the team. I concluded that by saying to my friend I would have to lose weight before playing, the coach was telling me indirectly he did not want me on the team. My friend might have exaggerated what the coach said or implied, yet I became convinced the story was true when the coach complained during a newspaper interview that his team lacked height. Yet there I was, a 6'2" kid, as tall as the tallest guy then on the team, who was reasonably good and wanted to play. One positive word, and I would have joined. My basketball career at Corinth was over, but my weight had only something to do with it.

While I never really played on a winning team at Corinth, I saw some talented athletes and impressive personal performances. The kid who comes quickly to mind is Jimmy Hopkins, a genuinely gifted three-sport athlete from the mid-1960s. With blazing-fast speed, nothing could get your heart racing more than watching Jimmy, who played halfback on the varsity football team, break a tackle at the line of scrimmage under the Friday night lights and run lightning-fast for the goal line. I remember that he scored four touchdowns during one of his career games. Jimmy was also the team's punter, and his kicks would most often be towering, majestic spirals that would travel 60 yards. Jimmy might have been the most naturally gifted Corinth athlete to set foot on the Main Street fields. I once heard the rumor that Jimmy got a tryout as a punter with a pro team after high school.

Jimmy's athleticism was grounded in his speed. I was on the track team with him as a freshman in the spring of 1966, his senior year. I participated in the weight events, so we had no direct interaction. Jimmy was undefeated all season in the Northern Conference in the 100 and 220-yard sprints, with a 100-yard time of 10.3 seconds, his best during the regular season. I recall the day at practice when it was rumored he was clocked unofficially at 9.9. In the 1960s, Corinth's track consisted of a fifth-of-a-mile-long white oval line in the grass the encirled the football field. Jimmy ran in leather shoes with steel spikes, standard track footwear at the time. His most significant moment that season, however, was at the Section II Runoff meet in Schenectady, where he won the 100-yard dash with a time of 10.0 seconds, his official best. It was a stunning performance. Jimmy Hopkins was a local hero for many boys interested in sports who came of age in Corinth during the 1960s.

I witnessed a particularly memorable athletic performance in May 1966 when the track team participated in the Section II Class C meet at East Field in Saratoga Springs. I did not compete that day but traveled with the team. Rain and lightning had delayed the meet, causing it to run over 4 ½ hours. The storm had turned parts of the track to mud, and several inches of water had pooled in a few places on its inside lanes. Two Corinth runners entered the two-mile run, which was scheduled toward the end of the meet but had been delayed by rain. One of the boys was a senior and a four-year track team member, a strong competitor in both the mile and two-mile. He was considered the team's best distance runner. He was well-liked in school and came from a well-known and highly respected family. The team's second two-miler had transferred to Corinth, arriving in town with his parents, who placed seven kids in the Corinth school system. He was in my 9th-grade class that year, although he was three years older than the rest of us. The children's jet-black hair, dark eyes, and swarthy complexions made them distinctive, perhaps of Native American descent.

The two-mile race began that day with a group running along the inside of the track. Water and mud splashed on their shoes and legs as they ran the eight laps around the quarter-mile oval. An obstruction briefly blocked my view from where I was standing, but as the runners came down the final stretch, I could see Tom pull out and move up to challenge the lead runner. As the leader approached the finish line, Tom launched forward, crossing it ahead of his teammate, placing second in the race. But as soon as he finished, Tom collapsed unconscious into a pool of water three to four inches deep. He was lifted from the track by his teammates and coach. A newspaper reporter wrote that he "almost became the first runner to drown at the finish line." Tom's second-place finish earned him a trip to the Section II finals, where his track career ended. Tom Collard left Corinth High School the following month.

Tom Collard led a troubled life after high school and, by most measures, became Corinth's most notorious former resident. During the several decades after high school, Tom was arrested on 21 occasions and convicted 14 times, once of a felony. In the late 1990s, authorities began to search for Tom's wife, whom her family had not seen for several years. By then, Tom had moved from his Minerva, New York, home to Alabama. In 2010, when the search for his wife resumed more seriously, New York State investigators tracked Tom down. When interviewed, he admitted to killing his wife and dumping her into a hole outside their Minerva trailer that had been dug for a septic system. He said he then bulldozed the ground to cover the hole and built an addition to the home over the site. Within three weeks of the confession, his wife's remains were found and verified by DNA. Tom pleaded guilty to first-degree manslaughter and was sentenced to 24 years in prison. Evidence at the trial showed that Tom's life went sideways right after high school and continued downward across several decades.

Tom was 18 years old at the Section II Class C meet in the Spring of 1966 when he fell unconscious at the finish line. He had yet to become the man his daughter would later describe as a "monster" during his trial for the manslaughter of her mother. On that rainy day at East Field in Saratoga Springs, over 40 years earlier, he showed character and determination when he placed second in the two-mile. When he finished the race, Tom was cheered as though he had won. Looking back, after learning about his life in the years that followed and the heinous acts that he admitted, I realize what I witnessed that day in 1966 might just have been the best day of Tom's tragic life. It could be he never rose higher than when he was face-deep in that pool of water at Saratoga's East Field. Thomas Collard died in prison in 2016.

19

LITTLE TOWN ON THE PRAIRIE

Corinth's Sesquicentennial was celebrated in 1968. The celebration sought to recapture the days of the Town's founding in 1818, even though Corinth got its start some 50 years earlier. The 1818 date was when the area that became Corinth was carved out of the Town of Hadley. Tradition holds that the community started to take shape after 1770, when the Jessup brothers are said to have begun logging operations in nearby Luzerne. The lands granted to them by New York's provincial governor were considerable. Ebenezer reportedly built a log cabin and erected a sawmill on a stream that flows into the Hudson from the east, about a mile upriver from Palmer Falls. While historical evidence is relatively scarce, it is believed that Ebenezer used a flat-bottom boat to ferry cut lumber from Warren County to the west side of the Hudson, landing it near the current Corinth Free Library, then transporting it by horse and wagon to place below Palmer Falls. River commerce that grew from this activity led to the small settlement of Jessup's Landing.

The Jessups were in the area for only six years, from 1770 to 1776. After the two brothers sided with England when the War for Independence was declared and abandoned their Luzerne homesteads, their lands were confiscated by the newly formed State of New York. After the American Revolution, young men began arriving with their families to settle and farm the lands in the southern and eastern sections of the future town of Corinth, in the valley between the Palmertown and Kayaderosseras Mountain ranges. The commercial activity that grew from this early settlement led to the founding of Chapman's Corners or Chapmanville, about four miles south of Jessup's Landing, which then was part of Albany County. By 1820, just two years after the Town's official founding, Corinth's population was nearly 1500.

The New York State legislative acted in 1818 to create the new Town of Corinth. The rationale for the formation of the township is lost to history. The honor of naming the new town fell to Abigail Chapman, wife of Washington Chapman, who operated a woolen mill on Kayaderosseras Creek in Chapmanville. According to tradition, Mrs. Chapman was inspired by the *Bible* to name the town "Corinth." The naming privilege given to Abigail Chapman underscores the importance of Chapmanville in 1818 relative to Jessup's Landing, a few miles further north. Arthur Eggleston affirmed this in his 1968 *Town of Corinth,* noting that Chapmanville was "the center of activity in the newly formed town, with voting and much of its business carried on in the settlement." Located near the many small farms east of the plank road that led south from Jessup's Landing towards Saratoga Springs and Ballston Spa, Chapmanville was also home to sawmills, a tannery, a woolen mill, and a tavern. Along with Porter's Corners, somewhat south and to the west, Chapmanville served as the commercial center for the many farmers who lived in the southern and eastern portions of Corinth. Another historical curiosity worthy of note is that when Abigail Chapman plucked the name "Corinth" from her *Bible,* her husband, Washington, was one of only two slave owners in the newly formed town.

At the time of Corinth's founding, Chapmanville was comparable in size to Jessup's Landing, whose commerce relied on the seasonal transportation of logs to sawmills further south on the river. Not long after the organization of the Town, Chapmanville began to lose its identity when the Federal Government opened a post office there in 1828 with the postal cover "South Corinth." South Corinth remained a commercial center within the Town of Corinth through the mid-19th century when Corinth was still primarily an agricultural community. The force of industrialization in the post-Civil War decades eventually shifted much of the Town's commerce north to the Landing and to the hamlet of Palmer Falls, where a fast-growing pulp and paper mill was gradually transforming the community. Although South Corinth could justifiably claim to have been central to the Town's founding in 1818, there is no record that a single Sesquicentennial event was held there in 1968.

Corinth's Sesquicentennial celebration allowed the community to engage in an entire year of nostalgia for old-timey days. While civic leaders supported the event, they did not want to pay for it. In March 1968, a public auction of "Sesquicentennial shares" was held in the Corinth High School auditorium to raise money for the planned celebration and provide its organizers with working capital. Citizens were offered sesquicentennial shares for $1.00 each. When the celebration was over, any remaining funds would be returned to the citizen investors based on the number of shares each held. The organizers were so concerned about the potential cost of the Sesquicentennial that the Village and Town of Corinth signed a joint resolution that banned individuals from selling or trading anything related to the celebration. Citizens were prohibited from hawking items like themed T-shirts, hats, or coffee cups that would compete with the Town's efforts. Any individual who sought to profit from the Sesquicentennial in any way required the written permission of the Sesquicentennial Committee, which would then issue a "Peddler's Permit" badge.

The scheme of selling shares to fund the celebration seemed too conniving to have been dreamed up by the organizers of a small-town celebration. The Sesquicentennial program committee, in fact, contracted with the Hooper Production Agency to scheme for them. The Town of Corinth's Sesquicentennial was not a unique affair, but it was just one of many similar town celebrations that Hooper planned and directed throughout the United States. A search for "sesquicentennial" on eBay will sometimes yield objects created expressly for town celebrations in states across the country, similar to what was produced for Corinth, all likely engineered by Hooper. In other words, much of the Corinth 1968 Sesquicentennial was a boilerplate celebration.

The Sesquicentennial provided grown men and women with a legitimate reason to pretend they were living in a time gone by. For the celebration, it was roughly the several decades before the Civil War. Some female celebrants wore long dresses with a bustle, fancy hats, and stylish feathers. Other women, who dressed more simply in gingham dresses and bonnets that emulated frontier fashion, looked like extras from the TV shows *Rawhide* or *Gunsmoke*. Men who were all-in on the celebration wore dark pants and vests and either a top hat or a derby, and many grew beards or mustaches for the occasion. A red or black Sesquicentennial-branded bow tie usually accentuated their white shirts.

The enthusiasm that some citizens showed for donning such get-ups is understandable, given how many TV shows set in the 19th century were on television then. By some accounts, over 100 different Western shows aired on American TV networks between 1950 and 1968. Most programs featured heroic, gun-wielding sheriffs who maintained law and order in rough frontier towns. Many shows included a romantic thread, so a woman or two was generally in the cast to offer domestication. It would have strained credulity even in Corinth if western hats and six-shooters had become part of Sesquicentennial attire, so what the celebration's organizers set as the model for apparel was as close as they could get to the Old West without having to schedule shoot-outs or hangings on Main Street.

But not everyone joined in on the historical hysteria. Photographs made of community groups in 1968 whose participants were engaged in official meetings of the Town and Village boards, the school board, or fraternal organizations show some men dressed in full Sesquicentennial costume sitting alongside peers whose only concession to the celebration was the event's branded bowtie. The celebration's outliers look as if they are cringing at the realization they are being captured in a photograph with men who, to them, must have looked silly in beards and top hats. Such images appeared in the *EMBA News* during the summer of 1968 when the celebration started to ramp up. Indeed, a photograph made at the annual party of IP retirees and men with 25 years of service that was held in August 1968 shows only five of the nearly 300 attendees with facial hair or dressed in Sesquicentennial attire. Most older Corinthians appear not to have been overly enthusiastic about participating in the Town's birthday party.

Corinth's Sesquicentennial organizers seemed uncertain about which historical past to celebrate. The word "frontier" was often used in press releases, but Corinth was hardly on New York State's frontier in 1818 when the Town came into existence. Someone had the brilliant idea the celebration should include the creation of small-scale human figures cut out of plywood in the shapes of an Indian and a white man who appeared in colonial-era garb. The cutouts were painted on both sides and attached to fire hydrants and other vertical elements throughout the Village. While the figures provided a decorative embellishment for the event, Indians and 18th-century Americans had nothing to do with the founding of the Town of Corinth. The solitary Indian figure placed at the entrance to Pagenstecher Park, however, might have been construed as an implicit recognition that nearby Indian Hollow was once used as a campsite for Mohawk peoples. Yet Corinth's official Sesquicentennial history, published in 1968, begins in 1775 with the "pioneers," not mentioning that Indian peoples had once lived in the Corinth area. So it was ironic then that the Sesquicentennial committee would utilize Native American imagery as part of its celebration.

The Sesquicentennial party of 1968 contained other ironies. The most conspicuous was the official Sesquicentennial seal that a Corinth high school student created as part of a competition. The circular design chosen featured the words "1818 Corinth 1968" within the outer ring of the seal, while the bottom of the same ring featured the Bicentennial's slogan, "Years of Progress Through Toil." Inside the circle were spare line drawings of prominent features of Corinth's landscape: the school, the library, a church, a small house, and possibly a plowed field or a river. It wasn't altogether clear which one it was. No toil was depicted on the seal, no farmer, no team of oxen, no paper workers, and no shirt makers. Images of the Hudson River Mill and Palmer Falls, which had provided the water power that created modern Corinth, whose custodian International Paper put $10 million into the local economy that year, did not appear on the official seal either.

One or more students who entered the competition might have included elements on their seal depicting Corinth's working-class and industrial heritage. Still, the winning design provided no so such evidence. It was as though the committee made its selection to distance the Town from its true history, preferring to accentuate symbols of Corinth's progress rather than the industry that was responsible for it. The exclusion appeared as a blatant act of self-denial. The omission of any visual reference on the Sesquicentennial seal of the role of the pulp and paper within the community's history was offset by Town Supervisor Arthur Eggleston, who devoted several pages to it in the history of Corinth he wrote for the celebration.

Corinth men seemed most enthusiastic during the Sesquicentennial and had a more public presence than Corinth women. Men organized fraternal organizations like the Brothers of the Brush, Keystone Cops, and the Kangaroo Kort. The Brothers even had a sub-chapter that called itself the Moonshiners. It was men who most often organized and participated in the events that were scheduled through the summer. Perhaps the most popular was the Kangaroo Kort. The Kort would convene after the Keystone Cops had determined that a Brothers of the Brush member had broken one of the Sesquicentennial's rules. The Cops would round up the offender, put him into a wagon, and then cart him through the village streets to a public location where his punishment would be meted out in front of a large crowd. Punishments administered in good fun included being placed in a stockade, getting doused in the Hudson River, or being forced to "dance a jig" on the corner of Main and Maple Streets. In one instance, a man found guilty by the Kort was required to wash the shirtless back of another man who sat in a claw-foot bathtub that had been secured to the bed of a Chevy pick-up truck. Some of the several hundred people on hand to view the spectacle surely cringed at the homoerotic nature of the unusual performance.

Adult Corinth women also played active roles in the Sesquicentennial. The Sesqui-Belles were perhaps the most conspicuous group. Their most public moment came when the Village Mayor led them in a "Sesqui-promenade" toward their place in the line-up for the big parade that culminated the celebration at the end of August. Younger women also played a role when they vied for the title of Sesquicentennial queen, an essential component of any self-respecting community celebration. Twenty young women, ages 17 to 22, were chosen to compete for the title. At least ten were still in high school or had just graduated. Fourteen candidates once appeared together for a publicity photograph wearing modest, contemporary knee-length dresses. The young women, a few of whom were classmates or friends of mine, at least had been spared the indignity of having to wear homespun outfits from the Laura Ingalls collection as a precondition for their participation.

The Queen and her court, each escorted by a young man, were chosen at an August coronation ceremony. The runner-up candidates became members of the Queen's court, and a Miss Congeniality was even named. The court rode in the parade with the Queen on a designated float while the remaining contestants rode in one of the parade's 100 antique cars. Although the Queen's competition suggested that Feminist thinking of the late 1960s had not yet made inroads in Corinth, the celebration's organizers must have believed they had to provide a compelling incentive for young women to vie for the title. The contestant who was ultimately crowned – a college student at the time – won an all-expense paid trip for two to Miami Beach, a costly prize that helps to explain why the Sesquicentennial's organizers believed they had to sell shares of stock to pay for the celebration.

While the Queen's prize did not expose the patriarchal character of the Queen competition, the award given to the runners-up did. Each of the five members of the Queen's Court received a set of electric hair rollers as their prize. To situate Corinth's Sesquicentennial Queen's competition in historical context, only a few days after the Corinth coronation, 100 women protested at the Miss America Pagent in Atlantic City to denounce the event as sexist. While Corinth's queen competition was not a beauty contest, and contestants did not have to appear in a swimsuit, it did suggest how far removed a provincial community like Corinth was from the emerging cultural sensibilities of the late 1960s.

The Sesquicentennial culminated in a lavish parade at the end of August. Some 20,000 people were reported in attendance. Numbering 12 divisions that consisted of numerous floats, marching bands, and fire departments, the parade lasted for over two and one-half hours as it snaked through village streets. The parade was taken so seriously that organizers arranged for the G.A. Trahan Company, a professional parade consultant, to come to Corinth to provide float planning assistance and to take orders for materials needed for float construction. The parade included floats created by nearly every organization in town and selected businesses from outside Corinth. Two New York State beer brewers found the parade a terrific branding opportunity. The famous "Schaefer beer train" was even in the parade. Seven or eight establishments in Corinth sold draft beer in 1968, so sponsoring a float probably represented a good investment for the beer companies. Stewart's Ice Cream, which had operated a store in Corinth since the early 1950s, planned to open a new store at the corner of Main and River Street to coincide with the peak of the celebration in August. The Saratoga-based private company reaped a public relations bonanza when one of their part-time employees was crowned Sesquicentennial Queen, and a photograph of her standing in front of the new store was published in the newspapers.

The parade marked the official end to Corinth's Sesquicentennial celebration. Its conclusion came in the symbolic "brush off," a competitive event when men in the community shaved off their celebratory beards and mustaches and received awards for doing so. Plaques and trophies were awarded in twelve different "bearded categories." Some men were happy to be clean-shaven again, for facial hair on men was uncommon in Corinth in the 1960s. Those who refused to grow a beard or mustache for the Town's celebration had been derided for their lack of participation. George Holland, the editor of the *EMBA News*, wrote an editorial in the Fall of 1968 after the glow of the Town's celebration had faded, suggesting that the Sesquicentennial had been divisive. Holland noted that "some persons did not share the enthusiasm of the many" while the celebration was underway, yet admitted that "the occasional participant in his zeal went a little overboard and offended some of those disinterested persons." Holland's editorial suggests that Corinth's Sesquicentennial celebration may have contributed to the community's unsettling in 1968.

20

— • —

BAD MOON RISING

Corinth of the 1950s and 1960s was the product of the Hudson River Mill's success. Nearly every family in the community was part of the food chain created by the local pulp and paper industry. The advent of coated paper manufacturing at the Mill in the 1940s ushered in a period of unparalleled economic growth and prosperity for Corinth that peaked in the mid-1960s. In 1958, when the No. 11 paper machine was installed to cement the mill's status as a leading manufacturer of high-quality coated papers, IP was still focused on manufacturing traditional paper products. Yet the decade that followed would bring significant change to the Company.

During the 1960s, IP developed new products and increased paper production by building new mills, many outside of the Northeast, and it diversified into businesses unrelated to paper. IP also expanded internationally while engaging in mergers and acquisitions, committing millions of dollars towards moving the Company into areas well beyond its core paper business. For the first time, the Company turned to executives outside the pulp and paper industry for leadership. Jud Hannigan, who began his career in the Hudson River Mill in the late 1940s, is believed to have been the last IP President who came up through the ranks within the Company.

By the mid-1960s, the Hudson River Mill was part of a corporation un-dergoing a dramatic transformation. These changes profoundly affected Corinth.

IP poured millions of dollars into the Hudson River Mill during the 1960s. The investments made at the Corinth plant were primarily for upgrading existing facilities that only marginally increased the amount of paper the mill could produce. Improvements made during the decade were designed to create production efficiencies. IP's "modernization" of the Hudson River Mill in this period translated into a loss of jobs and a reduction in the mill's payroll. With each passing year, the Hudson River Mill's aging paper machines, except for No. 11, forced the mill to compete with the paper made at newer mills that ran larger and faster machines. The Mill's other machines that produced coated paper - No. 3 and No. 4 - were built around 1906. They were slow machines with narrow 148-inch wires that were fast becoming obsolete.

Growing environmental concerns in the late 1960s affected Hudson River Mill operations. In the latter half of the decade, New York State and Federal Government began to mandate corporate action to protect the Hudson River. In early 1967, IP agreed to build a several million-dollar plant to treat the Hudson River Mill's liquid and solid wastes. IP was now required to mitigate the environmental damage that pulp and paper manufacturing had inflicted on the Hudson River for nearly a century. New regulatory environmental standards increased the cost of production at the Mill and influenced its future.

IP expanded operations in several parts of the country in the 1960s. However, the mills the Company scheduled for construction in other Northern Division communities were of most concern in Corinth. IP announced in 1964 that it would build a new mill in Jay, Maine. Located on the Androscoggin River, the mill was to run two paper machines, each with a 210-inch trim or width, and manufacture as much as 500 tons of kraft pulp daily, enough to supply three paper mills. IP planned to ship Jay-manufactured kraft to its Hudson River and Otis Mills by rail. IP's consolidation of kraft production in Maine resulted in the shutdown of Hudson River's sulfite mill that had been operating since the 1890s, and its Binderene plant, which had treated and recycled effluent from the mill's sulfite digesters for resale as an adhesive agent since 1916.

While the burnt sulfur that had fouled the air in the Palmer section of Corinth with the smell of rotten eggs for decades would not be missed, the jobs lost by the shutdown of the Sulfite Mill and Binderene Plant would be. Corinth village officials were particularly concerned that IP's announced plans for the expansion of its core papers business did not include an increase in production capacity for the Hudson River Mill. It was likely no coincidence that Corinth's civic leaders proclaimed "Paper Week" in Corinth in March 1965 to express the community's loyalty to IP. When announcing the planned event, the village mayor reminded both IP and local citizens that "the economy of our community is greatly dependent on International Paper Company operations." By year's end, the initial impact of IP expansion at Jay, Maine, and the corresponding shutdown at Hudson River had been felt in Corinth by the loss of several dozen jobs.

The construction of Jay's Androscoggin Mill did not initially pose a direct threat to IP's mill in Corinth because the machines installed there would not manufacture coated paper. But in 1966, IP committed another $39 million to Androscoggin with plans to construct a third paper machine that would produce 300 tons of coated paper daily. By 1967, IP had built a machine with a 306-inch trim at Androscoggin, the largest paper machine in the State of Maine. The new machine was 60% more productive than the Hudson River Mill's No. 11. By the time it was finished, IP had invested over $100 in its new Jay mill. The following year, in 1968, IP announced it would replace its existing plant at Ticonderoga, New York, another Northern Division plant about an hour north of Corinth, by building a new $76 million pulp and paper mill.

Civic leaders were discouraged that Corinth was being passed over. While the Ticonderoga Mill, like the Androscoggin and Hudson River Mills, was part of IP's Northern Division, it was considered an upstart within the Company since it had only become part of IP in 1925. To be built on a 1000-acre site, the new Ticonderoga Mill included 235-inch and 306-inch paper machines with a total yearly capacity of 207,000 tons. Although the new Ticonderoga Mill would not compete directly with Hudson River by producing coated papers, and IP announced it would not hire any employees above the 1,000 working at its old mill, the mill's construction was viewed as yet another instance of IP investment in manufacturing capacity other than at Corinth. Press coverage of the Ticonderoga Mill's construction noted that IP expected the yearly tonnage production at the new mill to be double that of its former mill while the number of employees would remain steady. A thoughtful reader would have understood that IP's investments in new technologies translated to job losses and reduced payroll.

IP committed millions of dollars to the Hudson River Mill in the 1960s. However, most of the money was spent on new, more efficient technology to keep the plant profitable. Between 1966 and 1971, IP expanded the mill's wood yard, erected a new wood room, and added a new steam plant. The mill's pulp wood grinders, which represented descendent technology from the original machines that first operated at Palmer Falls in 1869, were replaced by electric grinders that required fewer employees. During the same period, the Hudson River Mill's coating plant was closed, and the No. 1 and No. 2 paper machines were shut down. As IP installed new and larger coated paper machines at other mills, the two Hudson River Mill machines in 1896 had become obsolete. The No. 2 machine was brought back online briefly, but within a few months, it was shut down for good. The Company also built a plant to treat the Hudson River Mill's wastes for $2.8 million. The modernization projects at the Hudson River Mill in the 1960s, which approached $20 million, including the cost of the waste treatment facility, resulted in the loss of several hundred jobs over five years.

With IP's modernization program at Hudson River and outsourcing the Mill's kraft production to Maine, the number of Corinth mill employees declined sharply. With a peak of around 1500 workers shortly after the No. 11 machine began operations in 1958, the Mill's total employees fell to 1025 by 1970, a reduction of thirty-five percent in a little over a decade. Yet, due to the strength of the unions that represented paper workers at the Hudson River Mill, its payroll remained constant between 1965 and 1971, at just under $10 million per year. IP continued to pay about 60% of Village, Town, and school taxes. Competition from mills running larger and faster paper machines, coupled with technological improvements that had been made, contributed to the reduction in the Mill's workforce. By the end of the 1960s, the Hudson River Mill was no longer our father's paper mill.

Despite the impacts of IP's modernization program at Corinth and its production expansion elsewhere, Mill engineers and paper makers met the challenge. They continued to manufacture quality coated papers that were in high demand. In March 1967, the mill set a production record of 510 tons in a single day, with nearly 200,000 tons manufactured by year's end. Hudson River Mill paper was being used in major American magazines. Seventy-five printing companies representing over 100 publications used the paper the mill produced, including *LOOK, Saturday Evening Post, McCalls, The New Yorker, Glamour, Time, U.S. News, Newsweek, Scientific American, Good Housekeeping, and Popular Mechanics*. During this period, the demands of its customers varied so widely that Mill's chemical engineers had to create as many as twenty different base paper finishes and twenty-five separate coating formulations.

IP's earnings were trending upward, and the Company continued to diversify, slowly expanding away from its core business. Some of Corinth's civic leaders thought Jud Hannigan, a beloved former Hudson River Mill manager, would change the Company's direction in Corinth's favor. Hannigan, who had started his career at the Hudson River Mill in 1948 and had become its manager in 1961, was transferred to IP's home office in New York in 1963. He became a member of the IP Board of Directors in 1965 and its President by the early 1970s. Yet neither the Mill's production success nor Jud Hannigan's service as a member of the Company's management team assuaged the community anxieties that resulted from developments elsewhere within IP.

By the late 1960s, IP was committed to increasing production outside the Northeast. The Company announced plans for a new flakeboard mill in Arkansas, and it pledged $190 million in 1967 for two new bleached paper mills. IP was also planning new mills in Louisiana and Texas. Then, in early 1968, the Company indicated that it would build a new paper machine with 374-inch wire at its Vicksburg, Mississippi mill that would produce 1000 tons of paper daily. The news became a sober reminder that Hudson River Mill's No. 11, a state-of-the-art machine in 1958, was becoming dated with its 208-inch trim and 300-ton daily capacity. Later, in 1968, IP announced that it would enter the disposable fabric field when it purchased the manufacturing process for Confil, a non-woven German fabric that combined wood and polyester. IP said it would build two new mills to manufacture Confil, which it planned for use in disposable clothing.

The introduction of Confil by IP coincided with developments in Corinth that increased the anxieties of its civic leaders. In July 1968, New York State ordered the Village of Corinth to build a waste treatment plant to manage the community's sewage. Village waste had been emptied into the Hudson since 1900. Over 450,000 gallons were being discharged daily into the River by 1968. State and Federal Government agencies would pay 85% of the new plant's anticipated cost, yet the Village had to float a bond to pay the balance. The completed plant would then require the Village to budget $30,000 for yearly operating costs while requiring an increase in the tax rate on residents, estimated to be $6.21 per thousand. The unease felt by civic leaders over IP's development plans, understandable given the increased community costs anticipated in 1968, would intensify in just a few years when the $695,000 expected price of the treatment plant ballooned to $1,700,000 when it became operational in 1974. The added cost required the Village to float additional bonds and increase the tax levy.

At the time, Corinth was also trying to build a new hospital. The existing hospital was housed in the former Warren Curtis homestead on Palmer Avenue, and a modern brick addition was constructed in the early 1960s (The addition serves as the Corinth Town Hall). When Medicare began operating in 1965, the Federal Government determined that the Corinth Hospital did not meet minimum standards for patient care. As a result, care provided for Medicare patients would not be reimbursed. As Corinth patients were being moved to other hospitals, plans got underway to build a new 50-bed regional hospital whose costs would be shared among the Towns of Corinth, Hadley, and Lake Luzerne. After the three towns agreed to a plan, bids for the $1.5 million facility went out in 1968.

These circumstances prompted a community effort to persuade IP to build one of its planned Confil plants in Corinth. The Company was constructing new mills elsewhere in the Northern Division, yet it only intended to upgrade facilities at its Corinth mill. Jobs were being lost. By 1968, 1300 people were employed at the Hudson River Mill and the Cluett-Peabody shirt factory, down by 300 just a few years before. The two plants put over $10 million into the local economy each year through their payrolls alone ($87 million in 2024 dollars). Yet Corinth's civic leaders believed the community needed more jobs.

By late 1968, a public relations campaign was launched to persuade IP to build a Confil plant in Corinth. In the Fall of 1968, the Corinth Village Board authorized the Mayor to send a letter to IP President Edward Hinman and Corinth's Jud Hannigan, recently promoted to vice president, asking that the Company build one of its new plants in the community. The spirit of the mayor's letter was endorsed by an editorial published in the Glens Falls *Post-Star*. Corinth's civic leaders, who hoped that taxes and payroll from a new mill would help support the costs of the new hospital and the waste treatment plant, were shaken when Hinman wrote to the Village Board that Corinth would not become a site for the planned mill.

IP was proud of Confil and optimistic about the market for its use in disposable clothing. It launched a national advertising campaign in 1969 that featured high-profile actors Lloyd Bridges and Ali McGraw, the latter fresh from her starring role in the movie *Love Story*. Corinth's civic leaders undoubtedly viewed the much-sought Confil plant as a greater lost opportunity when the ad campaign was rolled out. It was with some irony that when the new Adirondack Regional Hospital opened in 1970, its window drapes, donated by IP, were made from Confil.

Having rejected Corinth as a site for a new mill, IP still brought a Confil road show to Corinth in the Spring of 1969. It included a stop at Corinth High School, where my senior classmates and I were ushered into the high school auditorium one morning in April to learn about the new disposable product. A young woman walked across the stage several times, modeling different dresses made from the fabric in each instance. We found the show entertaining, yet I don't think any of us understood at the time that Confil represented IP's shifting priorities, that nearly thirty-five percent of the jobs at the Mill had been eliminated in the previous ten years, or that civic leaders had sought a Confil plant to bring some of those jobs back.

While many of our fathers and some of our mothers worked at the mill and would occasionally speak about their work and Mill developments, they did not share their concern that more jobs would be lost unless the Company installed a new paper machine that would increase production. Senior management understood that the Hudson River Mill was becoming an aging plant, as did Corinth's civic leaders. By the late 1960s, old technology, new State environmental regulations, and the projected operating cost of the Mill's waste treatment plant were making the Mill increasingly less competitive.

Civic leaders, fresh from celebrating Corinth's founding during the Sesquicentennial celebration, were at the close of 1968 worried about the town's future. The Village mayor's concern over IP's reluctance to add new production capacity to the Hudson River Mill was reflected subtly in editorials George Holland wrote in the *EMBA News* in the latter 1960s. Civic leaders considered Corinth a progressive community and wanted to keep it that way, but doing so was expensive. An editorial that appeared in the *Saratogian* ticked off the Corinth community's achievements that had been realized in the 1960s: a new 50-bed hospital construction underway, a youth center in the works, a new Village water supply had been installed, an addition to the Emergency Squad building had been built, and a new building to house the Village's public works and police departments was just completed. The editorial also noted that Brookhaven Golf Course was adding another nine holes. The Village Hall, a historic former school on Main Street slated for demolition, had been saved, and the Village was constructing a waste treatment plant. Perhaps mindful of the mayor's plea to IP for a new mill, the editorial writer asked rhetorically, "What is left for Corinth to do?"

In early 1970, just after my classmates and I graduated, another display of fealty to IP was organized by a Corinth Citizen's Committee. It held a dinner to pay tribute to the Company, an effort that might have been considered an apology for the community's zealous attempt to land a Confil plant. The event, attended by 140, was an expression of the veiled anxiety growing in the community over the future of the Hudson River Mill. While the dinner had the appearance of an orchestrated groveling ceremony, with each Corinth speaker reciting some measure of the importance of that the paper mill held for the community, at least one guest got to the heart of the matter by saying that "without I-P Corinth would have long been a ghost town." Yet the IP dignitaries in attendance, some of whom appeared to gaslight their hosts, included Jud Hannigan, who then served as the Company's Vice-President for Manufacturing. Hannigan could offer no more than the gratuitous pledge that "I-P definitely plans to go down the road with the mill." No one at the time was willing to speculate where that road might lead. In 2002, the community would find out.

Three years later, the relationship between Corinth and IP would begin to head south. The Company filed a lawsuit against the Village in 1973, seeking a reduction in the valuation of the Mill and its property taxes. This development occurred while the EPA sought to enforce the Pure Waters Act of 1972 by ordering IP to cut its discharge of organic material into the Hudson at Corinth by 50 percent. A settlement was finally reached with the Village and the Town in 1975, and both agreed to substantial tax reductions. The Mill manager at the time, Richard O'Brien, stated that recent modernization programs still left the Mill with high operating costs and marginal profitability. Deteriorating business conditions led the Corinth Town Board to pass a resolution in 1978 pledging its support to the IP management in any practical way to ensure the continued operation of the Hudson River Mill. The support provided by the Town and Village and the extraordinary means employed by the Mill's engineers and paper makers miraculously kept the Mill running for another 25 years. Yet, If there were a time when Corinth's civic leaders might have considered the long-term implications of the shift in IP's stance towards the community and begun preparations for an alternative economic future, the 1970s would have been it.

As one of the thousands of kids who grew up in Corinth in the 1960s, I feel fortunate to have been raised in the community during its best years. I don't believe anyone living in Corinth during that time - civic leaders, business people, paper workers, or even Mill management – ever imagined they were witnessing the beginning of the slow, inexorable decline of the Hudson River Mill and Corinth itself. But this is precisely what was happening. Knowledgeable citizens surely understood the Mill was aging and that its shelf-life was limited without the addition of modern production capacity. I doubt many Corinthians at the time ever envisioned a day when the Mill would be shut down and demolished. As kids, we took the Hudson River Mill and our town for granted, never once imagining that we might return as adults to find the Mill gone and our hometown so profoundly changed. Perhaps our only consolation is that we lived in Corinth during the best of times.

21

— · —

Abraham, Martin and John

The Class of 1969 finally attained long-sought senior status when we returned to school in September 1968. Like many of the classes that preceded us, we had attended school with 12th-grade kids since we arrived in the 7th grade, sharing hallways, classrooms, locker rooms, and the cafeteria. We observed each successive class ahead of us, measuring their behavior and gauging how they carried their senior status. Now, it was our turn to the top of the educational pyramid.

Kids entering 7th grade attended school with seniors because Corinth lacked a middle school. When the new elementary school was built in 1936, a one-story wing was erected at the same time that connected it to Corinth High School, which had been constructed in 1936. So technically, 2nd graders and seniors went to school under the same roof. Of course, a 2nd grader never came in contact with a senior, but 7th graders rubbed shoulders with them daily. The small physical stature of many 7th graders and their generally impressionable and naive natures could make a kid feel like they were on top of the world when they became seniors at Corinth High School.

The year 1968, when our senior year began, was of great national significance, one of the most decisive twelve months in American history. Much of the 1960s since the assassination of JFK in 1963 had been tumultuous, its events seemingly driven by two powerful and transformative national developments: the Civil Rights Movement and the Vietnam War. The Beatles' arrival in 1963 proved to be an accelerant for a third development whose origins were in the 1950s. Rock music increasingly served as a force of cultural change for American youth, its songs reflecting both the angst traditionally felt by teenagers and opposition to the dominant American culture of the 1960s. These parallel and sometimes overlapping forces made 1968 particularly notorious. The assassinations of Martin Luther King Jr. and Robert Kennedy, the riots in 100 American cities that followed King's death, the Tet Offensive and the ongoing Vietnam War, urban rioting, and the chaos in the streets of Chicago during the Democratic Party National Convention all exploded into our living rooms, penetrating the bubble of our small-town life. 1968 also brought the War home when two Corinth boys, one of them a member of the Class of 1969, were killed in action in Vietnam.

Yet life in Corinth went on. The Town's Sesquicentennial celebration provided a temporary distraction from the national strife and local developments that had made civic leaders anxious. Some believed that growing restlessness among the community's youth needed to be managed and restrained, while others were growing concerned about the future of the community's pulp and paper mill. Some citizens understood that IP's continuing modernization of the Hudson River Mill would result in the loss of more jobs. The future was uncertain.

While Corinth celebrated its 150-year history throughout 1968 and appeared poised to maintain a progressive community agenda, International Paper – with a $10 million local payroll and a 60% contribution to the local tax base – was diversifying and expanding its operations, but not in ways that were adding jobs at the Hudson River Mill or increasing its payroll.

As teenagers, my friends and I were oblivious to these concerns and largely unaware of what was happening at the Mill. Yet the national chaos beyond Corinth's borders was palpable. Reflecting on that time, I think my closest friends and I turned to music, often to the songs of Simon and Garfunkel, Judy Collins, and Crosby, Stills, and Nash, to assuage the anxieties that we felt but rarely discussed.

The swirl of national and world events remained distant, seen chiefly through our TV screens and in the occasional *Saratogian* or Glens Falls *Post-Star* headline. My home was like most in Corinth, where there was little or no conversation about what was happening beyond our community. And there were no conversations at school either. Years later, we were told the high school administration had restricted our teachers from engaging in controversial social issues. This sad fact was disclosed by one affected teacher at a Corinth Alumni Association reunion in 1999 at a bar in the Saratoga Springs Holiday Inn. He divulged to a small group of us the prohibitions imposed when he taught at Corinth High School.

It was then I understood why, in this teacher's 11th-grade economics course, he encouraged us to participate in the purchase of General Dynamics common stock. He asked members of his two economics classes to contribute $1.00 each so we could buy a few company shares. If Corinth teachers were prohibited from discussing the Vietnam War in their classrooms, our economics instructor reasoned, by owning a part of a company and following its progress in the newspapers, economics students could at least understand that American corporations like General Dynamics were reaping huge profits from the ongoing conflict in Southeast Asia. I am not sure how many of us figured out what he was up to, but in my stored belongings, I still have a copy of the stock certificate and the names of every kid who owned General Dynamics shares.

My classmates and I had the War on our minds, even if Vietnam was not a classroom topic. Each year, Dick Stein, who taught 10th grade English at Corinth High School, assigned his students to write a poem which he then assembled into a four-page publication entitled "The Best of the 10th." The 1967 edition by the Class of 1969 contained 15 poems. Four of the poems were about war. My poem "War," among those published, offered the somewhat naive stanza: "Thru war and peace many men die, Though most do not know the reason why, Perhaps to defend a firm belief, But victory might end in grief." Classmate Ten Andrus railed forcefully against the Russians, but Anne Healy and Mike Butler exposed the rage many of us must have felt. Anne's poem included this stanza: "Vietnam is an ugly place; Men dying and leaving no trace." Mike's effort offered a broad diatribe against our parents and our teachers with lines like this: "Adults invented the dirty books. They are the ones that bought the guns" and then, "Is it really the child who is at fault? The ones who sit in the shop drinking a malt? Or is it the adult who is at fault?" Like our economics teacher, Dick Stein created a means to bring the Vietnam War, and more generally, generational angst, into the classroom.

When my senior year at Corinth High School began in September 1968, the year had already produced several events of great national consequence. In January, the Tet Offensive showed that America's adversaries in Vietnam could conduct damaging offensive operations despite the Pentagon's claim the United States had the upper hand. Tet moved Walter Cronkite of CBS News, then regarded as the most trusted man in America, to travel to Vietnam in February to observe the war firsthand. Cronkite's earlier newscasts helped shape public opinion supporting the war, but his Vietnam trip changed his views and reporting. When he returned to the air in early March, Cronkite proclaimed on an evening broadcast that the Vietnam War had become a stalemate and suggested the U.S. should negotiate for peace. In a comment allegedly made after viewing the broadcast, President Johnson said, "If I've lost Cronkite, I've lost Middle America." American opinion on the War began to change following Tet and Cronkite's prognosis. President Johnson saw his reelection hopes dim and, within weeks, declared he would not seek the Presidency in November.

The assassinations of Martin Luther King Jr. in April and Robert Kennedy in June had badly shaken Liberal hopes that America might become a more just society, free of racism and less willing to engage in needless wars abroad. The speech that RFK gave from the back of a flatbed truck in a Black Indianapolis neighborhood on the night of MLK's assassination would have earned him America's African-American vote had he lived to become the Democratic party nominee. RFK would have been difficult to defeat in November.

By most accounts, RFK's assassination in June eliminated Republican Richard Nixon's most threatening Democratic challenger. Anyone who has ever viewed the documentary film *"Ethel,"* made by Kennedy's daughter, Rory, which includes rare footage of RFK, has understood that American history would have taken a radically different trajectory if RFK had become President in 1968 instead of Nixon. The Vietnam War would have ended much sooner; there would have been no Watergate scandal; the nation would not have had President Gerald Ford or likely President Carter. And without President Carter, President Reagan, Newt Gingrich, and the Tea Party Movement would probably not be part of our history. This is not to say that the arc of history that would have begun with a Robert Kennedy Presidency would have landed us in a better place than we currently find ourselves. Yet, we certainly would have landed elsewhere than where the nation finds itself in 2024.

Race continued to be at the center of the national discussion in 1968. The Kerner Commission, charged by President Johnson to investigate the causes of the urban riots that had rocked the nation during the summer of 1967, concluded that systemic white racism had been responsible. Indeed, we had watched urban riots on our TVs since 1965 as the Black neighborhoods of cities like Los Angeles, Detroit, and Newark went up in flames. The 1968 Olympic games in Mexico City in the summer of 1968 provided sprinters Tommie Smith and John Carlos a forum to protest racial discrimination by boldly raising black-gloved fists as the American national anthem was played. Later, in November, Captain James Kirk and Lt. Nyota Uhura, characters on TV's *Star Trek,* performed what is widely regarded as TV's first interracial kiss.

The assassination of Martin Luther King eliminated the Civil Rights Movement's most influential yet moderate leader. Many Americans grew increasingly anxious with the rising prominence of the Black Panther Party following King's death. Some of the Party's well-armed members had been involved in violent police encounters that made the evening news. Much of the national discussion leading up to and during my senior year dealt with civil rights and race. However, these issues had little resonance in Corinth since our community had no African-American residents. And neither race nor Civil Rights were discussed in any high school class I attended.

The events of 1968 helped fuel a conservative backlash against the liberalism of the 1960s that began with the election of Richard Nixon to the Presidency. Nixon's election victory may have been sealed in August 1968 when Vietnam War protestors battled with Chicago police in the streets outside the Democratic National Convention, a spectacle broadcast live on national television. Some political observers said the debacle showed the nation that Democrats could not govern. Meanwhile, the Democratic party faithful were inside the Hilton Hotel working to suppress the voices of its anti-war delegates so that Hubert Humphrey, who had pledged to continue President Johnson's Vietnam policies, could receive the party's nomination. Conservatives who saw Vietnam protestors as un-American, even after trusted Walter Cronkite turned against the War in March, relished in the assault orchestrated by Chicago's Mayor Richard Daley, a Democrat, on the youth that flooded the city. Indeed, large swaths of American society – Democrats among them - still believed in the Vietnam War even after the Tet Offensive in January and despite Walter Cronkite's defection in March. It might be argued that the events of 1968 hardened American support for the War.

Richard Nixon recovered Middle America, which had become disillusioned with the Vietnam War. Nixon used an assortment of "dog whistles" to enlist his Silent Majority to support him in a presidential run. His campaign featured a law-and-order pledge against hippies, war protestors, Hollywood, and the media. Implicit in his messaging was also a palpable racism intended to bring Southern whites into the Republican Party. Conservatives supported Nixon because they believed there was too much change and the America they knew was slipping away. Hardline, uncompromising support for the Vietnam War soon formed. The 1968 release of John Wayne's *The Green Berets,* an unapologetic pro-Vietnam propaganda film, was a prime example of this trend. Wayne's film tried to make a case for the War as support for it was beginning to erode in some places. The film's narrative arc showed how a skeptical American journalist became a fervid war advocate after viewing the conflict first-hand. Wayne used a choral version of Barry Sadler's "Ballad of the Green Berets" for his film, a song that had been No. 1 on the music charts for five weeks in 1966.

The politics of John Wayne and Richard Nixon reflected the threatening potential of reactionary conservatism as we began our senior year at Corinth High School. The tendency was foreshadowed in Peter Fonda's movie *Easy Rider,* filmed in early 1968 yet not released until 1969. The film's final scene shows two Southern good old boys killing the two motorcycle-riding hippies, Wyatt and Billy, for no apparent reason other than they were hippies. The killings in the film suggested that some Americans might use violence against ideas that didn't conform to their own or against people not like them.

Less than a year later, in May 1970, the personal risk of threatening the status quo in America became real when the Ohio State National Guard killed four students on the Kent State University campus during a Vietnam War protest. A few days later, when protests against the Kent State killings erupted in New York City, 400 hard hat construction workers and around 800 office workers left their jobs to attack Vietnam War protestors in the Manhattan streets below. Young people finally realized that exercising First Amendment rights in America could kill you. The impact of Kent State and the Hard Hat Riot had only begun to sink in when Crosby, Stills, Nash, and Young released their song "Ohio." The song was banned in Ohio and some AM radio stations, but its lyrics "Tin soldiers and Nixon coming, we're finally on our own" resonated among American youth, infusing the popular expression, "America, love it or leave it" with a terrible new meaning.

Life and work in Corinth carried on against this turbulent background. As the Class of 1969 anticipated our final academic year in September 1968, one that would be rich with senior year activities and, for a few, the angst-ridden college application process, it was easy to ignore the world beyond. College acceptance was critical for a handful of boys, providing a deferment from the military draft and escape from the Vietnam War. Of course, the boys in our class who were not planning to go to college would not have the privilege of a draft deferment. Most would soon receive a 1-A classification from our local draft board office at 33 Phila Street in Saratoga Springs and be called to military service. Conscription numbers for 1969 were tracking similarly to 1968, which had brought almost 300,000 boys into military service, an average of 25,000 per month. So, the boys from our class who would not get a college deferment had to calculate the advantages of enlisting for three years of service or being drafted for two. It was widely perceived at the time that enlisting in the military would improve your chances of staying out of harm's way. At the time, boys who waited to be drafted seemed always to be sent to Vietnam.

Several of my high school classmates made this very calculation. Jeff Dodge, Ron McLeod, and David Thomson enlisted in the U.S. Army in March of 1969, three months before graduation. Like most of us, they had been watching the Vietnam War nightly on the evening news and understood they would undoubtedly get drafted after graduating since they were healthy and not college-bound. The three enrolled in a delayed enlistment program called the "Buddy System" that their Glens Falls recruiter promised would allow them to undergo basic training together. The recruiter's reassurance that enlisting was far better than waiting to be drafted supported their rationale for joining. According to Jeff, the recruiter made the military sound like the guys were joining something just a notch above the Boy Scouts, even suggesting they might spend their enlisted time in an air-conditioned office stateside. The recruiter gave Jeff, Ron, and David the impression that enlisting increased their chance of escaping combat and not being sent to Vietnam. They believed what they were told.

However, the experiences of my classmates did not match the Army's promises. After arriving at Ft. Dix, New Jersey, on a bus from Albany, the three were split up and assigned to different units. They did not see each other at Ft. Dix and were eventually deployed to Vietnam. Jeff landed in Cam Rahn Bay after a 29-hour flight via Hawaii. Sometime later, he met up with Ron, but he never saw Dave again until after the war, many years later. Jeff served for a year in the Signal Corps in South Vietnam's central highlands. Like most soldiers, he marked off his days in-county on a calendar, saving his earned R&R until the end of his twelve-month tour. When the time came, Jeff opted to spend his time off in Australia, but he was denied a seat on the plane because his worn uniform and ragged hair did not meet the regulations for travel out of Vietnam. Jeff was instead forced to spend his R&R in Saigon, where American soldiers remained vulnerable to Viet Cong attacks. After leaving Vietnam, Jeff served two more years in the Army before mustering out in 1972. David Thompson, who served in the Army for over a decade and brought the agony of war back home with him to Corinth, was hit by a car and killed in 1983. Ron MacLeod, who completed four tours in Vietnam from 1971 to 1975, spent his career in the Army. Ron died in 2021. Jeff Dodge is retired in Western New York, where he spends warm summer days on his sailboat.

Even the deaths of Corinth boys Carl Merchant and Bruce Colson, which brought the Vietnam War home in 1968, did not seem to alter the calculus of our indifference. Bruce had been our classmate before he enlisted in the Marines in late 1967, and Carl was the older brother of another of our classmates, Billy Merchant. By the time we began our senior year, I think many of us had become desensitized to the turmoil that the War had created. Our teachers could have shaken us from our complacency, but they did not. They remained silent on controversial issues – particularly the War - complicit in the high school administration's insistence that they not engage students in political matters. So, we never discussed the Vietnam War, the Civil Rights Movement, or the 1968 Presidential election in our classrooms. Far removed from the world we would soon inherit, many among us drifted thoughtlessly through our final year of public school, the last one that some of us would ever spend in Corinth.

22

— • —

WHAT'S GOING ON

C orinth's Sesquicentennial organizers sought to foster a celebratory atmosphere in Corinth in 1968. In a year when two Corinth men had been killed in Vietnam, two prominent national leaders were assassinated, and TV networks broadcast the Chicago police using clubs and tear gas to silence anti-war protestors during the Democratic National Convention, the most ardent boosters of the Sesquicentennial had remade Corinth into a 19th-century theme park. The coexistence of these disparate realities must have seemed incongruous to some of the community's more thoughtful citizens, so much so that growing a beard, wearing a derby, or fabricating a homespun dress to march in the Sesquicentennial parade might have seemed both corny or insensitive or both.

The dissonance between national affairs and the community's birthday celebration in 1968 was exacerbated by developments within Corinth that created community unease. Like most Americans in the 1960s, Corinthians had become hardened to a steady stream of troubling and sometimes alarming national news. Yet the community's history had shown that Corinth seemed always to be just one newspaper headline away from another tragedy, yet one more unsettling occurrence. Numerous disquieting community developments within the town in 1968 resulted in hand-wringing by those most invested in the town's future. Corinth's civic leaders were concerned by its exclusion from International Paper's announced plans for expansion and growth, and incidents of teenage delinquency and social disorder led some municipal leaders to believe the community had a "youth problem." Corinth had a long history as a community where almost anything could happen. And it usually did.

Several disturbing local events marked 1968. Early in the year, Mosher's Laundromat, which was located on a building that once sat on the northeast corner of Main and River Streets, was set on fire by an arsonist. Reports suggested its origin was similar to a fire that destroyed the former Burnham and Winslow's grist mill and feed store, a 165-year-old building on Mallery Street, in late 1967. The arrest of a 25-year-old man suspected of the crime was made only a few days later. Lent's Supermarket on Palmer Avenue also burned to the ground, nearly taking the legendary Star Hotel next door with it. In May, two 16-year-olds used knives to slit open 35 tires on cars in IP's Pine Street parking lot. The responsible boys were apprehended, tried, and sentenced to 90 days in the Saratoga County jail. Brust's Garage was burglarized in early June, and its safe was stolen. The safe was found three weeks later behind the Corinth rail depot, where two men had gone to take target practice. In a fashion characteristic of Corinth in those years, the theft of the safe was not made public until it was found. Even then, the public report failed to say if it had been opened and, if so, what had been stolen.

Also, in June, two men were arrested for crimes against local women. On June 17, a 22-year-old Corinth man was arrested for assault, accused of holding a knife to a woman's throat at her Hadley home. Only four days later, a 24-year-old Corinthian armed with a 16-gauge shotgun forced his sister-in-law from her home to a camp on the Hudson River north of the village, imprisoning her for three days before she could escape and contact police. The man received only a nine-month jail sentence after pleading guilty to a felony. In the Fall, FBI agents came to town searching for two Corinth brothers who were AWOL from the U.S. Army. Found holed up in a room at the Central Hotel in Corinth, they were both arrested for desertion. In October, a paper worker and friend of my Father, a man who used his old Jeep to plow our driveway after every snowstorm for just $1.00, committed suicide with a 12-gauge shotgun after reportedly finding his wife in bed with another man. Community tragedy continued as three Corinth boys, the youngest age 13 years old, committed suicide in the first five months of 1969. And these were just the events that were reported.

Several serious automobile accidents intersected these disturbing community events. Car wrecks severe enough to be published in the morning *Post-Star* would always draw the curious and the voyeuristic to Pike's Garage on Main Street, whose wrecker would usually be dispatched to pull the smashed-up vehicles into its rear parking area. Some mornings after the *Post-Star* had arrived on village doorsteps with the news of a car crash the previous day, a small crowd would gather around the wreck at Pike's. The most spectacular car crash that year was reminiscent of the tragic accident at the Aldous home on River Road in 1947, where a young woman lost both of her legs after a wood truck plowed through the front porch of her house. In 1968, a Ballston Spa man was killed when his car left Eastern Avenue at a high rate of speed and crashed, airborne, through the front porch of a house. Fortunately, no one was sitting out at the time. The vehicle knocked out each of the porch's five supporting columns before coming to rest 700 feet away in a grassy field. The crash was so horrific that a photograph of the demolished porch appeared in a local newspaper. And while there had been several fatal car-train collisions in Corinth's past, a 63-year-old resident narrowly escaped death in October 1968 when his vehicle was hit by an 82-car Delaware and Hudson freight train at the

Route 9N crossing just south of Heath Road. The driver of the totaled car, who reached the crossing well after sunset at around 7:30 PM, told State Police that the crossing's red signal light was inoperable.

Corinth's civic leaders became unsettled in 1968 and early 1969 by arson, vandalism, and youth suicide. Concerned that the growing use of recreational drugs nationwide would spread to the community, Corinth's police chief arranged for a New York State Police officer to present a program on narcotics to Corinth kids 12 and older. The program was evidence the pillars of the community wanted to be proactive, hoping that drug use would not become part of what some in Corinth had begun to believe was "the community's youth problem." While 1968 had provided multiple instances of unacceptable juvenile conduct, most of which never made it to the newspapers, concern for the perceived problem may also have been driven by the media's portrayal of youth in rebellion elsewhere in the United States.

In 1969, the Mayor of Corinth Village proposed the creation of a community youth center. Centers were popping up across the region in 1967 and 1968, so he probably thought that recent events in the community demanded that Corinth have one, too. Yet, citizens were not expected to pay for it. A fund was established to raise $6000 in donations to cover construction costs ($53,000 in 2024). The Mayor, who would not have suggested that a Village department hold a bake sale or car wash to raise the funds required, soon enlisted Corinth kids to participate in fundraising activities to pay for the center. He expressed confidence the youth center would help address adolescent misbehavior in the community. It must have occurred to someone that the young people slitting car tires and setting fires to Corinth buildings were unlikely to be rehabilitated by playing ping-pong and bumper pool.

The Corinth Youth Center project, which the community's adults sought but did not want to fund themselves, had an air of theater. It appeared to get launched because civic leaders thought it was the progressive thing to do. When the Center finally opened in 1970, the kids involved named it "The Establishment" without the slightest bit of intended irony. The center's name offered insight into the side Corinth kids were on during the culture wars of the late 1960s. Not long after the Center opened, it was featured in an issue of the *Youth Service News*, published by the New York State Division for Youth. The article cited the contributions made by the Village Mayor and adult community organizations yet did not name a Corinth teenager involved in the project. The article's writer, noting a lack of "enthusiasm and exuberance" for the Center upon completion, seems to have understood that its construction was an adult idea.

Besides the need to address the community's youth problem, Corinth's civic leadership grew increasingly concerned with International Paper's investments in new pulp and paper factories everywhere but Corinth. They were so bothered that the community lost its bid to get a Confil plant in Corinth that the Village Mayor complained directly to IP's President. Village and Town officials may have believed that Corinth was still in the running for IP's second proposed Confil plant when the roadshow it brought to the high school in the Spring of 1969 also made a stop at the Hudson River Mill, making a presentation to River Mill's Technical Association. Civic leaders and mill officials viewed IP's explanation of its new product in Corinth as indicating the company might still build a Confil plant in town after being passed over for the first mill. By then, thoughtful Town and Village officials understood that the Hudson River Mill would eventually lose its competitive advantage in coated paper manufacturing if it relied on existing technology. The Mayor's direct appeal to IP's President underscores the degree to which Corinth had grown increasingly dependent on the Company, seemingly unable to imagine how the community might survive economically without it. IP decided, however, not to build a proposed second Confil plant in Corinth.

Corinth's Mayor and other civic leaders, who perhaps sensed for the first time their paper mill might not be around forever, also became alarmed by a strike at the Cluett-Peabody shirt factory in January 1969. The strike, originating in Troy, put over two hundred Corinth shirtmakers out of work. The Village Mayor again inserted himself into corporate affairs, writing to both Cluett-Peabody management and the Amalgamated Clothing Workers Unions to complain about the adverse effect of the strike on Corinth's economy.

Corinth civic leaders in 1969 were virtuous in a way that would be unrecognizable today. Yet, as a businessman, the Mayor indeed considered his own economic well-being and that of other business owners in town. After all, the Mayor's family had buried nearly everyone who had lived in Corinth during the previous 100 years. Committed civic leaders were gradually beginning to realize that the "modernization" of the Hudson River Mill to which IP was committed was intended to improve production efficiencies and preserve Company profits. This meant Corinthians might still have their paper mill, yet the new technologies required to sustain the plant would inevitably result in lost jobs.

While 1968 is considered one of the most tumultuous years in American history, Corinth experienced unrest of its own. A small group of committed celebrants had orchestrated the Sesquicentennial celebration, yet most Corinthians preferred to be observers rather than participants. Community members who held homespun and facial hair in disdain sat on the sidelines. Corinth's teenagers and some of its young men created enough social unrest to persuade civic officials that the town needed a youth center, a reluctant admission the community's established guard rails had failed, and new ones were needed to avert future reckless behavior. For perhaps the first time, Town and Village officers considered in 1968 that they could no longer count on IP to sustain the community's economy.

It was ironic that O.B. Beyer died in 1968. Beyer had served as the Hudson River Mill manager for 25 years, overseeing the development of coated paper production following World War II. He was also responsible for installing the No. 11 machine in 1957, which was state-of-the-art technology then. O.B. Beyer was at least one old-timer who did not have to witness the beginning decline of the Hudson River Mill.

23

— · —

Hot Priest

M any of my closest friends were Catholic. Our association was not premeditated based on this commonality; it just turned out that way. Nearly all of us attended catechism classes at the Immaculate Conception Church offered by the parish's three nuns and its assistant priest from elementary through high school. Our earliest classes were co-educational and held once weekly and on Saturday mornings. My most explicit memory of those classes is an aggregate of the many hours spent in the lower level of the Parish Hall. This modest wood frame building served as the parish church from 1887 until the construction of the substantial brick church next door in 1905. During our elementary school years, catechism instructors were nuns from the Convent of Franciscan Sisters of the Atonement. They usually stood before us, flipping through the oversized pages of the tripod-mounted catechism chart, each page revealing a different lesson. I was often distracted during catechism, thinking how hot Sister Mary Ellen must have been in her ankle-length wool habit.

The pinnacle of our religious instruction came in preparation for Confirmation in May 1963, when my classmates and I were 12 or 13. As one of the Catholic Church's seven sacraments, Confirmation instruction was taken seriously, so the nuns held classes in the church instead of the Parish

Hall. With over 180 members, the 1963 Confirmation class was divided into smaller groups who sat in pews at the front and rear of the church on both sides of the center aisle. A nun taught each group. Sister Germaine, considered the gentlest and perhaps most naive of the nuns who lived in the convent, led our class.

The Last Supper was the topic in one of our sessions. Using the Socratic method of instruction, Sister Germaine, at one point, asked us, "What did Jesus say to his disciples when he took the bread, blessed it, and broke it for them to eat?" Complete silence. No one answered. She then repeated the question, this time with a notable indignant tone. "What did Jesus say to his disciples when he took the bread, blessed it, and broke it for them to eat?" After several seconds of silence, one of the boys, almost certainly my friend Dennis Moylan, blurted out, "Eat me!" Undeterred by several giggles and at least one howl, Sister Germaine responded excitedly, "That's right. Now, class, let's say the answer together." The group of perhaps 50 kids, some looking at each other in disbelief, dutifully did what she said, loudly affirming in unison, "Eat me!" The volume of our provocative response got the kids' attention in the other class groups, including Sister Joseph Adele, who promptly came to Sister Germaine's side and whispered something to her. Sister Germaine moved quickly to the next topic.

At some point, perhaps in the 9th grade, Saturday classes were discontinued, with boys and girls attending their remaining mid-week classes separately, just about when many of us entered puberty. The boys' classes were most often held on the upper level of the Parish Hall, an ample space whose north end, which had served as the altar when the building was a church, was a few steps higher than the main floor. With no fixed pews remaining from its time as a church, metal folding chairs stored along the walls were used for seating when needed. Girls had their classes downstairs in an often dark and musty basement. One might suspect that separating boys and girls had something to do with our burgeoning sexuality, yet I don't recall that any instruction in that area was ever offered, at least not in the boys' class. Regardless, with a few notable exceptions, most of Corinth's Catholic boys and girls I knew best were chaste.

Besides serving as a catechism classroom and the site of CDA bake sales, the upper level of the Parish Hall also became the setting for the Great Shoe Fight of 1966. It was one of those rare, spontaneous events when you were a kid that could never have been planned or imagined. The Parish Hall shoe fight remains memorable, an epic encounter between teenage boys and girls, fueled no doubt by our raging hormones. One weekday afternoon after catechism classes had ended, several kids lingered on the sidewalk outside the Parish Hall. Our priest and the nuns had returned to the rectory and convent, yet the door to the upper level of the Parish Hall remained open. A couple of the boys wandered back in to check out the large cardboard boxes at the front of the room stuffed with shoes and used clothing, the haul from a recent Catholic Daughter's clothing drive. Just about the same time that one of the boys pulled a shoe from a storage box, another boy came through the front door at the rear of the hall.

Likely without thinking about it, yet with purpose, the shoe in his hand was thrown toward the boy who had just entered. Missing its mark, the shoe was picked up and hurled back just as the first boy chucked a second shoe. The exchange of shoes and boots that continued between the two created a commotion that brought the kids outside back into the hall. Each one of them, boys and girls alike, quickly picked a side, some staying at the back of the hall while those who ran to the front hunched over to avoid getting smacked upside the head by an old boot. Soon, about twenty kids were in the Parish Hall hurling shoes and boots at each other. I don't recall anyone getting hit, but the heels of some heavier shoes left holes in the wall. The fantastic thing about the shoe fight was how aggressive and skilled the girls were. Some had excellent arms and gave as good as they got. A few kids got worked up, no doubt some primal reaction to the benign violence. Then, just as spontaneously as the conflict began, the Great Shoe Fight ended. The scattered boots and shoes were gathered and put back into the box, and we all went home.

The Catholic church always had two priests living in the rectory in those days. Father Hanlon, who baptized most of my classmates and closest friends born in Corinth, arrived at our parish in 1930. He served until 1958, when he suffered a cerebral hemorrhage and was replaced by Father Whelly. Father Walsh became the head priest in 1964 and was in charge of the parish when our co-educational catechism classes ended. He was also my "boss" during my first year as the Catholic cemetery caretaker. Father Meehan replaced Father Walsh in 1967, serving our church for 18 years until 1985. Our parish also had assistant priests, although I don't recall ever differentiating between them since they were both authority figures and wore similar liturgical clothing. The assistants usually taught catechism, so we got to know them better.

Father Polumbus was the first priest I recall the boys had for catechism class. He arrived at our parish in 1965. He was a modestly rotund man in his early 50s who was outgoing and walked with a slight swagger. His classroom was arranged so that we sat in metal folding chairs separated from each other by several feet, front and back, and side to side. Father Polumbus used the Socratic method, consistently testing our knowledge of the catechism we were to have studied. He would walk around the room in between the chairs, asking questions while carrying a yardstick he would use to strike the upper arm of boys who gave the wrong answer or the wrong look, using it like Sister Mary Stigmata did in *The Blues Brothers* when she used one to whack Jake and Elwood. Some of the boys called him "Father Yardstick."

Another teaching method used by Father Yardstick was not as corporal as swatting a kid, yet it did result in some pain. Sometimes, when he would walk down an aisle in between our chairs, there was not enough room to swing his yardstick and smack one of us without taking out an innocent kid behind him. He would instead grab his victim by the cheek with his thumb and two forefingers, admonishing him as he forcibly pulled the boy up and out of his chair into a standing position. After a minute or so of nose-to-nose verbal abuse, the kid was pushed back down to his seat, his face red from embarrassment, our priest's finger marks still visible on his cheek. Father Yardstick succeeded in terrifying us while ensuring we would not learn anything of lasting value in his class, theological or otherwise.

Father Polumbus passed away in early 1968. The assistant pastor who took his place was a slender man in his mid-40s. He was soft-spoken, sensitive, and deliberate, not the sort of priest who would use corporal means to instill catechism into us. He could have been mistaken for a Yoga instructor or a Buddhist monk. We soon realized our new priest seemed to be amid a nervous breakdown. During one of our first class meetings, he told us that he had quit smoking, but he then took out a cigarette that he mouthed off and on throughout the entire class without ever lighting it. This was not too long after the Surgeon General issued his epic warning linking cigarette smoking with lung cancer. A few classes later, he removed his black jacket as soon as class started and continued to strip off his clerical garb so that he was down only to his black trousers and white undershirt. He pretended to smoke an unlighted cigarette and speak to us about Catholicism while he disrobed, not once making eye contact with anyone in the class. My closest friends and I thought his actions were odd, but we weren't bothered by them. As kids, we were so used to hearing about or observing unusual behavior in Corinth that having a priest go off his rocker in catechism class didn't seem all that out of the ordinary. The next thing we knew, he was gone without explanation.

Our third assistant pastor in four years arrived shortly after that. I refer to him here as Hot Priest, a name inspired by the recent BBC TV series "Fleabag," where a priest becomes objectified by a 30-year-old female parishioner. The priest is not given a name in the series but is known only as "Hot Priest." Our Hot Priest arrived in Corinth in June 1968, driving a green pick-up truck with a horse saddle in the bed. He was a man of medium height, wiry, and in his mid-20s. He was outgoing and irreverent. He often said mass in blue jeans with cowboy boots visible under his vestments. Not long after he arrived, Hot Priest began to perform in a local coffee house, singing folk songs and playing the banjo. He also rode in a local rodeo on weekends. He was not exactly your run-of-the-mill Catholic priest, especially for Corinth. Catholic girls thought he was cute, and the guys thought he was cool. I think it is fair to say that some girls had a crush on him.

I don't remember Hot Priest teaching catechism, so perhaps classes for high school boys had ended towards the end of our junior year, or my parents had released me from the obligation. He was, however, a strong advocate for the parish's teenagers. Hot Priest proposed that we create a Catholic Youth Organization (CYO) in the lower level of the Parish Hall to provide a place where kids could hang out. At about the same time, Corinth's civic leaders decided that our town needed a community youth center; Hot Priest's CYO idea was born in that atmosphere. The CYO plan was embraced enthusiastically when it was hatched in the Fall of 1968, initially by the girls and soon by the boys. The boys realized the crush that some girls had on Hot Priest complicated our efforts to get their attention, yet we liked Hot Priest too, primarily because of his irreverent nature. He could get away with what we couldn't.

Members of the Classes of 1969 and 1970 didn't need a new place to congregate. We had 313 Center Street, the home of my classmate, Sandy, whose parents always seemed to be out on Saturday nights. They were the most social of my friend's parents. Many of our weekend nights were spent there. Sandy's sister Fran, who was four years older, also went out on Saturday nights, so we had the house to ourselves. Besides Center Street, we had Kayo's downtown on Maple Street. We always put several tables together when we went there, eating pizza and nursing Cokes through the evening. Kayo's had a jukebox, so there was always music, three songs for 25 cents. Nettie Kehoe, who owned and ran the place, never seemed to mind that we used her restaurant as a hang-out.

The kids who got behind the CYO project were not seeking a "Catholic" place to go, although a few of the boys involved had been altar boys. When we told our parents about the plan for the Center, they thought it was a great idea. Before long, the basement of the Parish Hall was full of donated couches, chairs, and tables. The Center was a secular space. There were no statues of the Virgin Mary, no crucifixes on the walls, and no one ever spoke about God or the Gospel. We didn't even have any communion wafers to snack on. My memory of the CYO project remains vivid, but the only specific experience I can remember was a mixer that Hot Priest organized with kids from the CYO at St. John the Baptist Church in Schenectady, where he had served before arriving in Corinth. The mixer was a debacle. There wasn't the slightest chemistry between the two groups of kids, one from the city and the other from a backwater mill town. While I don't remember returning to the Center after that event, Hot Priest remained popular with many kids throughout our senior year. In the end, some of my senior classmates determined that we would rather spend the weekend nights of our final year at Corinth High at 313 Center Street, going to

Kayos or just walking the streets rather than sitting around in an old church basement.

While activity at the CYO center diminished for some of us, Hot Priest kept busy outside his parish duties. He performed regularly at a coffee house in Ft. Edward. The local newspapers reveled in his novelty, referring to him as "the singing priest." Hot Priest also developed a local notoriety by riding in the weekly rodeo in Lake Luzerne. A popular figure at the Painted Pony Ranch and other venues where he competed, Hot Priest was named Rookie of the Year for 1968 by the Adirondack Rodeo League. He became a local celebrity. I always wondered what the Bishop of Albany thought or if Father Meehan, the priest superior to him at our parish, supported his extra-priest activities. If any Catholic priest could push past the clerical profession's normative constraints, it was Hot Priest.

Things soon turned sideways for him. When I returned home from college in May 1970, following the completion of my freshman year, the Corinth rumor mill was churning out stories about Hot Priest. Each rumor had in common the belief he had been forced out of the parish after being caught in a compromising position. After departing from Corinth's Immaculate Conception Church, the "singing Priest" seems to have left the regional coffeehouse circuit. Not long after, Hot Priest was seen tending a bar in Stony Creek by two of my friends who were part of the CYC Center project.

I heard nothing about Hot Priest until 30 years later, in the summer of 2000. I was in Corinth for a weekend to help my Mother. One night, I visited a close friend from the Class of 1969 who still lived in town. We were sitting on their front porch, and before long, two other high school friends arrived, both members of the Class of 1970. We had been part of the same social group of about twenty kids in high school, and all four of us had worked with Hot Priest on the CYO Center project. The conversation quickly turned to a memoir that Hot Priest had recently published that one friend there had just read. A mother with children of her own by then, she became impassioned when describing the memoir's account of a young woman she thought to be from Corinth, who the author said visited him when he was in Mississippi in August 1969.

I retained a vivid memory of that evening, but I didn't think about it again until some 20 years later when I was preparing to write about growing up Catholic in Corinth. I began to reflect on Hot Priest and his influence on my friends and me. I also thought about that summer night in 2000 when my high school friend had become furious when discussing his memoir. It was about the same time someone told me they heard that Hot Priest had a Facebook page. When I could not locate the page, I wondered about the memoir and what Hot Priest might have written about his time in Corinth. I was particularly interested in how he might have described the kids – my friends and me – who worked with him on the CYO Project. How did he view us, I wondered? What did he have to say about his Corinth experience? What was his view of the community in 1968 and 1969?

After some research, I finally located a copy of his book. As soon as I read it, I realized one of the reasons why my friend had become so enraged over it 22 years earlier. The memoir leaves out a lot. It does not mention the nearly two years that Hot Priest spent in Corinth, nor does it describe any of the kids he knew during his tenure there, whose lives, like mine, he had touched. The adult reflection of our teenage selves I expected to see in the memoir was nowhere to be found. Like many of my closest friends, I held Hot Priest in high regard. We all looked up to him. So, it was a great disappointment to discover the memoir had nothing to say about us. It became another troubling realization that as teenagers growing up in Corinth in the 1960s, we might not have meant much to the adults we most liked and respected.

One of the memoir's chapters describes the time Hot Priest spent in Mississippi engaging in clean-up work after Hurricane Camille hit the Gulf Coast. The opaque account of that period also describes the arrival of a female visitor with whom a relationship is implied. I found myself returning to the chapter after I discovered that Camille made landfall in August 1969. I was working in the Mill and getting ready to head to college, and my Class of 1970 friends were preparing for their senior year. The memoir itself does not provide the dates for the time spent in Biloxi, nor does it explain that the writer was then the Assistant Pastor at the Immaculate Conception. Nor is it mentioned that he resumed his clerical duties in late August following his return to Corinth.

I now understood there was another reason why my former high school friend had become so enraged after she read the memoir in 2000. Apart from being bothered by Hot Priest's omission of his work with her and other kids on the CYO Center project and the failure to mention he was a priest when he lived on the Gulf Coast in August 1969, the memoir's disclosure of his Biloxi visitor was something my Class of 1970 friends – many of whom remained close to him after the Class of 1969 moved on – probably did not previously know about. The memoir fueled speculation that the young woman who visited Hot Priest in Mississippi in 1969 and the one whom the rumors circulating in Corinth in early 1970 implicated were one and the same.

I sought Hot Priest's memoir while writing my own because I believed it might offer a perspective on life in Corinth in the 1960s. I wondered what he thought of my friends and me. I was disappointed, for not a sentence was written of his time at our church. Yet the short period he spent in Corinth seems to be present in the memoir nonetheless, laying at the heart of a transformative personal experience that is alluded to but never described. That he leaves the priesthood is implicit, but the memoir does not explain why or when.

Hot Priest writes that with the help of the Bishop of Albany, he was given a second chance by the Bishop of Gallup, New Mexico, without explaining why he sought or needed redemption. It appears the effort at resuming his career was brief. He complains in the memoir there were just too many rules to being a priest; everything was black or white. Noting that he was married in 1974, Hot Priest might have written that celibacy was one of those rules. Hot Priest's memoir seems to have been crafted in the hope it would be cathartic, yet because some of the most determinative events of his life were seemingly left unexamined, it is not clear that his writing brought him the peace he sought.

The memoir reveals a charismatic man with a big heart and a deep sensitivity to the human condition. As teenagers, my friends and I saw these qualities in Hot Priest when he arrived in Corinth in 1968, and for that reason, many of us idolized him. He was the only adult we knew who was "cool" and who acted as irreverent as many of us felt. His memoir suggests he was more a man than a man of God. Even though Hot Priest was unwilling to acknowledge in his memoir the Catholic teenagers in Corinth who thought so much of him or to explore his fall from grace, I think most of us would have accepted him for his shortcomings. What we admired most was the man, not the priest.

24

FIVE O'CLOCK WORLD

By mid-summer 1968, I had left my job at Gaslight Village in Lake George to begin work at the Grand Union supermarket on Main Street in Corinth. I had grown weary of commuting to Lake George for my 2 PM-10 PM shift, working hours that made it difficult to play golf except on my days off. Besides, operating the Round-Up myself for eight hours got boring and fast. My uncle Charlie, who lived in Corinth and knew about my situation, spoke to the local Grand Union Supermarket manager to see if I might work there. At the time, my Uncle Charlie was the undersheriff of Saratoga County and was well connected within the Republican Party, which ran everything in the county and within Corinth. I was surprised when he said I had a job at the Grand Union if I wanted it.

While I missed working with Tom and Bob at Gaslight, I made the switch because I believed I would have the option to continue working at the grocery during my senior year. Although I was planning to play football in the fall and basketball in the winter, I imagined there might be a way I could work and also play sports. When I started work at the Grand Union the following week, I was assigned to the produce department, which turned out to be a more appealing job than running the ride at Gaslight Village that I had begun to refer to as the "Throw-Up." I might have to swat a fruit fly or two at the Grand Union, but I wouldn't have to dodge flying vomit.

My Grand Union job paid the same $1.60 per hour minimum wage as my Lake George job, but it provided social engagement that was often missing at Gaslight Village. Work in the produce department required dealing with shoppers regularly since there was no self-service in the 1960s, at least not in Corinth. A shopper would first select their fruit or vegetables and place each selection in separate brown paper bags. I would then put the bags on a scale, determine the weight of each one, and then find their cost on a chart based on their weight and the per-pound cost. I marked the price on the bag with a giant black crayon.

I met many new people working produce, especially visitors who vacationed at our nearby lakes. The occasional teenage girl would come in with her mother, which was a satisfying distraction. However, I was always guarded about my actions while working on the floor since the door to the produce room in the back of the store had a window. Occasionally, I saw the produce manager looking through the window to check on me. I never thought he liked me very much, concluding that the store manager required him to hire me as a favor to my uncle.

The Grand Union was far less busy after Corinth's summer visitors went home on Labor Day. Many locals refused to shop at the market in July and August because its aisles were clogged with people on vacation. Corinth's summer visitors owned homes nearby that were generally referred to as "camps," the common descriptor for summer housing in the region. Most were on Hunt, Efner, and Jenny Lakes in the Western part of town, off Route 10 or West Mountain Road. It was the only area in town that might make a credible claim to being "Adirondack.". Some camps were situated on the Hudson River north of the village, although technically, they were in the Town of Luzerne. Still others were on the Sacandaga Reservoir further west in the Towns of Day and Edinburg.

Summer residents would drive several miles into Corinth Village each week to restock their pantry shelves and fill their gas tanks. There had always been some animosity in Corinth for those who summered on local waters and shopped in town. Even my Mother, one of the kindest people I have ever known, refused to shop at the Grand Union during the summer because it was so busy with "campers," the pejorative she used to describe the people who vacationed near Corinth. The long-standing aversion that Corinthians have had for outsiders of all stripes might have originated from their interactions with local "campers" in public places like the Grand Union. In 2007, the *New York Times* columnist David Carr subtly noted Corinth's provincial nature. Acknowledging that his family owned a cabin nearby, Carr remarked that Corinth "has always been its own little place, insular and isolated by choice and geography." The community has often been cold to outsiders, and even native sons like myself are viewed with suspicion, if not indifference, when we return to town.

Some of Corinth's visitors in the summer of 1968 came from the Sacandaga Reservoir, a 29-mile-long body of water with 115 miles of shoreline that became the setting for an increasing number of summer homes, the result of the renaming of the Sacandaga Reservoir to the "Great Sacandaga Lake" in the 1960s. The name change was intended to promote tourism and real estate development, a strategic move that obscured the water body's origins which had been created by damning the Sacandaga River in the late 1920s. The construction of the 4000-acre reservoir put many large family farms and several communities underwater, forcing the destruction or removal of 12,000 structures, the relocation of over 1000 people, and the reburial of nearly 4000 graves. While creating the reservoir was touted as a "public benefit," the corporations that used their political capital to persuade Albany legislators to develop the Hudson River-Black River Water Regulating District – the Hudson River's hydro-electric plants and pulp and paper companies like IP who paid 95% of the reservoir's costs - benefitted the most from the construction of the Conklingville Dam.

After Labor Day, 1968, the Grand Union's manager moved me from produce to grocery. The produce manager could handle his entire department alone in the off-season, so I was no longer needed. I was okay with the move, for I worked 12-15 hours per week through my senior year, stocking grocery shelves and filling the milk and beer coolers, usually two evenings a week and a weekend day. I was called a "grocery stocker." Today, I would be called a "grocery associate." It's the same job, just a more dignified title. And there were no "teams" then; we had "crews." Sports metaphors had not yet penetrated American work culture in the 1960s. Working grocery was a more solitary job, lacking the social interaction of the produce department.

Stocking grocery shelves required some training and was often done under the watchful eye of the Grocery Manager. This guy took his work seriously and was more hard-core than the Produce Manager. His elevation to Store Manager at Corinth or at another store required it. Sometimes, he directed our work like a foreman; other times, he worked with us. He showed me how to use a box cutter, how to work the pricing tool, how to stock shelves correctly, and where to dispose of empty cardboard boxes. After I had finished stocking shelves, and when I was not called up to the registers to bag groceries, I was expected to go down each of the store's aisles and pull items to the front of each shelf so that the store had the look of abundance which, I was told, made people want to buy more groceries than they would if the shelves appeared empty. It sounds counter-intuitive, yet this is what consumer behavior studies have shown. During my work at the Grand Union, I learned the entire retail industry in America was constructed on the psychology of consumerism, a thoroughly studied aspect of human behavior. Even in my small hometown of Corinth, national corporate strategies were being used to encourage us to buy and spend more.

Working at the Grand Union was a good experience. The exception was those days when my hours overlapped with the shifts worked by two guys who had graduated from Corinth High School a few years before and held full-time, "career" jobs at the store. Then, work could become political. These guys liked to exercise their seniority to boss around another part-timer and me. Nothing harsh or cruel, but their desire to assert their superiority was palpable. After all, a guy whose career goals included someday becoming the assistant manager of Corinth's Grand Union first had to demonstrate his managerial skills. Part-time high school grocery stockers were the perfect foil for testing one's supervisory ability. Once the store organized a "night crew" to stock shelves, I rarely interacted with its full-timers since they started work very late in the day and worked all night. So, I most often worked alone during 5-9 PM shifts. Sometimes, only the acting manager, a cashier, and I were in the store on a slow midweek night. After I arrived for work and put on my white apron and Grand Union name tag, the manager usually showed me a cartload of grocery items I was expected to shelve that night.

Working through the cart required a price stamping tool, a box cutter, and a price list. A price stamper, the most vital instrument in a 1960s grocery store, is now a vintage item, having been rendered obsolete by barcode technology. A few weeks ago, I saw about ten stampers on display at a small New Hampshire antique shop. The stamper, about eight inches long and made of heavy gauge stainless steel, had a straight bar handle about four inches long attached to a small open frame that held an oblong wheel with several small rubber belts attached. Each of the belts, which had numbers and symbols, could be rotated to set the price of an item. Once a price was set, the tool's head moved into the stamping position when you pushed the device's handle down. When you released it, the wheel rotated back, so the numbers were inked in the stamper pad at the top of the tool. The stamper was then ready for action.

Before it became the favorite tool of airplane hijackers and terrorists, the box cutter was intended to do just what its name suggests: cut boxes. We used the box cutter to remove the tops of shipping boxes to expose the tops of canned or boxed goods inside so they could be priced. Using the cutter required a degree of finesse if the box contained items like cereal or instant potatoes. Cut the shipping box too aggressively, and you slice the grocery items inside. While the tops of shipping boxes must still be cut off in today's supermarkets, grocery associates take the items out of the box and put them directly onto shelves. Their price is already marked on the item in a bar code. The cost for the item is generally posted on the edge of the shelf where the item sits, so if there is a price change, only the shelf's price tag must be changed. It's hard to believe that grocery stockers today have been promoted to "associates" when shelving items is all they do.

Changing the price of a grocery item was sometimes complicated. The cost of the product to be shelved first had to be located on a printout. If the price was unchanged, the work was much easier than if the price had gone up or down. You set the current price on the stamper, stamp every can or item in the box, and then put the item on the shelf. There was more work if the cost of an article had changed. Each canned or boxed item on the shelf had to be removed and repriced. That's right, existing groceries were often shelved at one price and sold at a higher one, just like at the gas pump where Mobil fills its tanks and sets the pump price at $3.29 per gallon, but then if the price of oil per barrel goes up on the international market, so too does the price of gas already in the tank below the pump.

Changing prices of already shelved items was a pain. If the price of a canned item at the Grand Union had to be changed, steel wool was used to rub off the old inked price so that the new price could be stamped. If a box required a new price, a blank adhesive label was used to cover the old price. After steel-wooling the old prices from the cans and covering them up on boxes, the stamper tool was used to mark the new price. As the most tedious job at the store, the pricing process was straightforward, only carrying the hazard of ending the job with blue-black ink all over your hands as the pad that held the ink in the stamper tool had to be refilled periodically. The occasional call by the manager to the front of the store to bag groceries provided a welcome relief from the monotony of stocking cans of peas and evaporated milk.

My job at the Grand Union required me to work part-time one morning a week to help unload a semi-truck that delivered the store's weekly grocery order. The only problem was that the semi-truck that brought our goods arrived at 6 AM. So, every Wednesday morning before I went to school, I worked with four other guys unloading 2000 units of canned and boxed grocery items. The semi would first back up to a door on the west wall of the store's back room. Inside, we would position several sections of a metal conveyor track with small moving wheels that stretched from the back of the truck through the store room, past six or seven rows of tall, metal storage shelves. The truck's driver would push the boxed items down the track. When a box reached the appropriate row, one of us would stop the box, pick it up, and carry it to a shelf for storage. On a few occasions, one of the full-time employees, a burly Corinth graduate from the class of 1963, would stand along the track, pulling off boxes and tossing them to us as we stood several feet away in one of the aisles. Some packages, like those that held instant potatoes, were easy to manage, but those containing canned goods could weigh 40 pounds or more. Catching a box containing

12 half-gallon grapefruit cans required strength and finesse. Work on those Wednesday mornings was non-stop for two hours, as box after box came down the rack until the 53-foot-long semi-truck was empty. After I clocked out around 8 AM, I went directly to school.

I observed a profound expression of kindness while working at the Grand Union that I have never forgotten. I had been filling the milk and beer coolers during a routine weeknight shift. Around 7 PM, I climbed up a makeshift wooden ladder in the back room that led to the top of a room-size dairy cooler. That is where I took my permitted break, 15 minutes every four hours. At the top of the cooler, a one-way window looked out and down into the store, presumably built to watch for shoplifters and to monitor young workers like me. I was up there drinking a Coke when I saw a disheveled man acting oddly at the near end of the grocery aisle below me. When I looked carefully, I saw he was stuffing cans of tuna fish into the pockets of his baggy trousers. I climbed down from my perch and found the store's meat department manager, Seraphine John, who was that night's on-duty store manager. I told him what I had seen. I pointed out the man I had observed and watched Seraphine walk slowly to the store's front and position himself near the cash registers. I returned to my lookout above the cooler to finish my break.

A few minutes later, Seraphine and the man I had reported came into the backroom, unaware I was sitting above, hidden behind some boxes. I remained still. I presumed that Seraphine had confronted the man with the canned goods in his pockets. Seraphine, short and wiry with thick black hair and a dark complexion, had worked for Grand Union since 1940. I heard him gently interrogate the man who told him he had taken the food for his family, who had little to eat. After a few more questions, I watched Seraphine take out his wallet and give the man the money to pay for the food he had taken. He put his wallet back, placed his arm around the man's back, and walked him out of the storeroom and into the central part of the store. I continued to watch the two of them through the one-way glass, and while I could not hear what was said, I could tell that Seraphine was offering the man some tender words of consolation before they parted. Corinth has always been a community with kind and generous citizens. The expression of compassion and generosity I observed that night at the Grand Union 1968 remains an inspiration.

25

— . —

WINNERS AND LOSERS

F all football practice began in August 1968, just as Corinth's Sesqui-centennial celebration was winding down. I decided to continue at my job at the Grand Union at least until Labor Day, having arranged work to fit in and between our twice-daily scheduled football practices. In the Fall of 1968, getting to practice required that players run from the boys' high school locker room to a field at the far western end of Eggleston Street, roughly a mile away. The Eggleston Street fields, which once held a baseball diamond, were used for football practices to preserve the grass on the Main Street athletic field that got badly torn up only a few weeks into the season. The required run to the fields was also intended to improve player conditioning.

Eggleston Street, situated on the western frontier of Corinth village in the 1960s, had a God-forsaken quality. The street emptied into a broad expanse of dirt at its western terminus, an open landscape that served as the runway of the old Corinth airport. Its western end seemed so desolate you might expect to see tumbleweeds blowing down the street. If you were a kid in the 1950s and 1960s who lived on nearby Center, Oak, Walnut, Beech, and Ash Streets, you could quickly have gone to the store that was situated on the eastern end of Eggleston Street near its intersection with Main, but otherwise, there was no reason to go out there.

Practice on the Eggleston Street field began in the mid-1960s. It required team members to suit up in the locker room, sling their spikes over their shoulder pads by their laces, and then run in sneakers to the field. Sneakers in those days were typically Converse Chuck Taylors, the low-cut version that lacked foot and ankle support that is common in athletic footwear today. The route to the field from school was west on Oak Street to First Street, then over to Beech, down Beech to Main, then a quick turn to the south and right onto Eggleston. Coaches, blocking sleds, footballs, and water coolers awaited players when they arrived. After changing into spikes, our sneakers were thrown into a pile on the side of the field that the school's maintenance crew had marked out in hydrated lime. The run to the Eggleston Street field was more challenging in 1968, probably because I had done less preconditioning than before the 1967 season. All I had been doing during the summer when I was not working was playing golf at Brookhaven. I might have walked five miles if I played 18 holes, but I needed more than that to get into shape for football.

As soon as I arrived at the Eggleston Street field, I thought back to what the area had been like not many years before. The airport at its west end had served as the base for the local Twin Falls Flying Club since the late 1930s on land owned by Joe Seppa. The dirt airfield and large quonset hangar were still there in 1968. When the Club was most active in the 1950s, it held "fly-ins" with pilots from other clubs in the region landing their planes at the airport to compete for prizes, sometimes with as many as 500 spectators looking on. Watching small planes take off and land was a form of local entertainment in Corinth in the decade after World War II. It was up there with spending an afternoon shooting rats at the old Corinth dump near Gabriel Road and Wall Street. In 1948, Corinth's airfield was the site of a field day and picnic sponsored by International Paper as part of the Company's 50th-anniversary celebration. It was a massive celebration with some 4500 people reportedly in attendance. But Corinth's airport had fallen out of use by 1965, its most avid pilots having died or just grown too old to fly. The idea that the airfield could be shaped into a housing development that occupies the area now had not yet taken root.

The location of our pre-season practices on the fields behind the houses on the south side of Eggleston Street had once been the site of a golf course. It was not an actual course, but one some of us kids built. The idea for the Eggleston Street course came from playing the golf holes set up during the summer on the Main Street athletic field. The Corinth Youth Commission, which offered some terrific summer activities for kids in the 1960s, would sometimes hold "pitch and putt" golf tournaments on the field. I still have the little plastic trophy the Youth Commission gave me for winning the tournament the summer I was 11 or 12. And I recall the year when an older boy, who knew I was a good golfer for my age, offered me five dollars to let him win. During one of those tournaments, I met up with some boys who lived on Eggleston Street and liked to play golf as much as I did. Kids from Center Street like me never played with Eggleston Street kids, even though an old road through the woods connected the two streets. Eggleston Street kids had a reputation for being mean, but the boys from Eggleston Street that I got to know were a lot like me. So together, we decided to build a golf course.

The Eggleston Street kids said we could use the fields behind their homes for our course. We all met up one afternoon to figure out where the holes would be located and then used their fathers' lawnmowers to cut the field's knee-high grass. I think we made about three golf holes in all. We lowered the mower height adjustments for the greens, although the grass was still too tall for accurate putting. We got some one-pound metal coffee cans for the cups and ski poles for flag sticks. The area was large, so the holes were long enough for us to use actual golf balls rather than the plastic balls required in our more space-restricted neighborhoods. We played together there several times but eventually lost interest because our experience was not enough, like golfing on an actual course. But we still had fun playing. A residential neighborhood with a dozen homes that encircles a street called Wiley Way now exists where our course was laid out. Besides my memory of a few creative boys getting together to play, all that remains of our boyhood golf course are the coffee cans we used for holes. They are probably rusting away under the lawns being mowed by the people who live there now.

As soon as drills began on the first day of football practice, I could tell it would be a challenging season. No one was serious. There was an awful lot of joking and fooling around. There was a new, untested head coach that year, so that could have had something to do with the behavior I observed. Yet if the coaches were concerned, they didn't show it. Compared to the character of the previous year's varsity team, I didn't think enough guys were committed to playing the game to make the 1968 team one that could win. Graduation that June had cut the heart out of a good 1967 team, one that was much better than its 4-4 record. Its quarterback, Bruce Healy, was a strong leader in whom everyone had confidence, often more than we did our coaches.

I recall one practice during the 1967 season held on the lawn that used to be in between the former elementary school on Oak Street and the high school gymnasium. An addition to the school now occupies the site. Our coaches, both prone to temper tantrums and yelling, became so angry at the team for some reason or another that they stormed off the field mid-way through practice and returned to the locker room, leaving the team dumbfounded. So Bruce took charge of the team, and we had a good practice. I thought we were better with him leading us. But Bruce had graduated in

1968, and sadly, none of the guys vying to win the quarterback slot had his skills or temperament. The 1968 team did not have anyone who could step up and lead.

Within the first hour of practice, I had the growing sense that the coming season would be a disaster. I began to feel a sense of impending doom. I had become so tired of playing on losing teams at Corinth High School that I didn't think I could stand to play on another one. The 1967 varsity football team was the winningest team I had ever been on. Simply having an even record felt good, in part, because everyone was playing their best. The track teams I was on from 1966 to 1967 had winning seasons, but track – except for the relays – comprises individual performances. It's not a team sport in the traditional sense.

By the end of football practice on the first day, I had decided to quit the team. I did not have the heart to endure the season I foresaw. I had made a purely intuitive decision. I didn't speak to my parents about it first or ask my friends what they thought. I didn't calculate the implications. I just knew I had to turn in my gear.

I returned my practice uniform, pads, and cleats to the athletic director, George Spieldenner, right after practice. He had previously been the much-respected varsity football coach until a heart attack forced him to cut back his coaching. He was a good man and a fine coach. I never once saw him rage when one of his players made a mistake. And he treated me similarly when I told him I was quitting. All he said was I would be letting my teammates down. Maybe, I thought. But I had not been a valued player the previous season as I had been passed over when variety letters were awarded. Besides, I hated being a lineman. I never had any interest in playing tackle, defensively or offensively. I did not have the heart or the aggression for the position. But I was over six- feet tall and 200 pounds at the time, and the line was the only position the coaches imagined I could play. I didn't like the position and wasn't good at it, but I wanted to be on the team. So, I had little choice but to play where I was told. Yet even when presented with a glimpse of my ability to play other positions, the coaches continued to see me as just a big kid, a lineman. That's the thing about high school. You are often pigeonholed as being one thing or another, and it is nearly impossible for teachers and coaches, even your friends, to see you another way.

I recalled a few practices during the previous 1967 season when I had the opportunity to show I could do more than be a large body on the line of scrimmage. One day, the back and ends were off doing some drills. Bruce, our quarterback, was looking for something to do, so he asked some lineman standing around to help him practice by taking passes. I was one of the players who did. I went out for 12 to 15 passes and caught every pass Bruce threw. Bruce made a big deal about it to one of the coaches, saying, "He caught every ball I threw to him." The coach just shrugged his shoulders.

Another time, we were preparing to play Hudson Falls, a perennial football powerhouse in the old Northern Conference. They had a fullback who was about my size, so our coaches thought giving our defense some practice tackling a 200-pounder was a good idea. So, I became a tackling dummy for a day. I was put in the backfield and was given the ball every time it was snapped. No plays were run, so the defense knew precisely where the ball was going every time. Nonetheless, I gained at least three to four yards with every carry. It must have crossed the mind of one of our coaches that they should try playing me in the backfield. Yet this would have required a change to the offense, the elimination of a half-back, and seeing me as a fullback rather than a tackle. It didn't happen. Seeing me as something other than an obstacle on the line of scrimmage was too much of a stretch. I returned to the line and stayed there.

Quitting the football team after the first practice must have appeared to be a selfish act. Maybe it was, yet I don't recall anyone saying anything about it. I could not ignore the fact I did not believe a team assembled from the guys I observed in practice could win. And our new coach wasn't all that impressive either, evidenced by the fact that he said nothing about all the goofing off on the first day. Most of the team were good guys; some were my friends, but many did not appear committed to playing winning football. Nor was I, perhaps. Maybe I saw my lack of will reflected in my teammates.

In retrospect, I don't understand how I dared to quit. Even as a senior, I was not immune to peer pressure; although admittedly, few of my closest friends were football players, I knew none would hassle me for quitting the team. While I still felt guilty for bailing out, I knew the season would not end differently if I were on the team. I would not have carried or caught the ball, and a lineman was rarely seen as team leader material.

Two months later, in November, my decision to quit was validated in a bittersweet way. The varsity football team finished the season winless. The team scored its first touchdown in the fourth game, then just one more touchdown in its remaining games, for 13 points for the entire season. During one game, the offense gained negative three yards. While it took some time for me to be at peace with my decision, only years later did I come to understand that quitting the team was only partly related to my reluctance to play on another losing team. Sure, I should have been content with just playing the game. Yet by the fall of 1968, I was ready to move on from Corinth High School, and quitting football was merely a manifestation of an emerging sense of personal autonomy, a growing determination not to conform to what was expected of me. Ultimately, I realized that leaving the team after the first practice was an act of self-preservation.

Quitting the football team had another benefit. Some of its more rowdy members started riding around town on weekends in the back of the large truck, causing mischief. Not all of them, but some of them. One night, they came upon two varsity cheerleaders, both friends of mine, near the corner of Oak and First Streets, provoking them in a way that frightened both girls. The purpose of confrontation wasn't apparent to the two, yet they fled down the alley between Oak and Walnut Streets, thinking it odd – as one of them told me - football team members would affront the very girls who cheered for them. The two did not report the incident. A week or two later, the older brother of one of the cheerleaders allegedly told someone he hated football, which was then conveyed to a team member, probably as hating Corinth football. Something more offensive must have been said to trigger what occurred the following weekend.

A pick-up truck with some football team members riding in the back drove to the boy's Ash Street home. The truck parked at the curb in front of his house. My friend's sister, the cheerleader, saw the truck pull up and heard players shouting her brother's name. One guy, nicknamed "Animal," jumped out of the truck, raced up the front lawn, and leaped onto a brick planter along the house's foundation. He pushed his face against the window, leering in as my friend, her brother, mother, and grandmother sat inside, shocked in disbelief at what was happening before them. It was told later the team members in the truck were bent on some form of retribution. Animal and his teammates finally relented, continuing to shout epithets as they drove off.

The following Monday, Coach Spieldenner, who lived only two doors away and probably heard the commotion, spoke in all boys' gym classes, lining everyone up along the sideline on the east side of the football field, assailing the conduct of the football team's members and issuing a condemnation of such behavior. I don't recall if any varsity team members who participated in the stunt were punished, but the sister of the boy the team was pursuing quit the cheerleading squad that week. Some members of the football team had proved that night they were better thugs than they were football players.

26

— • —

WE GOTTA GET OF THIS PLACE

The Class of 1969's senior year began right after the formal conclusion of Corinth's Sesquicentennial. The only kids I knew who had been involved in the celebration were several female classmates who competed for the title of Sesquicentennial Queen. A few boys in our class tried to grow a beard or mustache for the celebration, but not very successfully. Of course, they could not stop shaving until after the close of the previous school year in June, for our principal would never have permitted a boy with facial hair into school. Yet the Sesquicentennial was mainly an adult fantasy, with only a few activities for children and teens. A few young boys could be seen around town wearing derbies and Sesquicentennial ties, and some young girls posed for the cameras in homespun dresses and bonnets. Except for the Queen's contest, the Sesquicentennial was a playground constructed primarily for adults.

The main events of Corinth's Sesquicentennial were the same week as the 1968 Democratic National Convention in Chicago. So, after a day spent reenacting life in the 1820s, shooting muskets, firing cannons at the Clothier sand pit, or watching the Keystone Kops arrest and punish a member of the Brothers of the Brush for violating Sesquicentennial regulations, Corinthians could go home, turn on their TV's, and watch mayhem unfold in the streets of Chicago. The violence during the Days of Rage" that left 500 protestors and over 100 non-participants injured, including 152 police officers, occurred on August 28 in the middle of the Sesquicentennial's final celebration week. Corinth was such a thoroughly Republican town at the time that most citizens would likely have preferred to watch re-runs of *The Beverly Hillbillies* or *Here Come the Brides* – which were usually broadcast on TV on Wednesday nights in the summer - then tune into the Democratic Convention. Since the networks canceled regular programming that week, Corinthians had little else to see on TV but the Convention. However, watching a bunch of Hippies get clubbed by Chicago police did have some entertainment value.

So there we were in late August 1968; the Class of 1969 was about to begin its senior year of high school. The community's adults were preparing to leave the 19th-century world they had created to celebrate Corinth's 150th birthday. Civic leaders remained anxious for the future of the Hudson River Mill while simultaneously seeking to tamp down the restlessness of the community's youth. A thousand miles away on the shore of Lake Michigan, the world was being turned upside down. The Presidential election between Richard Nixon and Hubert Humphrey was about to begin in earnest, and the Vietnam War raged on. The year 1968 would be the War's deadliest, with 16,592 American men and boys killed. Among them was our classmate, Bruce Colson.

Like most of my friends, I lacked the political awareness at the time to appreciate the events broadcast in our homes that last week of August. I was still trying to process my decision to quit the football team, gradually beginning to understand that my action represented the beginning of my withdrawal from life in Corinth. While I still hung out with my closest friends on weekends, I don't recall attending many school events during my senior year, certainly not football games. I continued to work at the

Grand Union on weeknights and Saturdays. I can recall very little else from my final year in Corinth other than my growing disinterest in school that caused my grades to crater. I realized that my senior year at Corinth High marked the end of the life I had known. Something brand new was about to start. While I had no idea what was to follow, I was cautiously ready to move on.

My senior year at Corinth High School was unremarkable. There were several ritual senior events that year, and while they each seemed ever so important at the time, I cannot recall a single one in any detail. That's the thing. When you are in high school, maybe more so when you are senior, you think you and your friends are the most important people in the world and that nothing matters but what makes you happy and satisfies you. It is a selfish time in one's life. The most cheerful among us were likely the college-bound, especially the boys free from the immediate concern of being drafted and shipped off to the hellhole of Vietnam. You have no idea until you are older how meaningless your high school years are in the larger scheme of things and that some of the most honored kids in your class would never accomplish all that much despite the gifts they were given. Or that the jocks, those who many envied in high school, peaked at age 18 and would never again gain the personal recognition they enjoyed on the high school football field, basketball court, or baseball diamond. The adults in the room knew all this, but no one told us.

I had to look at our class yearbook to remember what I was involved in that year. Not all that much, really, and certainly nothing of enduring value. I was a member of a few of the school's service groups, like the Stage Crew and Assembly Announcers, and I served as stage manager for the Drama Club. These groups mainly consisted of good friends, so socialization rather than service was probably my objective in participating. Predictable rituals punctuated our final year at Corinth: enjoying senior status, receiving our class rings, awaiting the arrival of the yearbook, and trying to figure out what came next—only about 20% of our class planned to continue their education, while the remainder would soon be looking for a job, planning a wedding, or preparing to go into the military.

Most of Corinth's graduating seniors who had come before us probably had similar senior year experiences. However, the young Corinth men who had donned their caps and gowns while an American war was raging – World War I, World War II, Korea, and for us, Vietnam – indeed graduated with more anxiety than those who graduated in peacetime. What was probably not familiar to the experience of the classes that came before us were the three teen suicides in Corinth that occurred early in 1969. I don't recall anything being said or done about it in school. If such events happened today, the school system would bring grief counselors into school. Maybe that happened in the spring of 1969, but I never heard about it. We were just expected to deal with the tragedies and move on.

Quitting the football team had put me into self-imposed sports exile until spring, when I rejoined the track team. I did well that year, but I was on another losing team. Only two of us on the team won our events consistently that season. Yet what I remember most about the team occurred off the track. During a meet at Granville High School, perhaps a dozen team members were headed to a nearby mom-and-pop store to buy snacks when we came across a Volkswagen Beetle parked in front of the school on the street. It was a pre-1968 model whose front and rear bumpers had a thick chrome bar running along its top. As if on cue, we all stopped, looked at each other, and immediately surrounded the car. We grabbed a front or rear bumper, which served as a handle, picked up the VW, carried it to the school's front lawn, and left it there. It was a relatively benign form of delinquency, yet it might have been the greatest success we had as a team all year.

While our team was hapless at every meet, it had a great spirit. Joe St. John, who always seemed to take first place in the high jump, brought his guitar along on every road trip. When we were ready to depart from a high school after an away meet, all the windows on the bus were pulled down. Joe would sit at the back of the bus and start strumming his guitar. The team would sing the 1967 Box Top's song, "The Letter," in our loudest voices. We continued repeating its lyric, "Ain't time to take a fast train, Lonely days are gone, I'm a going home," as the bus moved through village streets. The bus driver drove very slowly as if to prolong the intended effect of our singing. We sometimes sang the Animal's 1965 song, "We Gotta Get Out of This Place," repeating its refrain until we were out of town. If we couldn't be known for our athletic prowess, at the least, the citizens of towns where we traveled might remember us for our spirit. Singing together made team members feel good despite all the losses we endured.

June 1969 graduation provided a ceremonial ending to our school years while offering an opportunity for reflection. At least it did for me. The event was held in the high school gymnasium, where a platform had been erected at its west end. Graduates sat in folding chairs below the platform, segregated by gender in the color of the robes they wore: white for girls and black for boys. I seem to recall that each girl was given a red rose. The arrangement was standard gendered protocol for the 1950s and 1960s. This practice continues to this day in many American high schools, particularly in rural areas of the country that are not ready to abandon the patriarchal thinking that is signified when the school system prescribes white gowns for graduating female students.

It wasn't always done this way. Members of the Corinth Class of 1946, for instance, girls and boys alike, wore the same black caps and gowns, but before long, senior women wore white and boys black. The reason for the shift to white gowns for women is unknown, yet remarkably, the practice continued well into the 21st century. Photos of Corinth's 2022 and 2023 graduation ceremonies reveal nearly all female graduates wearing white, with only a few in black. None of the boys in 2023 wore white.

High School graduation is one gauge of how much Corinth has changed. Graduation is the type of event where community rituals are preserved, although it should be open to re-imagination by the current graduating class. After it all, it is their graduation. But who imagined the 2023 graduation ceremony? It may have been difficult to notice the colors of the graduate's caps and gowns for the humungous American flag that hung above the stage from the Fire Department's ladder truck, a version of Old Glory that visually consumed the event. Corinth's 2023 graduation might have been mistaken for a firefighter's rally, as the entire north end of the athletic field was consumed by Corinth fire department vehicles, including three fire trucks, a rescue truck, and its white Chevy Suburban. Did Corinth's graduating seniors request their presence, or was it a production of the administration? Regardless, a high school graduation with three fire trucks and an American flag large enough to have its own zip code would have been unrecognizable to a Corinth graduate fifty years earlier.

The problem with the American flag is that it no longer means what it used to. It remains a recognizable symbol but carries different meanings for different people. Much of this is the product of post-9/11 hysteria that resulted in the American flag being flown everywhere and anywhere. It became common for the Flag to be painted on barns and rocks, flown from the bed of a pick-up truck, and used for car upholstery. It was placed on caps, t-shirts, and coffee cups. In contemporary culture, the people who distrust government, who are disposed to believe in conspiracy theories, who are convinced the United States Government is run by a "deep state" are often the Americans who fly the flag the highest. Do these American flags represent the same thing as those that unfurl from the top of a flag pole? Given the differing representations of Old Glory that have become common in the past 20 years, what did the American flag represent at Corinth's 2023 graduation? What values was it intended to confer on the event?

The use of the Old Glory at Graduation in June 1969 was far different. Guests who sat fanning themselves as they sat on the gym's hard wooden bleachers probably did not even notice the American flag that stood un- furled and discretely positioned at the rear of the stage. If there ever was a time when the American flag might have been purposefully displayed, perhaps to rally Corinthians to support the United States government and an unpopular war, June 1969 would have been a good time. Yet the flag was not appropriated for that purpose. Nonetheless, our graduation ceremony was replete with all the pomp and circumstance expected of such a community ritual, yet no fire trucks were in sight. Music was played, platitudes were expressed, and awards were given. The high school's music groups performed, mostly in key.

Even before the ceremony started at 7:30 PM, I began to disengage from the experience. Looking around the gym as guests filed into the stands, I recalled several events in that large room. The obvious ones came to mind: the gym classes when the boys played basketball, volleyball, or the occasional game of crab soccer. Perhaps the strangest gym classes I could recall were the single weeks each year when boys' and girls' classes were held together. It was during those classes we learned how to square dance. Not exactly one of the most valuable social skills a teenager could acquire in the 1960s. While it is understandable that our gym teachers would be reluctant to promote contemporary dance styles like the Twist, the Jerk, or the Dirty Dog, teaching kids how to waltz would have been much more practical.

Two of the events in the gym that I remembered were severe accidents. Sitting there, I looked at the steel chains attached to the gym wall and connected to the ends of the climbing ropes and rings used in gym classes. When the gymnastics equipment was to be used in a class, the chain would be unlocked so the attached ropes could descend toward the gym floor. A chair was used to stand on to reach the hooked tenon that locked and unlocked the chain. While looking at the ropes overhead that night, I could not help but recall the day in high school when a boy, two years older than me, tried to get the tenon to lock the chain into place. But rather than stand on a chair or be lifted to reach it, he reportedly jumped up to slap it shut, and when he did, he got his class ring caught on the hook end. One of his classmates told me he hung there momentarily, two feet off the gym floor. The weight of his body partially severed his finger, which had to be amputated. There were several stories about what happened that circulated the school. Afterward, it was hard to pass the boy in the hallways and not look for his missing finger.

A few years earlier, the other end of the gym was the scene of another accident. During a varsity basketball game in the winter of 1964, when I was in the 7th grade, a plucky guard on the varsity basketball team tried to grab a ball going out of bounds at the lobby end of the court. He crashed into one of the gymnasium doors, putting his right forearm through its window. The game came to a crashing halt while he was whisked away to the hospital by the Corinth Emergency Squad. It took thirty stitches to close the wound on his forearm. In the following weeks, he could be seen in the hallways, his arm fully bandaged and in a sling, a badge that testified to his heroic effort in the game. He returned to the court later to be part of the team's winning season and Section II victory over Cobleskill.

The gym held only a few personal memories for me, most of them unpleasant. Yet, there is one that I think of from time to time. The moment in the gym I remember most clearly occurred during my final period 7th-grade gym class on November 22, 1963. I cannot recall what sport we were playing when the principal's voice came over the school's PA system to announce that President Kennedy had been shot in Dallas. When we were changing our clothes in the locker room after class ended, the principal reported JFK was dead. I was sitting on the wooden bench in front of locker No. 73 with Kris Boerner, my best friend at the time and with whom I shared the locker, when the news came over the loudspeaker. The atmosphere in the locker room was quickly subdued. No one knew what to say or do—the several days of national mourning that followed the assassination only ensured that every member of the Class of 1969 would never forget where they were that Friday afternoon.

On graduation night in June 1969, I recalled that November day only a few years earlier. I also thought of Kris Boerner, as I have every November 22 in the 60 years since, triggered by the memory of what happened in Dallas. Kris became seriously ill the following year and died of leukemia at 13. He was a polite and quiet boy with a keen interest In the sciences. I recalled that we once worked on a project in elementary school, identifying and placing local rocks on a display board. I also remembered that shortly after Kris's death in early June 1965, one of the coaches who also taught gym class asked me to clear Kris's belongings from our shared locker. So, every November 22, I think of my 7th grade gym class and the day I had to gather Kris's shoes, socks, shorts, and tee shirt into a small pile to be sent home to his parents. I still have the postcard Kris sent me somewhere from Florida, probably around 1962, where he and his family had traveled for a vacation.

It was easy to let my thoughts drift during the graduation ceremony since I was not expecting to be called to the podium except to receive my diploma—no awards or scholarships for me. Given my terrible senior year, I was surprised I was even invited to graduation. After I had gained admission to two colleges before Christmas, I just coasted through my senior year. The neglect of my studies wasn't purposeful; it just turned out that way. Looking back, I understand that I was ready to move on. Among my classmates who made one or more trips to the stage to be recognized for academic achievement or to receive a scholarship were the kids planning to go to college. They had all the accolades and the scholarship money locked up. Of course, the boys going to the Hudson River Mill to begin their work lives wouldn't need any financial support. And my classmates, who would soon enter the military and then go to Vietnam, didn't need a scholarship. The Federal government would pay all their expenses.

I was engaged enough that night to hear some of the speeches offered by my most honored classmates. Each kid was a model student, clean-cut, hard-working, and driven to achieve and to please. Our teachers loved those kids. Yet their speeches were reportedly pre-approved by the administration. Our principal was unwilling to take the chance that one of them might utter an irreverent word or phrase and ruin the whole evening. He would have the School Board to answer to if anyone did. Or worse, what if a scholarship recipient shouted out one of the resonant slogans of our time, like "power to the people," "kill the pigs," or "make love, not war." What our class's valedictorian said that night was forgotten by the time everyone had exited the gym, but if he had raised a black-gloved fist into the air as Tommie Smith had done at the 1968 Summer Olympics, people would be talking about it to this day. But there was a greater chance of JFK appearing as a commencement speaker that night than any of these imagined scenarios happening.

27

GHOSTS AND ELEPHANTS

The graduation ceremony for the Class of 1969 was detached from the world we lived in. The lack of references that night to the chaotic events that had played out in the background during our high school years - particularly those from the seismic year of 1968 - should have come as no surprise. Our teacher and the school's administrators remained largely silent on most contemporary issues, especially Vietnam. Any discussion of the War in 1969 would have been problematic in any case, for American attitudes towards the conflict in Vietnam had become increasingly divisive. By February 1969, 60% of Americans agreed that sending US troops to Vietnam was a mistake.

Support for the War had been a challenge for many because Vietnam did not fit into the prevailing American myths instilled in us since elementary school, particularly the idea of American exceptionalism. While most Americans had been willing to believe the War in Southeast Asia was part of the larger fight against communism, Vietnam lacked a "Pearl Harbor moment" that would have provided self-evident justification for waging war against the Vietnamese people. Despite the presumed legitimacy of the conflict and the enormous firepower that the United States brought to Southeast Asia, there was no evidence by June 1969, the month of our graduation, that the end of the War was in sight.

Most Americans did not understand the United States had thrust itself into a civil war when it went to Vietnam in the 1950s. After a century of colonial control by the French, Vietnamese nationalism emerged during World War II under Ho Chi Minh in the belief that the Allied Powers would relinquish their colonial outposts around the world at the war's end. But the French were so demoralized by the quick Nazi conquest of their country in 1940 and its subsequent occupation into 1945 that the United States and Great Britain consented to the French determination to reoccupy Vietnam after the war, having been dislodged from the country by the Japanese in 1939. The French political officials and the military that returned to Vietnam in 1946, in their effort to suppress Vietnamese nationalism, were aided by Vietnamese people living in the southern provinces who spoke French, were raised Catholic, and saw a personal opportunity in their support for the reassertion of French colonialism.

Vietnamese resistance to French control, driven by a powerful desire to create a Vietnam nation under one government and one flag, extended throughout the country. The French fought the Vietnamese unilaterally until the United States considered the war against Ho Chi Minh and the Vietminh as part of a global fight against communism. Once the French opposition to Vietnamese nationalism was considered an extension of the Cold War, the United States began in 1950 to fund France's military efforts in Vietnam. The French army failed despite American support, ending with its epic defeat at the Battle of Dien Bien Phu in 1954.

As French forces left the country, a conference at Geneva temporarily partitioned Vietnam into North and South. It also scheduled national elections for 1956 so the Vietnamese people could determine their future as a nation. The elections were never held. Between 1956 and 1960, the United States moved to fill the void left by the departed French by providing political and military support to a movement centered around Saigon in the South that opposed unification with the North, which Ho Chi Minh and the Vietminh controlled. The United States opposed Vietnamese self-determination and inserted itself into a struggle between two competing Vietnamese factions with radically different visions of their country's future.

As high school students, we might have learned about 19th-century colonialism in our 10th-grade World History classroom, which would have explained how and why the French were in Vietnam in the first place. Or we could have been taught about the 1954 Geneva Conference and the fact the United States was not a signatory to the agreement reached by other attending nations that promised Vietnam's self-determination. The circumstances that led to the passage of the Gulf of Tonkin Resolution in 1964 and the initial deployment of combat forces to Vietnam in 1965, widely reported by the press, could have become classroom discussion topics. We might have been taught some or all of this at Corinth High School, but we were not.

It was also easy to ignore the Civil Rights Movement and Martin Luther King Jr. in our high school classes, no matter how just the cause or how inspiring King's rhetoric on fundamental human rights was. There were no Black families in Corinth in the 1960s, yet it's hard to imagine that our high school curriculum would have been any different if there had been. King was assassinated early one evening in April 1968, so our principal never had to face the decision of whether to announce his murder during the school day over the PA system as he had done with President Kennedy.

However, Corinthians knew something about Blacks and their history, even if none lived in our town. How else would the Corinth chapter of the Catholic Daughters of America have a history of performing minstrels with members in Blackface? Even in Corinth, TV made it challenging to unsee film footage of Black American neighborhoods going up in flames in the 1960s. The riots that broke out in several major cities across the country were studied by the Kerner Commission, which issued a report in 1968 citing systemic racism as the primary cause. The cities where they occurred – Watts, Detroit, Newark – must have seemed like foreign countries to some in Corinth. While the causal factors cited for the riots by the Commission were pervasive throughout the nation, they had nothing to do with life in Corinth. So, they, too, were easy to ignore.

Graduation is called "commencement" because it marks a beginning. The beginning of life after school, the beginning of life beyond our family and community, the beginning of a life we would have to make for ourselves. But did our education prepare us for the world beyond Corinth? Hardly. The determinative events of the day that would impact our generation and the ones that followed us were never mentioned on graduation night in June 1969, just as they had barely made it into any of our classrooms during our years in high school. Normalcy and maintaining the status quo were paramount in a conservative community like Corinth, where graduation was a place for speeches about hard work, leadership, inspiration, and dreams. By shutting out the world around us, the graduation ceremony in June 1969 proved only that our school had succeeded in turning the Class of 1969 into smiling and complacent members of the Pepsi generation.

Despite the commencement ceremony's platitudes, handshaking, and big smiles, the Vietnam War was the elephant in the high school gym that night. The deployment of American ground troops to Vietnam increased rapidly after President Johnson used the Gulf of Tonkin Resolution to increase the U.S. presence. There were 23,000 troops in Vietnam in 1964 when my classmates and I entered the 8th grade. By the time we were juniors in 1968, the number exceeded 535,000. To America's Cold War-riors, Vietnam seemed like a sure thing. After all, if you were going to take on communism, it was better to oppose Asian peoples who fought in uniforms that resembled pajamas than to take on the Russians who had nukes to throw around. What could go wrong?

Plenty, it turns out. The guerilla tactics used by the Viet Cong, the environmental devastation caused by the American use of Agent Orange, the napalm that leveled villages in the South that were thought to harbor guerrilla fighters, the millions of Vietnamese who became refugees as a result of the search and destroy missions in the South, and the My Lai Massacre, were not what Americans wanted from their wars. And then there was the relentless, three-year bombing campaign against North Viet-nam, which did not affect the policies of its leader, Ho Chi Minh, who continued to send well-trained troops to the South, as many as 10,000 a month, over the Ho Chi Minh Trail. The Vietnam War, too messy to serve even as a teachable example of American exceptionalism, was MIA during our graduation ceremony as it was during our high school education.

If the Vietnam War was the elephant in the gym during graduation, our fallen classmate Bruce Colson was its ghost. Bruce had quit school in December 1967, in the middle of our junior year, to enlist in the Marines. He was just 18 years old. After completing basic training at Parris Island in April 1968, Bruce was first sent to Camp Lejeune, then to Camp Pendleton in California for deployment to Southeast Asia. While still at Pendleton, Bruce met up with a distant relative he had never before met. His girlfriend set Bruce up with a blind date, and the two couples drove north to Ana-heim to visit Disneyland, where they stayed until the park closed that night. Soon after, Bruce left for Vietnam. Just 25 days later, he was killed in the Quang Tri province along the demilitarized zone. Bruce's fate offered an abject lesson to the boys in our class who sat in black graduation robes that night in June 1969 on how quickly the Vietnam War could end your life.

Carl Merchant was also killed in Vietnam in 1968. Carl graduated from Corinth High in 1963. He was the older brother of my high school classmate, Billy Merchant. I recall the day in March 1968 when Billy came to track practice after school and told me that his brother Carl had been killed in Vietnam. I don't recall what I said to Billy or that we even practiced that day. Many years later, when I saw Billy for the first time since graduation, I brought up the track practice when he told me about Carl. I learned then that Billy had only found out about his brother's death the same morning. He said his father had come to the high school to ask that our principal get him out of class so he could be told about Carl. Billy opted to remain in school that day rather than go home. Later that afternoon, in a lonely corner of Corinth's athletic field where Billy and I threw the shot together, little could be said that might have consoled him for the loss he felt by his brother's death.

Bruce and Carl were the second and third young men with Corinth roots to die in Vietnam. The first was Willard Durham in 1967. Willard was born in Poughkeepsie and graduated from Saratoga Springs High School, yet his parents lived on Main Street in Corinth at the time of his death. A fourth local young man, Floyd Andrus, would lose his life in Vietnam in 1970. Although three local boys had been killed in Vietnam by 1969, I don't recall any of them being mentioned during our graduation ceremony. However, Bruce Colson was justifiably honored in our class yearbook. Maybe it was because American sentiments towards Vietnam had shifted decidedly in the months since Bruce was killed in 1968, with more Americans increasingly questioning the War. The week after we graduated, *LIFE* magazine published its iconic June 27, 1969 issue that featured an article entitled "The Faces of the American Dead in Vietnam."

The magazine included the photographs and names of the 242 men killed in Vietnam in just one week. The photos revealed that many were just boys. *LIFE* June issue was highly controversial, further widening the divide that had been forming around the war.

I never heard the word "Vietnam" spoken during graduation, yet the War was on our minds that night in June 1969. I recall a few of us kidding around before the ceremony – all college-bound guys, of course – wondering "what if" when we exited the gym later that night, we were met in the parking lot by U.S. Army soldiers who took our caps and gowns and issued us sets of fatigues in exchange, then ushered us into the back of a green military truck to be whisked off to basic training. Such an imaginary scene was not all that far from reality. Since less than a fifth of the boys in my class – about 8 of 53 - were planning to attend a four-year college and could count on getting a college deferment, the others knew they would get drafted if they did not enlist first.

Richard Nixon had been in the White House since January 1969. He subsequently created a plan for an "honorable peace" to get the United States out of Vietnam without admitting defeat. Nixon called for the "Americanization" of the war by shifting military responsibility to South Vietnamese army regulars so that American boys could be sent home. Over 500,000 troops were still in Vietnam when we graduated in June 1969, and deaths averaged 2,000 a month. It is not altogether surprising, however, that I never heard any male classmates express enthusiasm about the Vietnam War or suggest they wanted to do their patriotic duty by enlisting.

On the contrary, many boys felt conflicted, wondering why they did not feel the same patriotic fervor that their fathers felt during World War II. By quitting high school to enlist in the Marines, Bruce Colson may have been the most patriotic kid in our class. My male classmates, who did not enjoy a deferment by going to college, found themselves in a precarious situation after graduation. The President had declared that the United States would retreat from Vietnam, yet boys were still being drafted and sent to Southeast Asia. After Nixon's Americanization plan was underway, kids sent to Vietnam risked being the last American soldier to die there.

28

—— · ——

LOVE IT OR LEAVE IT

The Class of 1969 took its final classes at Corinth High School just as America reached a cultural crossroads. Since the Tet Offensive and Walter Cronkite's turn against the Vietnam War in early 1968, a sharp line had been drawn that separated Americans who fully supported the War from those opposed. *LIFE* magazine's June 1969 issue contributed to the unsettling of American attitudes towards the conflict. By the time of our graduation, well-more than half of Americans believed the War was a mistake. The public disclosure of the My Lai Massacre that came in November 1969 further widened the divide. Yet admitting the nation was wrong to be in Vietnam and managing an exit would be difficult.

Somewhere between the chaos of the 1968 Democratic convention, the indictment of the Chicago 8 in March 1969, and the student uprisings at Berkeley, Harvard, Columbia, and Cornell in the Spring of 1969, middle America had become weary of America's youth protesting the Vietnam War and otherwise showing contempt for most things cherished by Greatest Generation. Richard Nixon successfully channeled this anger when he asked for political support from America's "silent majority." Nixon, an early master of the politics of resentment, convinced millions that America was right, even if the Vietnam War was wrong. Conservatives began solidifying their support for all things American and precipitated a shift to the political right. The expression "America, "love it or leave it'" echoed more loudly across the land. Led by President Nixon, conservative Americans doubled down on their support for the War.

The TV networks seemed to understand that a culture shift was in the air. In the spring of 1969, as we were about to finish our final semester at Corinth High, CBS canceled the controversial *Smothers Brothers Comedy Hour,* which had been brutal in its satire of President Nixon, the Vietnam War, and anything representing our parent's generation. The show was heavily censored because network executives were reluctant to let the show's irreverent view of the nation's dominant culture rattle its advertisers. As the Smothers Brothers left TV, two new shows premiered aimed at America's heartland, *Hee-Haw* and the *Johnny Cash Show. Hee Haw*, especially, expressed middle-America values with country western music and all its rural trappings. CBS first aired *Hee-Haw* in June 1969, creating the imaginary "Kornfield Kounty" and populating it with Buck Owens, Roy Clark, and Minnie Pearl, who brought country songs and rural humor into the nation's living rooms each week. *Hee-Haw* tapped into a growing interest in traditional Americana that became a characteristic of the 1970s, serving as a counter-force to the progressivism and moral relativism of the nation's 1960s youth culture.

The appeal to the American heartland represented by *Hee-Haw* also found expression in the political strategies of Richard Nixon, who continued to speak to his "silent majority." Segments of American society increasingly aligned themselves with Nixon after 1969 and began to express their opposition to America's youth, whom the President deemed insufficiently patriotic. Nixon believed that millions of Americans had become weary of those who aggressively opposed the Vietnam War. Although the youthful protestors Nixon detested were expressing their First Amendment rights,

Nixon argued that doing so was aiding our enemies. At the core of Nixon's appeal to conservative sentiments was his belief Americans were required to defend their country even if they disagreed with its President.

At about this time, police nationwide began to attach American flag patches to their uniforms to show solidarity with the War and the President. Politicians also started to place American flag lapel pins on their suits to show their patriotism, a gesture that became a tradition that endures. Growing segments of American society increasingly aligned themselves with the President. They began expressing their hostility to anti-war protestors whom Nixon deemed an enemy of the nation's fight against communism in Southeast Asia. The extreme expressions of solidifying opposition to America's counter-culture were represented in the imaginary scenes in *Easy Rider* and the real-life killings at Kent State.

The resistance to the type of change represented in the advent of American youth in the 1960s found a singular voice in the character of Archie Bunker on the TV show *All in the Family*, which premiered in 1971. In dealing with nearly every controversial issue of the time, Archie represented the values of Nixon's silent majority, giving voice to how the World War II generation viewed the American youth and what they represented. The degree to which conservatives, like Archie Bunker, resisted even the most benign change was brilliantly represented in numerous shows, but none quite so good in the classic "Sock-and-a-Sock, Shoe-and-a-Shoe" episode, where Archie schooled his left-leaning son-in-law, Michael, on the tradition that both socks are put on first, then both shoes, not sock-shoe-sock-shoe. The popularity of *All in the Family* (1971) proved that reactionary conservatism had become widely recognizable in the culture during the Nixon years.

Corinth's civic leaders had been alarmed by signs of adolescent rebellion and delinquency observed in the community. Their push for a community youth center in 1969, while plausibly a product of unacceptable teenage behavior in town, was as much fueled by the fact that many similar centers had already been opened in towns and cities throughout the region. But most kids in Corinth in the late 1960s were relatively conservative, politically and socially. There was drinking, of course, and the occasional hooligan acts, which usually peaked on Cabbage Night each year, but I don't recall ever hearing that someone in town was using recreational drugs before 1970. However, I had some personal exposure to Illicit substances before then. Sort of.

My good friend, Tom, spent the summer of 1967 working at a children's camp in Maine. His family had moved from Maine to Corinth when he was very young. He missed Maine, so his grandmother, who still lived there, got him a job at the same camp where she worked as a pastry chef in the summer. Tom and I wrote to each other a few times, but one letter I received – perhaps the same one where he told me his Father had bought him a car - was quite cryptic. In one sentence, he complained that "Mary Jane is pretty scarce around here." I wondered, "Who the hell is Mary Jane?" We didn't know anyone named Mary Jane. Then I thought perhaps Mary Jane was an old Maine friend or someone he had met at the camp. I never asked about Mary Jane in my return letters, and I neglected to bring her up when he returned to Corinth. Only several years later did I learn that Mary Jane was a euphemism.

I don't think Tom brought any marijuana home when he returned from Maine, but the summer sure got more interesting once he was back. After dark one night in late August, a few other guys and I followed him to the Main Street athletic friend, where we proceeded to walk out to the second base on the baseball diamond, far enough from Oak and Main Streets so that we would not be easily seen. We didn't know what was up, but I suspected it was something that could get us into trouble. Tom then pulled out a large brown paper bag from one pocket and a tube of airplane glue from the other. He opened the tube, squeezed a huge glob into the bottom of the bag, and then put the bag over his head, tightening its opening around his neck. I don't recall anything after that, if he got high by inhaling the glue or if any of us tried it. But I can recall a small group of teenage boys standing around 2nd base after dark watching our friend demonstrate an exotic activity that none of us had ever heard of.

The 1960s that our parents read about in *LIFE* magazine and saw on the evening news never made it to Corinth, at least not during that decade. Sure, most of us were listening to rock music anywhere and everywhere, made possible by the ubiquitous transistor radio. It was well known that the lyrics of many songs were coded so that our parents would not understand their messages about sex, drugs, and individual freedom. So rock was, by its very nature, a form of rebellion. Yet many kids were also listening to Judy Collins and Simon & Garfunkel. One measure of the cultural aptitude of the Class of 1969 can be seen in its choice of "Love is Blue" by the Paul Mauriat Orchestra for its junior prom theme song. The choice exposed the romantic inclination many Corinth kids still possessed.

My high school classmates and I came of age during the 1960s, a turbulent era of significant change that impacted each one of us in innumerable ways. Some of its effects were immediate, while others were realized only years later. At the time of our graduation, the excesses of the 1960s had precipitated a reactionary movement that resulted in the emergence of Richard Nixon, marking the beginning of a national tilt to the political right. Yet the same student protests against the Vietnam War and the growing opposition to the conflict by influential adults that had lifted Nixon to the Presidency had also contributed to making Vietnam a diminished factor in the lives of many young men.

By the end of 1969, Congress ended college draft deferments, instituting a lottery system that put college boys into the draft for the first time, making it less likely young men not attending college would get called up. Then, in early 1973, the Pentagon announced the creation of the all-volunteer military. Of course, ending the draft was also seen by some as a shrewd political calculation by the Nixon administration to reduce student protests of his Vietnam policies, which continued to send young boys back home in body bags. Sadly, the growing opposition to the Vietnam War and the changes that it brought came too late for Willard Dunham, Carl Merchant, Bruce Colson, and Floyd Andrus.

29

FRIENDS AND STRANGERS

igh School graduation in 1969 was a ceremony that separated my classmates and me from the world we inherited and the world we would have to create for ourselves. While every generation faces the same transition, there was considerable uncertainty in the late 1960s about what the future might hold. The continuing Vietnam War, unresolved matters of Civil Rights for Blacks, a growing reactionary conservatism under President Nixon, an emerging environmental awareness, and shifting gender roles resulting from the Feminist Movement all made for an unstable present and a precarious future. Regardless, graduation festivities carried out in the high school were conducted with little to suggest what might be in store for us—after thirteen years in the Corinth schools, our last night together ended with a half-dozen kids standing around an empty beer keg, trying to figure out what came next.

Celebrations of our achievement began at home in the late afternoon on graduation day and wrapped up early the following day on a beer-soaked lawn on Lower Ash Street. For nearly 24 hours, the thoughts any of us had about the uncertain times in which we lived were wholly suspended. Many of my classmates were the guests of honor at graduation parties held at our homes, where parents, aunts, uncles, cousins, and neighbors gathered. At my house, gift envelopes were placed on a table next to a large graduation cake with "Congratulations Steve" written across its white icing surface in a gooey blue gel. My Mother was all smiles in the kitchen while my Father sat on the back porch drinking beer with my Uncle Freddy. I spent an hour or so receiving congratulations and being told how proud my parents were. I would periodically eye the slowly growing pile of envelopes on the table, knowing the gratuitous Hallmark cards inside probably held a lot of cash.

The party was uneventful. There were no Benjamin Braddock moments that might have been mistaken for a scene from *The Graduate*; no one approached me with advice about "plastics" or to offer any forward-thinking, this-will-make-you-rich scheme. No one there could be mistaken for Mrs. Robinson; they were just well-wishing relatives and neighbors. After all, nearly everyone at the house was the son or daughter of an immigrant whose greatest aspiration was to get a good job. No one in my family ever expressed ideas about their desire to make a lot of money. Come to think of it, I cannot recall a single Corinth friend ever saying they wanted to be rich or famous.

All the guests at my party were cut from the same humble cloth. Most had spent their lives working in mills of one kind or another or had worked unpaid as homemakers. For them, going to college and preparing for a professional life had never occurred to them. While most had quit school, they understood that graduating from high school had become a necessity. Many there, like my Mother, believed that getting a college degree was the best way to avoid spending a life in a factory. While I got caught up in the recognition offered at my party, I didn't know then how trivial and inconsequential high school graduation would be in a much larger life that would take me far away from Corinth. But at the time, high school graduation seemed like a big deal. I was irreverent then but not yet cynical, so I basked in the adulation received that night because I was still one of them.

The after-parties were surely more anticipated than graduation itself. Although the novelty of drinking had worn thin by graduation, many of us planned to hit specific houses, for we knew which kids' parents would have beer kegs on hand. Anheuser-Busch emerged in the 1960s as the nation's leading distributor of beer. Still, regional brews like Genesee, Schaefer, Knickerbocker, Rheingold, and Piels were plentiful and were popular with Corinth's paper workers. So, the party kegs tapped on graduation night might have contained any of these brews. No one seemed to care which ones.

The legal drinking age in New York State was eighteen in 1969, so some boys in my class had been drinking in bars for much of their senior year. Those who were older, boys held back a year or two in elementary school, started ordering beer at the Belvedere or Star Hotel when they were juniors. There were at least eight bars in Corinth in the 1960s, ranging from Dutchies, an authentic neighborhood bar on Mill Street, to Beck's Bar and Grill on Palmer Avenue, right around the corner from the Hudson River Mill. The most raucous of the bars was at the Central House, at the corner of Maple and Center Streets. Once an upstanding 19th-century hotel heralded for its fine dining and used as the site where local citizens voted to incorporate the Village of Corinth in 1888, the Central House, by the 1960s, had fallen into disrepair and was considered a dive.

One memorable exception to the popularity of local beers comes to mind. At least one parent of a Class of 1969 member drank Michelob, a European-styled beer that had only recently been introduced by Anheuser-Busch. Kids who organized the junior prom held in May 1968 obtained several dozen. The Michelob bottle, whose original version won a design award in 1962, was appealing for its unique teardrop shape. So a small group of kids met at 313 Center Street one night in 1968 to plunge about fifty empty bottles into a bathtub of hot water to remove their labels. The clean bottles were then dried off, stored, and transported to the elementary school gym on Oak Street, where the prom was to be held. There, the bottles served as candle holders on tables across the floor. I never learned which of our parents had a taste for Michelob, a beer that would have been considered exotic for Corinth in 1968.

Many members of the Class of 1969 convened at one final party on graduation night. It was the Ash Street home of a classmate who was a notoriously wild, completely uninhibited guy who might say or do almost anything. I recall standing in his backyard, deep into graduation night, watching other kids move around in the darkness, their bodies outlined by the light streaming from the house windows. Not being able to recognize anyone from their silhouette seemed like an apt visual metaphor, for even in the daylight, I didn't know most of the kids there, nor did they know me. Not really. Of course, I knew who they were, but I didn't know much about them. What did they believe in? Were they happy? What did they want to do with their life? I didn't have a clue. It was somewhat surreal to realize that after thirteen years together, most of the kids I graduated with were strangers to me and probably to each other. It was now too late to get to know them.

I don't remember any music playing at the Ash Street party, but I am sure it did. There were very few "couples" in the Class of 1969, but that night, you would occasionally see a boy and girl go through an outside door to the basement of the house and emerge ten minutes later, smiling, their faces flushed. Kids talked, and promises were made to get together again the next day, but I cannot recall that any of them were ever kept. Graduation wasn't like the junior prom, where several picnics were planned for the next day to spread the ritual event across the weekend. No, this final graduation party was it. Over a decade of attending school together came down to drinking beer out of a paper cup in a crazy classmate's backyard and trying to converse with kids you never really knew. I did not realize it then, but graduation night would be the last time I would see most of my classmates again for fifty years—some I have not seen since that night in June 1969.

The party was raucous early on, but people started to drift away from the party around 1 AM, maybe later. I left with two of my closest friends with plans to drive to the New Way Lunch on South Street in Glens Falls to get something to eat, the only place we knew would be open at 2 AM on a Sunday. Our trip to South Street that night was a way to delay the inevitable, to create a means for our senior year to continue just a bit longer. We wanted to sit down together and recall memorable times, only hinting at our uncertain futures. The New Way Lunch was perfect for such conversations; as the writer Jack Kerouac would say, it was "beat." The diner had a soul, having thus far resisted the winds of modernity. There was no place like it in Corinth, not even Bud's Diner.

Entering the New Way Lunch transported you to another time. On the left side of the narrow space were about six booths, their dark stained wooden benches covered in red vinyl. Small silver Seeburg jukeboxes were anchored into the wall end of each white Formica table top. A single booth stood on its own at the end of the room. On the right, stainless steel circular stools with red vinyl seats were evenly spaced in front of a long white plastic counter. Several pies and cakes were spread out under separate plastic covers. Black steel napkin dispensers sat in between them. Behind the counter, tall stainless-steel coolers with glass doors held beer and soda. To the right of the coolers and on the wall over the cash register, the New Way's menu was posted along with an assortment of single-use personal items, each packaged on its own cardboard display: handkerchiefs, aspirin, plastic combs, and fingernail clippers. You could tell by the prices and faded colors that some items had been there for years.

I learned about the New Way Lunch from my parents. As a kid, I went to the diner on the occasional afternoon when my Father and I drove to Glens Falls to pick up my Mother from work. He would park in front of the Clark Brother's Glove factory on Elm Street, and I would go in. Once I was inside the factory and walked to the second floor, the noise from its hundreds of sewing machines was daunting. Someone usually greeted me politely in the hallway and then went to find my Mother. After she gathered her belongings and we walked to the car, we drove to the New Way just around the corner on South Street.

I would also go to the New Way whenever my Father drove me to Glens Falls for bi-weekly appointments with Dr. Forrest, my humorless orthodontist whose office was on Upper Glen Street. In the hallway that led to several rooms in his office, glass cases were built into the walls on both sides with shelves that held plaster "before-and-after" casts of the teeth he had straightened. Some of the "before" casts were downright scary-looking. If you have even seen the mouth of an Atlantic Wolfish, you'll know what I mean. While the casts were no doubt intended to show the magic Dr. Forrest could do with even the most crooked teeth, it was unsettling to see all those mouths without the faces that went with them.

My Mother, who spent much time in Glens Falls before she married my Father, called the New Way "Dirty Johns." The diner, which had been around since 1919, was famous for its hot dogs, which some people called "rot dogs." Yet it was the diner's palpable, gritty character that did much to explain its nickname. Hot dogs were always cooking on the large grill adjacent to the restaurant's front window whenever I went there. People walking down South Street would stop and watch them sizzle. The diner was often so busy that twenty or more hot dogs were usually on the grill simultaneously. The buns the New Way used had squared, solid ends with narrow slits to hold the dogs. They never used buns with rounded ends, at least not in the 60s. The buns, heated in a metal bin built into the counter, were accessed through a sliding, stainless-steel door. A small cloud of steam arose from the container whenever the door was opened to remove the buns.

The popularity of the New Way's hot dogs was due to their secret sauce that was dispensed from a grimy bean pot that sat on the grill's edge. It was a dark brown, watery sauce with tiny pieces of meat ladled onto the hot dogs with a wooden spoon. If you sat or stood at the end of the counter nearest the grill and cash register, you could watch all this action close-up, which we often did since my parents' orders were always "to go." We usually ordered ten dogs for dinner. The counter person would place each one in a sturdy box, two rows of five dogs, one on top of the other. The toppings were always placed on the dogs before they were put in the box, so the buns on the top row would be stained with meat sauce and mustard from the ones below. I only ate dogs with mustard when I was a kid, but my parents ordered the works: mustard, onions, and the secret sauce. Hot dogs were 15 cents each then, so dinner for the three of us only cost $1.50. By the time I was in high school, my tastes had matured. When I had ordered my dogs with "the works," I knew I was becoming an adult.

When my two classmates and I arrived at the New Way early in the morning after graduation, the thick smell of the New Way's meat sauce hit as soon as we walked through the door. We were the only ones there, except for the counter person in the back corner of the diner, leaning back in an old wooden chair, asleep. Only a few hot dogs lay warming on the grill. A thin ribbon of steam rose from the bin under the counter that warmed the rolls. A few slices of cake and pieces of pie were appetizingly secure under clear plastic covers. We sat down in a booth and ordered hot dogs and Cokes. Eventually, we played music on the small jukebox at our table.

We ate and talked for about two hours. I can recall only one of the two friends I went with that night, but it may not matter that I forgot the other one. Nor can I remember what we talked about. Not exactly. We were each going to college in the fall, about to start the next chapter of our lives. We were pensive, even wistful. We knew we had reached the end of something, although what would be next would not be apparent for years, at least not to me. I don't think we understood, sitting there under the New Way's florescent lighting, dimmed by years of accumulated dust and grease, that we would never again see each other in the same way as we did that night. Our lives after Corinth would transform each of us. Significantly.

Our collective past eventually became a nostalgic touchstone where some of us went to escape the lives the future brought. Yet our shared history grew increasingly obscure and elusive as the years passed. Our connections became more tenuous, complicated by distance, marriage, children, and sharply divergent political sensibilities for some. Then, other life events complicated reunion efforts, some of them tragic. Sadly, I now learn these things from emails whose subject lines typically read: "We've lost another one."

30

— • —

MIDNIGHT COWBOYS

I came to the realization on graduation night that I did not know most of my classmates, but not until years later did I discover that some of them were gay. Not acknowledging or even knowing in high school you were gay was understandable in the late 1960s. Homosexuality was considered a mental illness by the American Psychiatric Association in 1969, and sodomy was treated as a felony in every state except Illinois. There were numerous reasons a kid would suppress an emerging homosexual orientation in that era, for it was considered both a sickness and a crime. And Corinth, at that time, was not the sort of town that would be accepting of a teenager who tested the boundaries of the community's normative sexual culture.

Many of my classmates found full-time jobs the week after graduation, while others began summer work until college started in September. Several guys found employment to keep themselves busy until they were drafted or decided to enlist. Less than a week after commencement, the Stonewall Riots occurred in New York City. The Stonewall Inn in Greenwich Village was one of the few bars in New York City where gay people – primarily men - could assemble without fear of arrest. The Mafia owned the Inn, the Genovese family to be precise, who paid the police to leave its customers alone. However, the City officers would still patrol Stonewall periodically and hassle its customers. When they did on June 28, 1969, Stonewall's patrons resisted, and a riot ensued. The confrontation at Stonewall is widely regarded as the beginning of the Gay Rights Movement in the United States.

The Stonewall Riots were not considered significant when they occurred. The event did not get any closer to the front page of the *New York Times* than page 22. Indeed, no one in Corinth read about it in the *Post-Star* or the *Saratogian*. In the late 1960s, the words "homosexual" and "gay" were not in use in our town. I do not recall hearing a friend, classmate, or adult use either term. The word "queer" was in common usage, although as a kid, I never understood its meaning. But our fathers did, probably because of service in World War II when, as small-town boys, they found themselves serving with young men from major American cities who had both seen more and done more in their young lives. On the rare occasion when I heard my Father or one of his drinking buddies refer to another man as "queer," I understood that it was a pejorative term. Some of my friends probably knew more about it than I did.

My understanding of what it meant for a man to be "queer" increased dramatically just before graduation when I saw the film *Midnight Cowboy*, released on May 25, 1969. The film was inviting because it appeared to be about a cowboy - an American character that boys my age had grown up with on TV - but it was also provocative because it was an X-rated movie that required viewers to be 18 years old. I recently had my birthday so I could gain admission to a Glens Falls theatre as an adult and see the film. I cannot recall who I saw the movie with, but I quickly found it was not a traditional Western. The main character, cowboy Joe Buck, having failed to prosper as a gigolo in Times Square after arriving in New York City from the West, was forced into male prostitution to survive. His efforts were not shown graphically, yet they were presented vividly enough so that even a naive viewer like me could understand what it meant to be queer. Although the film received an X-rating for its depiction of homosexuality, it won the Oscar for Best Picture.

The social and cultural context of our graduation – the Stonewall Riots and the release of *Midnight Cowboy* – are historically meaningful because at least three of my male friends from the Class of 1969, two of its women, and at least two of my high school teachers were, in later years, known to be gay. There could have been more, and there probably was. None of the boys, each of them within my social orbit, ever had a girlfriend I can recall, although they did have dates for the junior prom, an event, quite frankly, that found more platonic couples in attendance than romantic ones. I didn't socialize with the girls who were gay, so I knew less about them. Not only did we not question a classmate's sexual orientation, or our teachers for that matter, but I don't believe many of us knew much about homosexuality or its implications. While the late 1960s was an era known for the sexual liberation of heterosexuals, most homosexuals remained in the closet, particularly in a small town like Corinth, where everything you did was known around town. A rare exception may have been the fathers of two of my classmates who were lovers, something I did not learn until many years after leaving town.

New York State did not de-criminalize same-sex sexual activity until 1980. Known or suspected homosexuals were commonly accepted in the late 1960s workplace as long as they did not wear their orientation on their sleeves. Our gay teachers were likely accepted by the high school administration and their colleagues on this condition. For example, the gay male teachers in Corinth High School were respected and admired, and each took active roles in the school and their communities. Yet they kept their personal lives private. While the rescinding of anti-sodomy laws, the advent of gay marriage, and protections provided by the U.S. Supreme Court have made homosexuality normative in the 21st century, people who were gay in the 1960s were compelled to deny who they were and, in many ways, forced to live a false life.

Most homosexuals remained closeted during the 1960s, particularly in rural communities. Yet homoerotic experiences that provided the opportunity for feelings of desire without the confirmation of one's homosexual orientation were available. A few were even offered in Corinth. The most evident was in the boys' locker room at the high school, where boys were required to take showers with other boys after gym class. Girls had private shower stalls in their locker room, but boys had to strip off their gym shorts several times a week and shower naked with twenty or twenty-five other boys. A gang shower experience, which for a 7th-grade Corinth boy began as early as age 12, could be uncomfortable for many reasons. Nonetheless, at Corinth High in the 1960s, like many schools in the region, the boy's locker room was a place where a teenager might have felt the first passions of his sexual orientation.

The modern tradition of communal showering dates to late 19th century France and originated in the United States in the military and boarding schools. The first gang shower in a public school began only in 1900, so by the 1950s and 1960s, the cultural practice was relatively new. While some accounts suggest that communal showering began over concern for public hygiene, it does not explain why boys were forced to shower in mass while girls were traditionally given privacy. Communal showering by boys remained a common practice across the United States until the 1980s and 1990s. Only with the AIDS crisis was the homoerotic potential of gang showers realized, prompting parental worries they invited undesirable viewing that could lead to homosexual behavior. Some American schools altered the practice by no longer requiring showers after gym class.

The other place in Corinth that offered the potential for a homoerotic experience in the 1960s was the Hole. Located below the Curtis Dam on the Hudson River, the Hole had long been used by Corinth boys for swimming in the nude. While I never went to the Hole myself, several guys I knew swam there regularly in the summer. While the homoerotic nature of the tradition cannot be dismissed, the ritual of swimming without any clothing may also have been a simple expression of adolescent rebellion, teenage boys doing what they weren't supposed to do. A recent Corinth community Facebook post about swimming at the Hole in the 1960s suggested that it was also a fraternal experience that included an initiation ceremony. Whether rooted in fraternal acceptance or adolescent rebellion, the writer noted twice in the post that it was all done while "naked." With its dark grey ledges and deep pools, a typical day at the Hole might have looked much like Thomas Eakins's 19th-century painting "The Swimming Hole," which features six teenage boys swimming nude in a rocky environment. Eakins' painting, often considered the best example of homoeroticism in American art, could easily have been painted in Corinth.

Our teachers, who we learned in later years were gay, certainly understood their orientation. I had one of them as an instructor. He was an extrovert, very funny, and prone to sarcasm. He was active in local theatre and once attended an award ceremony – possibly the Academy Awards - where he met the actress Elizabeth Taylor. He spent nearly an entire class period when he returned from the event raving about her beauty.

There was one instance in 10th grade English when this teacher might have suspected that I knew about or suspected his sexual orientation. We were assigned to write and submit a science fiction story. I don't recall what my story was about or where its inspiration came from, yet I named the main character "Captain Anus." Frankly, I had no idea what I had done. I didn't know what an anus was then since we spent little to no time on the human body in biology class. Besides, that body part would never have been mentioned in a Corinth classroom. I thought I had just made the word up, but I must have heard it somewhere. When my teacher returned the paper to me, it was full of red marks, including a comment that suggested I had been irreverent in naming my story's main character. Oddly, I think I still have that paper somewhere. Years later, after learning about the teacher's sexual orientation, I wondered if he had a good laugh upon reading my character's name in the story or if he thought my use of the term was a cryptic allusion to his sexuality.

The sexual orientation of my gay classmates only became common knowledge in later years. Two of them went off to college and left Corinth behind for good, except for periodic family visits. The third remained in town and worked locally. I would often visit with him during my college vacations. He was just about the only part of our larger social group who remained in Corinth. At the time, he lived in a sad little trailer on Gabriel Road. My friend, who drove a green Ford Maverick, could often be theatrical and was bitingly sarcastic. His perfectly coiffed jet-black hair was his signature feature, every hair kept in place with a heavy, near-lacquer hair spray.

His concern for his appearance was far more pronounced than it was for most guys our age. While I never had the slightest suspicion at the time that he liked men, the giant poster he kept in his trailer might have been a clue as to what was happening with him. While most guys in the early 70s had posters of Farah Fawcett or Catherine Bach on their walls, my friend displayed a large poster of a shirtless and ripped Sylvester Stallone on his refrigerator.

The purpose of the Stallone poster was lost on me, as was our visit to my friend's favorite bar. One night, after I arrived at his trailer for a visit, he insisted that we drive to an out-of-the-way place called the Driftwood Inn at the end of Dix Avenue in Glens Falls. We hung out there for a while, had one drink, and then left. I didn't get why the place appealed to my friend, although I did notice that its customers were all men. Several years later, I shared the account with a female classmate who had also visited the Driftwood with our mutual friend. Knowing the place to be a gay bar, she told me that after they were there for a short time on one visit, the front door opened, and one of our gay male high school teachers came in. He abruptly reversed course and left when he saw two former Corinth students sitting at a table.

Now that I am much older and prone to thinking about my life history, I think about what it might have been like for my gay classmates growing up in Corinth. I wonder if they had yet acknowledged their sexual orientation while still in high school. If they had attained any measure of self-realization during their adolescence in Corinth, there was nowhere to turn; no organization offered support in those days. And, of course, I also wonder about the teachers we had who were gay. Both of the known male teachers are now dead. I recently read obituaries for each and was moved by what they had made of their lives. Both were active and highly recognized for their school and community work. The administration and some of their colleagues surely knew about them, yet I could not help but imagine the challenges my teachers and classmates faced in the late 1960s.

Two of my three gay high school friends are now gone, too. The one who brought me to the Driftwood Inn committed suicide in 1992 at age 41. He was a tormented soul with demons few of us knew about. Another of my gay classmates died in 1990 at age 38 from what many believed was AIDS, although we never knew for sure. Few had ever heard from him after he settled in Boston after college. The third friend, who we learned was homosexual, faced the loss of a beloved partner and has survived a life-threatening illness. He has lived away from Corinth for most of his adult life. He and I were very close throughout high school. I reached him by phone a few years ago and then again as I wrote this memoir. We spoke for over an hour last fall. Each of my five high school classmates and our teachers lived part of their lives in an era of intolerance that would be incomprehensible to adolescents today. I cannot help but wonder how different their lives might have been if the progressive winds that kicked up at the Stonewall Inn in 1969 and gained strength over the following decades had arrived earlier.

31

ALL IN THE FAMILY

A job at the Hudson River Mill was a coveted summer job for a recent high school graduate heading to college. It was simply the best place to work for a student who needed to pay tuition, room, and board. It was also a good, short-term place for a guy to work in 1969 until he enlisted into the military or was drafted. Temporary summer jobs at the Mill were offered to fill the openings left when regular paper workers took summer vacations. Mill management took pride in being able to hire kids from the community for summer work, as the *EMBA News* often reported the total number employed in most years during the 1960s. But only some kids could get a job at the mill. Jobs went to boys and typically first to the children of IP employees. Guys whose fathers did not work for IP did get work, but usually not until after the sons of Mill employees were hired.

Summer work at the mill was a male privilege in the 1960s. Although adult women had worked at the paper mill, in its offices and the finishing room, since the 19th century, I never knew any graduating female senior who got a summer job there during the years I worked. A few might have gotten office work, but no one I knew did. Instead, many girls in my class did secretarial work in town during the summer, waitressed at a local restaurant, or traveled to Lake George for a job at Storytown. The minimum wage was the best that could be earned in those jobs. Both boys and girls could also get jobs at the Saratoga Race Course. Working there was a good deal, even at minimum wage, since the track was only open for August in the 1960s. Kids who worked at the Saratoga Race Course called the "Track," loved it because they could tell their parents they had a summer job, yet they had until the end of June and all of July free to hang out. You made only a little money working for just a month, but you had so much free time.

Getting a job at the Track was a political exercise. While it was operated by the non-profit New York State Racing Association, the Saratoga County Republican Party was somehow able to influence local hiring. I was always told a Corinth kid seeking a job at the Track first had to go down to a law office on Main Street, where the firm's principal served as the treasurer of the Saratoga County Republican Party. The lawyer was reportedly the Party member in charge of distributing political patronage in Corinth. From there, you were supposed to go to the Track's office on Union Avenue in Saratoga Springs to complete a perfunctory application.

As long as summer work at the Mill was available, I had no interest in working elsewhere. Yet in the 1970s, IP had a few bad years when orders for the Hudson River Mill's coated papers were down. During a downturn, the Mill did not hire summer replacements for its vacationing paper workers. When I failed to get a call to work during one of those summers, a friend urged me to seek a job at the Track. I went through the process: I met with our local Republican party official and then went to the Union Avenue office to complete the application.

I was very disappointed when I failed to get hired. I thought you had a job if you got sent to the Track. But for some reason, I didn't. I had plenty of prior work experience and even a recommendation from our parish priest. So, what was up? Only years later, when I discovered the extent to which the Republican Party controlled Saratoga County and the Corinth community, did I suspect I might not have been hired because someone found my Mother was a registered Democrat.

While a job at the track had its appeal, work at the Hudson River Mill was more valued. For most of my years there, the lowest hourly wage was three times the federal minimum. Some serious money could be made at the Mill, particularly from working overtime. New York State law then required an hourly paid worker to be compensated time-and-half, or 150% of his hourly wage, for every hour he worked after eight hours in a single day. So, an 8-hour extra shift resulted in 12 hours of pay. Working two consecutive eight-hour shifts at the Mill, called a "sixteen," resulted in 20 hours of total compensation. Working two shifts in a row on a Sunday was even more rewarding. The union contract paper workers held required they be paid "double-time" for each hour worked a Sunday, or 200% of the hourly rate. So, a "sixteen" on a Sunday resulted in 32 hours of compensation in just one 24-hour day.

You could also earn double time during the other six days of the week. If the "sixteen" you worked were the 11 PM-7 AM and 7 AM-3 PM shifts, clocking in at 11 PM the following night triggered another stipulation, resulting in double time for that shift. Some paper workers disliked paying union dues, yet they appreciated the sweet overtime deal the labor unions had negotiated. So, if a college kid like me worked five regular eight-hour shifts and two sixteens in the same seven-day tour, he would be paid for 80 hours. If one of those "sixteens" were on a Sunday, the number of paid hours would jump to 84. During my final week at the Hudson River Mill, I worked three "sixteens" and came home with what I considered an enormous amount of money.

My Mother's political affiliation might have prevented me from getting a job at the Saratoga race track, but my Father's long history at the Hudson

River Mill guaranteed me a job there. Most of the men in my family had worked for International Paper at one time or another. On my Mother's side, my grandfather, Benedetto Rea, had worked at the IP mill at Ft. Edward as early as 1915. His sons Harry, George, Alfred, and James had each worked as paper workers. My other grandfather, John Cernek, began work for IP at the Hudson River Mill in 1918. His other sons - John and Martin – had worked there. My grandfather and Father, Paul, were the longest in the Company's employ, working for IP for a cumulative 87 years. So, when I started working at the Beater Room in 1969, I became the 3rd generation and tenth member of my family to work for International Paper. The Human Resources office at the mill could not have known about my family members who worked for the Company, yet they knew my Father very well.

Of all the men in my family employed by IP, apart from my Father, I knew the most about the work experience of my grandfather, John Cernek. He was still working at the mill when I was born, and through the years, he and my grandmother, Zuzanna, cared for me at their house on Heath Street while my parents worked. They became my second parents. My grandfather was a quiet man, yet I got the impression from my Father and uncles that he had been a heavy drinker and a gambler in his youth. John was strong and hard-working. He once told me when he was out of work during the 1921 Paper Strike, a local farmer hired him and a friend to put up some firewood. My grandfather said that in one day, the two men cut, split, and stacked two cords of hardwood. In a time when only axes and hand saws were available for the job, putting up two cords of wood in one day was a formidable achievement. I think of my grandfather and the story of him cutting firewood for a Corinth farmer every time I see his old cross-cut wood saw hanging in my shed.

After arriving in the United States in 1911 and working for several years in a New York City saloon, John and Zuzanna moved with their first-born son, John, to Corinth in 1918. John sought work at the Hudson River Mill, where a cousin, Stephen Cernek, was already employed. My grandfather started working the day shift in the physically demanding wood yard. His primary responsibility was using a picaroon, a 24-inch long, wood-handled tool with a sharp, slightly curved steel hook at the end. The device was used to pull four-foot-long pieces of pulp wood from the rail cars brought into the woodyard along the spur line and move them onto a conveyer that transported the wood to the top of the yard's large wood piles. My grandfather and other wood handlers often pulled wood for their eight-hour shift.

My grandfather worked in the woodyard until he turned 60 years old. He then worked as a watchman until his retirement. This job was often given to an aging man with a long work history to end their years at the mill. Being a watchman was much easier on his body, only requiring him to walk an established route around the mill every two hours. As a watchman, he carried a round, black leather watchman's clock slung over his shoulder. The device was about eight inches in diameter with a small clock dial. Below the dial was a hole into which a key could be inserted. At each of the designated stops on the watchman's route, a small steel box was attached to the wall, and inside, a key was attached to a short chain. The slightly raised number at the end of the key identified the stop or station. When the key was inserted into the clock, the stop's number would be recorded on a circular piece of paper inside the device, marking the time of day the watchman was at each station. While this provided proof that the watchman had completed his round, it was also required by the insurance company holding the policy on the plant. The route had some 20 stations and took about 40 minutes to walk each hour. I learned all of this not from my grandfather but from a single week when I worked the same job during one of my Hudson River Mill summers.

My grandfather worked at the mill until he was 67 years old. For many years after that, well into his 70s, he was the custodian for the U.S. Post Office when it was located on Maple Street. He walked daily from his home on Upper Heath Street to the Post Office, arriving by 7 AM each weekday and finishing work at 10 AM. Then, he would walk back home. My grandfather never owned a car and never learned how to drive. When I was out of school in the summer, I would sometimes drive around looking for him, often finding him walking along Palmer Avenue, almost always opposite the Indian Trail, where steel posts and railings were set into the sidewalk on the north side of the street. Whenever I stopped to give him a ride, he would ask me to go back downtown so he could get a copy of the New York *Daily News* at Holmes's Newsroom. After we picked up the paper, I would drive him home and sit with him at the kitchen table to drink coffee.

Of course, I only knew my grandfather after he was in his sixties, so by then, all his youth had been drained out of him. When he was not working at the Post Office, he tended his large garden or sat on the porch and smoked his pipe. It was there where he often read the sports section of the *Daily News*, particularly the daily entries at the Yonkers and Aqueduct race tracks. I often wondered if he picked up the habit from his son, John - an avid follower of thoroughbreds who my Father said had once won $3000 from Corinth's best-known bookie – or if my grandfather had passed the practice to his son. Yet, on more than one occasion, my grandfather asked me to drive him to Saratoga Springs so he could place a bet with the bookie who operated at the back of Baldy's Newsroom on North Broadway. Corinth had a few bookies back then, but I think my grandfather preferred to use the one in Saratoga so that word would not get back to my grandmother that he was spending part of his Social Security check or his Post Office earnings on the horses.

My Father began working at the Hudson River Mill in 1937. He was a bright and conscientious student. I still have the framed "perfect attendance certificate" he was given at the close of one academic year. I cherish that document because my Mother discarded the dozen perfect attendance certificates I received from Kindergarten through the 11th grade. When my Father was 15 years old, he began a *Saratogian news*paper route, and the following year, he won a subscription competition that sent him on a trip through the Adirondacks with other winning *Saratogian* carriers. In 1938, he received a certificate from Corinth High School for preparing and exhibiting posters supporting National Air Mail Week. He played varsity soccer and baseball, winning letters from 1935 to 1937. My Father never mentioned any of these activities to me growing up. I had to learn about them from reading old newspapers long after he passed away. He did tell me that he quit school at the end of his junior year, and I have a fuzzy memory that it had something to do with the fact that his mother would not let him play varsity soccer anymore.

My Father was drafted into the Army in 1942. He served in the 5th Air Force in the Pacific as a radio operator on B-24s. Not until after his death, when I found his discharge papers, did I learn he had been credited for participating in ten Pacific theatre battles. It also mentioned he contracted malaria and was hospitalized for three weeks. He never talked about the war. Ever. Yet my Father did describe coming home to Corinth after the War ended in October 1945.

He told me he arrived at the Corinth station alone by train from Saratoga but then hitched a ride into the village. He had to ask people downtown if they knew where his parents lived. They had recently purchased their first home, moving from their White Street tenement, where they had lived since 1918, to a house on the corner of Heath and Hill Streets. My Father's story always struck me as profoundly sad for its anticlimactic quality: a young man coming home after three years, having fought in a war 10,000 miles away, and there was no one to greet him. He then walked a mile to a house he had never seen before that would be his new home. I have often tried to imagine what it might have been like to have been in my grandparents' kitchen the night my Father came home from the War and walked through the back door. One of my biggest regrets is not asking my parents more about their youth.

My Father returned to the Mill to work shortly after his discharge, taking a job in a pulp and paper lab. The lab's primary function was to test and determine the quality of the wood pulp and paper manufactured at the mill. I worked in the lab for two summers in the 1970s and became familiar with my Father's work. Because lab work was shift work, sometime in the 1950s, after I was born, my Father secured a transfer to the Time Office, a day job.

My Father was one of several men in the Time Office whose tally of the hours the Mill's 1500 employees worked each week served as the basis for weekly paychecks. All this work was done manually, aided only by monstrous Monroe electric calculators. In 1971, he became payroll supervisor for the Mill. It was not uncommon for him to get a phone call from a paper worker at home on the day when checks were issued, claiming their pay was a few hours short. The mill's payroll was computerized in the late 1970s, a transition that required the Time Office to be relocated down the hill near the Mill's other administrative offices. Finding the complexity of the new payroll process too stressful, my Father retired from the Hudson River Mill in 1982 when he turned 62, after 44 years of service.

In June 1969, I began working at the Hudson River Mill for the first of five summers. I became one of the thousands of Corinth boys who followed their fathers and grandfathers into the pulp and paper mill during the one hundred years it had been in operation. The sons of 19th-century farmers who did not see a future in agriculture were the first in their families to enter the mill. Then, the young men came to Corinth from long distances, many of them immigrants from Europe. Many sons of immigrants and farmers entered the Mill when they were 13 or 14 years old, some retiring fifty years later, never working elsewhere, except maybe for Uncle Sam. My Father and the many boys who came of age in 1910-1940 quit school and became paper workers to help support their families. Four generations of Corinth men and boys had worked at the Hudson River Mill by 1969.

My classmates and I, the sons and daughters of the Greatest Generation, came of age in the 1950s and 1960s when earning a high school diploma was essential. Yet a college education, beyond many's financial reach, was considered unnecessary in an International Paper Company mill town like Corinth. Some boys who came of age in the decades that followed World War II began their careers in the mill shortly after graduating. It was still believed then that a job at the Mill was for life. For kids like me, working at the Hudson River Mill offered a chance to participate in the family tradition of becoming a paper worker. Yet my summer work represented an inauthentic participation in the generational ritual because the few weeks I spent in the mill represented a temporary detour on the road towards a life that would send me far from Corinth.

32

TURN LEFT AND COUGH

I t was a sunny morning on the Monday following graduation when I went to the Hudson River Mill to complete a formal application for summer work. I left our house early, got into my white 1962 Corvair, and headed down Center Street. I turned right onto Mechanic Street, left on Main, and left immediately at the Shell Station to enter Palmer Avenue at the Baptist Church. I drove past the field on the left that Darius Fenton farmed in the early 19th century. I could see the beginning of the well-worn path to my right that passed across the steep slope that rose south of the railroad tracks. What Corinthians then called "The Indian Trail" could well have been a section of the Kayaderosseras Trail that Native Peoples had used for centuries to ford the Hudson above Palmer Falls. Then, over the Palmer Avenue rail crossing where, in 1921, striking paper workers blocked the arrival of a train thought to be carrying strikebreakers. For decades, a paper worker had been stationed at the crossing throughout the day to stop traffic on Palmer Avenue whenever a train entered or left the Mill yard. That day, the watchmen had yet to arrive.

Then, I drove past the High School Hill, Indian Hollow, and the Pagenstecher Park entrance. Just east of the High School Hill, Palmer Avenue straightens out and widens after its intersection with 2nd Street. At 3rd

Street, the Hudson River Mill's vast supply of pulp wood first came into view on the left, looming mountain-like behind the houses on the north side of Palmer Avenue, all the way to 5th Street. As I passed 3rd, I looked left to see the old coal pocket where a half-dozen kids from the Class of 1969 played spin-the-bottle during their 9th-grade picnic at Pagenstecher. I passed quickly by the Mill Manager's House, Hudson River Credit Union, Immaculate Conception Church, Star Hotel, Lent's Market, Mandigo's Florists, and Al Madison's, where I got my first haircut.

Al' Madison's, one of two barber shops in the Palmer section of Corinth in the 1960s, was popular with paper workers. Its big windows looked out on Palmer Avenue, allowing a full view of the comings and goings at Lent's Market and the Star Hotel across the street. The rear of his shop had a door through which his customers periodically passed. I never knew what was on the other side of the door, but other kids said men went there to place bets on horse races and to play poker. I never learned the reason for Al's impairment, but he had lost the full function of one of his legs, making it difficult for him to move deftly around his customers as he cut their hair. His limitations became evident whenever he needed to reach his counter to grab another pair of scissors or the brush he used to remove hair from clothing.

Al developed a clever way to compensate for his disability. A black steel collar had been fabricated to fit loosely around the base of his barber's chair. From the collar, a single steel bar extended about three feet from the chair, six inches off the floor. Two small wheels were attached to the bottom of the bar. Attached to the horizontal bar, directly over the wheels, was a vertical post on which a black bicycle seat was attached. Al sat on the bicycle seat as he cut hair, the wheels beneath permitting him to shuffle his feet left or right to position himself around the chair depending on where his customer's hair needed to be cut. He moved around effortlessly this way, cutting hair, chewing gum, and talking, all at the same time. Al Madison, a memorable Corinth character and confident of many who barbered in Corinth for 38 years, died in 1975 at age 60.

I turned left onto 5th Street, just past the building that once housed Abe's Diner, and parked opposite the Mill's Wood Room. INTERNATIONAL PAPER COMPANY was spelled out in large silver letters along its side, large enough to be read several blocks away. It was a short walk to IP's Administration Office, often called the Time Office, where most paper workers entered and departed the mill. The building that housed the Time Office was constructed in 1905 as International Paper's principal office in an era when the Hudson River Mill was the Company's flagship plant and was well-known as one of the largest pulp and paper mills in the United States.

IP's Administration Building was designed and located to represent an essential civic structure. Its strategic placement first required that Pine Street's east and west sections be joined by land-filling the ravine that separated them. Burleigh's 1888 birds-eye view of Corinth is the only known documentation of Pine Street's early geography. Once Pine Street became contiguous, the new building's entrance was sited with a direct view of Heath Street, which then reached only the south side of Palmer Avenue. As the IP building was being constructed, Heath Street was extended across Palmer Avenue to intersect Pine so that it ended opposite the entry to the new building. Sidewalks were built on both sides of the Heath Street extension. At the same time, the Mill's original 6th Street entrance was relocated to Pine Street, and the Village of Corinth abandoned Elm Street, which ran nearly parallel with Palmer Avenue to the north. The remains of Elm Street lay entirely within the mill yard after 1905. One of Elm Street's original houses, perhaps built by the Hudson River Pulp and Paper Company before 1888, survives in the Village today, largely hidden and unknown to all but a few residents. The positioning of the IP Building at the terminus of Heath Street, with sidewalks installed on either side, made for a dramatic arrival for Mill visitors after they turned off Palmer Avenue.

The Administration Building that IP built in 1905 served several purposes. Its upper-level exterior was distinctive, clad in red brick with an elevated staired entry and two ornate oval windows facing Pine Street. The building's upper floor contained a large room with a fireplace at one end where the Company's Directors met in the early years. The center of the upper floor contained two small offices intended for secretaries and a large open waiting area with two bathrooms. The floor's east side served as office space for the Mill's accounting and purchasing departments. Oak-paneled wainscoting covered most of the lower walls of the upper floor. By the late 1960s, much of the oak had been painted white, the walls covered with gaudy wallpaper, and steel partitions installed to create smaller office spaces. The upper floor's original twelve-foot ceiling had been lowered with the installation of white acoustic panels.

The exterior of the building's lower floor, clad in rough-surfaced granite, was designed in sharp contrast to the more refined red brick upper level. This level was used by workers who entered through one of two doors located under the steps leading up to the building's main entry. Once inside the doors to the lower level, two short sets of steps led down to an ample space that spanned the width of the building, with several offices on either side. One of the offices had served as the original office for the Hudson River Mill Credit Union, and another as storage for work boots – Red Wing, I believe – that paper workers could purchase at the Mill. Each of the small offices had been added over the years, for there were none in the architect's original plans for the building, just a large room with several long wooden benches along its edges and in the center. The lower level in the 1905 plans resembled a train station lobby. The presence of the benches in the original plans suggests that its architect, who likely designed the building on a New York City drafting table, imagined that paper workers would use the benches to hang around the mill before or after work. How little the architect understood industrial workers.

The Time Office, elevated from the rest of the lower level, occupied the middle of the building. Unchanged from the building's original design, the Time Office resembled a "cage." It was made of heavy gauge steel, designed somewhat like a chain link fence yet much heavier and stiffer. The Time Office had two doors and windows that permitted timekeepers to interact with paper workers. The Time Office had no ceiling, so the "cage" was open at the top. From the signage on its exterior, you could tell that the Time Office had once dispersed the Mill's weekly payroll, which was paid in cash in the early days. There were narrow corridors on either side of the Time Office where workers passed to reach the time cards and time clocks in the building's rear, single-story extension.

I spent numerous hours in the Time Office as a kid. My father had been working as a timekeeper since the late 1950s, so after catechism at the nearby Immaculate Conception Church, I would walk down Palmer Avenue and over to Pine Street to catch a ride home with him. While I waited for his work day to end, I explored the office, sometimes pounding on typewriter keys or pushing buttons on the big Monroe calculators. My Father's boss, Ken Kendall, and his co-workers, Earl Wait, Nate Ide, and Dick Balcom, were always very nice to me when I was there. At the end of each week, the timekeepers would collect worker time cards from the racks adjacent to their office, tabulate the hours clocked on each one using the Monroe's, and then record the totals. The hours worked at the employee's hourly rate would then be processed by accounting so that paychecks could be issued.

The Time Office was moved from the lower level of the IP office building to the administrative area in the lower part of the mill sometime in the 1980s. This occurred when the Company installed an IBM mainframe to handle the Mill's payroll, building a sizeable air-conditioned room that resembled a set from Stanley Kubrick's film *2001: A Space Odyssey*. Sometime in the 1990s, the former Time Office in the Pine Street building was gutted and replaced by a large utility room that held the building's new electric service and propane furnace. The time card racks and the time clocks were also torn out, with bathrooms and a storage area built into the space that held them. Sadly, only a few photographs of the Time Office interior survive, in addition to the building's original architectural plans, which are now stored in an archive.

After I passed through the rear door of the Administration Building that Monday morning, I entered the Mill Yard, where there was always activity, particularly early in the day. If you entered at 6:30 for a 7 AM-3 PM shift, you would see wood trucks parked, waiting their turn at the nearby Scale House, where loads of four-foot-long pulp wood were measured to determine how much IP would pay for the delivery. The trucks continued from the Scale House into the wood yard to be unloaded. Depending on the time of the day, a freight train might enter or exit the yard on the spur leading from the central Delaware and Hudson line. This occurred three to four times a day. And there was usually a truck or tractor being driven through the yard by the Outdoor Miscellaneous crew. Of course, other workers would be going to work the same time you were, maybe 600 men on the day shift in the 1960s. The early morning was the busiest time at the Hudson River Mill.

I first went to human resources, where I filled out some paperwork. There, I was told I would have to join the United Paper Workers International Union after 30 days of employment to remain employed, a requirement of the closed-shop agreement the unions negotiated with International Paper. My signature on the application represented my permission to have monthly union dues removed from my paycheck. It was a pretty good deal; my union wage at almost $5.00 per hour in the summer of 1969 was three times the $1.30 minimum wage in 1969, the rate many of my friends were earning elsewhere. Union dues for me were $20 weekly, about four hours of pay. While union membership has declined in recent decades, Corinth had a strong labor movement that dated to the late 19th century when Samuel Gompers of the American Federation of Labor endorsed the Corinth Allied Trades Assembly. Union bashing is a common sport these days, even in Corinth. Yet, the labor unions in the paper industry were responsible for the good wages that were paid at the Hudson River Mill for the 65 years before IP shuttered it in 2002.

From human resources, I went to the Mill's suite of medical rooms to get a physical from the International Paper Company doctor. This family practice physician also served as the doctor for the Corinth School system. He had been practicing in Corinth since 1929, was well-respected, and was a pillar of the community. I received the standard physical, which included the never-really-understood procedure where the doctor holds a boy's testicles in his hand like a pair of ripe walnuts and has him cough a few times ostensibly to see if he had a hernia. This routine made sense when a guy was in his late teens, but this type of exam had been practiced even when boys got physicals in the nurse's office during elementary school. When I coughed that day, I wondered why third-grade boys had to be checked for a hernia. When, in later years, I relayed the story to a female classmate, she told me her childhood Corinth dentist convinced her parents to let him give their daughter shots of Vitamin K in her buttocks. And when I told that story to someone else, I was told that boys got the shots, too. I found it remarkable these stories still got traction almost 60 years after the events occurred.

My first day of work at the Hudson River Mill was the same week as my physical. So, I had only a few days of summer freedom before starting my job. I was told I would be working in the Beater Room and to report for the 3-11 PM shift later in the week. The 3-11 shift was one of 3 8-hour shifts at the Mill that divided the 24-hour work day. The shift changes were inherent to the "tour system" operating at the Mill for decades to keep the paper machines running 24 hours a day, seven days a week. The tour system required that you work seven consecutive days on each of the three shifts: 7 AM-3 PM, 3 PM-11 PM, and 11 PM-7 AM. You got at least one day off between tour changes and four consecutive days off once a month. When you finished the 7th day of your 7 AM-3 PM tour, you clocked out of the Mill on Friday afternoon and resumed work at 11 PM the following Tuesday. Having four consecutive days off every month was great, but shift work was the price paid for the benefit.

The dramatic change in working, eating, and sleeping habits every seven days – the primary characteristic of shift work - adversely affects the life of an industrial worker. As the summer wore on, I found the 11 PM-7 AM shift most difficult. Keeping awake all night was not a problem, for the Mill was a world unto itself. Its bright lighting and intense noise were sure to keep you awake. What I found most challenging was trying to get ready for work at 10 PM just as my parents were heading to bed. It just seemed so unnatural. Still, shift work as part of the modern tour system was preferable to how Corinth's paper mill was run in the 19th century when a work day consisted of an 11-hour day shift and a 13-hour night shift. The six-day work week at that time consisted of either a 66-hour work week or one that lasted 78 hours. So, the 8-hour day – a product of labor union persistence – was a welcomed reform, even if shift work was required.

33

—·—

THE BROKE HUSTLERS

I arrived for work a half-hour early, at 2:30 PM, on my first day of work in the Beater Room. I did so because my Father told me it was customary for paper workers to show up for their shift thirty minutes before the hour so the man who did your job on the prior shift, the person you relieved, could go home when you arrived. This practice was a critical element of the Hudson River Mill's culture, contributing to a sense of camaraderie among paper workers. The courtesy you extended to the man you relieved was reciprocated at the end of your shift by the man who relieved you, also thirty minutes before the hour. Everyone still worked an eight-hour day, but the practice created a community among paper workers and gave them the feeling they were getting out of work early. But it did something else. By informally instituting early departures from the mill, paper workers signaled they were anxious to go home. That summer, I would learn why.

When I arrived for my first 3-11 PM shift, I joined a steady stream of workers who walked briskly from their cars to the Time Office to clock in. My Father and grandfather had each done the same thing for four decades. At the time, I didn't consider this fact, but now that the Hudson River Mill is gone, I have come to appreciate the meaning of that day. I quickly found my time card and "punched in." While I had often been in the Time Office, I had only been into the heart of the mill a few times. So I needed my Father to give me directions to find my way to the Beater Room. The route was not direct.

After I exited the Time Office through one of two doors at the rear of the building, I entered the mill yard. It was a vast industrial space intersected by railroad tracks and roads leading in several directions. Only from within the yard itself did you get a real sense of the Mill's vast scale. The fastest route to the Beater Room from there was over an enclosed bridge that began just past the Clay Shed and spanned the distance between two large mill buildings. Once over the bridge, you walked through a large storage room and across heavy, corrugated steel flooring. The building's interior had been painted several times, but many of the building's original red bricks remained exposed. At the end of the room, a set of stairs led down two stories to the west end of one of the mill's oldest surviving machine rooms, where the No. 1 and the No. 2 paper machines were located. Once I left the stairwell and could view the Mill's production areas, the decibel level increased considerably. Before entering the machine room to my right, I watched an inspector examine a finished roll of paper before it was wrapped for shipment. It was Jack Moylan, the father of one of my classmates.

The machine room where the Nos. 1 and 2 paper machines were located was a substantial red brick building with steel girders overhead. The building was one of several that were part of a late 19th-century expansion by the Hudson River Pulp and Paper Company. The two Fourdrinier paper machines, each with 148" wires, sat adjacent to each other with a twenty-five-foot wide "alley" in between. Both were installed in 1896 for $10,000,000 in 2024 dollars. When I walked through the machine room on my first day of work in 1969, only the No. 2 machine was running. The machine lacked on-machine coating technology similar to that used on the

Nos. 3, 4, and 11 machines, so it was nearly obsolete. The No. 2 ran for the summer of 1969 but was permanently shut down soon afterward.

The Beater Room was in a separate building most easily accessed from the north end of the Nos. 1 and 2 machine room. Because the Beater Room prepared wood pulp for use by the Mill's paper machines, it was situated perpendicular to the two machine rooms that held the Nos.1-4 paper machines. Large passageways between the end of both rooms and the Beater Room made it seem like they were all part of one structure. The Beater Room was a cavernous red brick structure built adjacent to the Hudson River in the 1880s. The building was constructed close to the Hudson, only a few feet from a large stone flood wall to the north designed to protect the Mill from the Hudson's heavy Spring run-offs. The early managers of the Hudson River Pulp and Paper Company that developed the site in 1869 learned early the Hudson high waters could be very damaging. After only a few years of operation, the Company was forced to construct stone walls to keep the River at bay after its pulp mill had been washed away. Over the years, they were upgraded and reinforced with concrete.

The Beater Room building, where I worked in 1969, was demolished in 2011. It can be seen in Burleigh's Birdseye View of Corinth, a lithograph published in 1888. It also appears in several other photographs and illustrations of the Mill in the late 19th and early 20th centuries. The building was conspicuous to anyone who visited the vantage point created on the Warren County side of the Hudson that provided a view of the River, the entire Hudson River Mill, and the hydroelectric plant at Palmer Falls. The Beater Room building can be seen on the rear cover of this book, to the right of the prominent dark circular structure at the river's edge. The construction of the viewing area underscores that even in the late 20th century, a view of the Hudson River Mill was considered an aesthetic experience. Today, a visitor to the site would see only a concrete void where the Mill once stood.

A visitor to the viewpoint before the Mill's 2011 demolition would have recognized the Beater Room's distinctive, north-facing gable that featured three side-by-side arched windows. It was one of the Mill's few 19th-century architectural details that survived until the early 21st century. The window's graceful arched top – inspired by Romanesque architecture in vogue in the post-Civil War years - spoke to the aesthetic investment Victorians made in industrial structures. After IP built its principal office on Pine Street in 1905, the Company tended to construct unremarkable structures for the remainder of the 20th century. IP built a few interesting buildings after 1905, using brick to construct the Binderene and the Core Plants in the first decades of the 20th century. But in the case of the machine room built to house the No. 11 machine in 1957, the resulting building was nothing more than a massive brick box.

More than thirty years after my first summer spent working in the Beater Room, I had the opportunity to learn more about how the original custodian of the mill – Hudson River Pulp and Paper – built things. In 2002, when I had the chance to explore the mill's sub-basements, I was stunned by what I observed. Enormous yet graceful granite arches had been built over the passageways between rooms, and vaulted brick ceilings could be found in some smaller spaces. The sub-basement walls were made from massive granite blocks. The scale of the construction was overwhelming. These extraordinary architectural details are now entombed beneath the concrete slab that was poured by IP in 2011 after the Hudson River Mill was demolished. Sadly, none of this industrial archeology was documented before demolition. Not until many years later did I understand the Mill's history or the architectural significance of the building where I worked.

When I arrived at the Beater Room on my first day, I was happy to learn I would be part of a crew of guys my age. Bruce was the oldest among us. He had just finished his undergraduate coursework in art education at SUNY New Paltz and was to return in the Fall to complete his student teaching. He was intelligent, athletic, and animated, always seeking to engage the rest of us in conversation. His walk was purposeful and energetic. I viewed Bruce as the leader of our crew. He had the most life experience and the best ideas. I also looked to him for guidance as I contemplated my first year of college in the Fall. Bruce was from Lake George, so he sought to gain a familiarity with Corinth, which I tried to supply.

Paul was the next oldest among us. He was a year ahead of me, graduating in 1968. His sister, Karyl, was in my class, where we had been good friends throughout high school, hanging out with the same gang since the 9th or 10th grade. Paul and I had been teammates on the 1967 varsity football team. Although Paul was over six feet tall and slender, he played tackle. In shoulder pads and a helmet, he appeared formidable. Paul was shy and soft-spoken, always happy to do whatever our crew decided. His father worked in the paper mill, so he knew a bit about what he was getting into. Paul was a full-time employee at the Hudson River Mill for many years after the summer of 1969.

Terry had just graduated with me the week before. He was about 5-10 and, like me, overweight for his height. Terry was a great kid, kind and thoughtful, yet he could act recklessly sometimes, behaviors that were often amplified by alcohol. He could be unpredictable and willing to take chances. Terry was also the most irreverent among us, barely adhering to social convention. One time, I ran into him at The Inn on Palmer Avenue. He stood before me, beer in hand, wearing an off-white, long-sleeved, insulated tee shirt. Where the hemmed crew neck of the shirt had once been, there was now a series of jagged, saw-like cuts in the fabric that went all the way around his neck. When I asked Terry what had happened to his shirt, he said the collar itched his neck, so he got a razor blade and hacked away at it until it was separated from the rest of the shirt. He did this while wearing the shirt. Terry seemed not to care much about what others thought about him.

Pierre was my age, tall and thin, with dark wavy hair. His family initially came from Quebec, but he grew up in Glens Falls. His father worked for IP, in charge of its forest operations. Kids whose parents worked for IP elsewhere often came to the Hudson River Mill in Corinth for a summer job. Pierre was smooth-talking and fluid-like in his movements. His name fit him perfectly. Pierre's speech was measured and polite, a product of his attendance at St. Mary's Academy, a Catholic high school in Glens Falls. Like Paul, he was quiet and soft-spoken. All five guys on our Beater Room crew worked well as a team and became friends that summer, sharing experiences that would teach us different lessons.

Our foreman, Ken Bailey, was in his late 50s. He married Alice Bailey, a 4th-grade teacher in the Corinth schools. His wife was born in Corinth, but Ken was born in Brooklyn, joining the ranks of the men and boys who had left the city to find work at upstate paper mills. It was not uncommon for a Corinth woman, who as a teacher was considered a professional, to marry a paper worker. No one ever thought it odd. The pool of eligible men was limited to a Corinth woman who returned to her hometown after college, consisting primarily of mill workers. However, a worker at the Hudson River Mill might have been considered a "good catch," for the Mill operated nearly all the time, providing plenty of work, and its union contracts ensured that wages were good. Ken was a pretty relaxed guy who we thought would leave us alone as long as we did our work. That's exactly how it turned out.

Ken had us gather around him near the Beater Room office so he could explain our job. He told us that the Beater Room prepares wood pulp before it is pumped to the paper machines. Chemicals are added to the pulp in the Beater Room to whiten the pulp and strengthen the paper. Pulp preparation did require some skill, but our crew would not be doing any of that. Our occupation was listed as "beater helper," which put us at the bottom of the Mill's food chain. He told us that we would perform the beater room's other principal function: to process manufactured paper of inferior quality, called "broke," back into pulp. In the early days, our crew would have been called "broke hustlers," but the term became a pejorative, so it was replaced by "beater helper."

Our work did not require any skill, or thinking for that matter. Our job was purely physical, although we would have long periods of inactivity, typical of work at the Hudson River Mill. There was often nothing to do at the Mill when the paper machines ran smoothly. The machines did all the work. Some of our tasks were undertaken in the Beater Room itself. But we were also required to venture to other parts of the mill to retrieve previously manufactured paper that had been returned by a customer, rejected by a paper inspector, or left over after a rewinder cut a roll down to a size ordered by a publisher. These were typically called "cull" or "broke" rolls. We were also sent to clean up paper after a paper machine "break." This stuff was called "broke." Nothing about our jobs was monotonous except for the occasional long, hot shifts spent pushing broke beneath the No. 3 and No. 4 paper machines—more on this in another chapter.

Ken showed us the dry-broke beater at the northern end of the beater room, where we were to bring the cull rolls. The beater was the size of a small bedroom, made of heavy gauge, dark green steel, and shaped like an upside-down cone with its point cut off flat. The beater resembled the Mercury Freedom 7 space capsule that Alan Shepard used to become

America's first man in space. The dry-broke beater was perhaps 10-12 feet tall. On one side was a chest-high observation window about five feet wide. On the other side was an even larger opening to the floor. A tilting steel table was built into the concrete outside this beater opening. A powerful Black and Clawson hydraulic roll-splitter was positioned over the table and anchored to the floor.

The splitter was a remarkable piece of equipment. It featured a wide steel blade that worked like a guillotine to slice up to four-foot-wide cull rolls through to their core. Before the installation of the splitter in 1967, cull rolls were hand-cut with a power saw or a roll skinner, a primitive wooden tool used in 19th-century paper mills. Cull rolls were moved to the roll-splitter by forklift or a hand cart. On days when the paper machines were running poorly, as many as a dozen rolls could be lined up waiting their turn with the roll-splitter. Once a cull roll was placed on the table below the splitter blade, the operator pushed a button that operated the hydraulic, and the blade edge came down slowly, cutting through perhaps three feet of paper like a knife through warm butter. After a cull roll was split, the operator removed its core. The steel table would then be tilted at the push of another button, and the split paper would fall into the beater.

Sometimes, when work was slack, I would watch the action of the beater through the observation opening. As the splitter cut the cull rolls into slabs that fell into the beater, water flooded into its bottom, and a wide circulating blade would revolve inside, breaking up the paper into smaller and smaller pieces. I would often lean on the chest-high rim of the opening and peer into the beater. I could feel the motor's power that drove the beater blades vibrate from below, through the concrete floor, and into me. I was mesmerized by the slow, methodical churning of the beater as large pieces of broke were gradually reduced to smaller and smaller pieces and finally into a thick, soupy mixture. The beater's slow mechanical motion created a hypnotizing pinwheel of milky wood pulp, offering a compelling diversion from our Beater Room routine.

Once the cull rolls were wholly beaten, the resulting pulp was piped from the vat to the Hollander beaters at the south end of the Beater room on the basement level to be prepared for possible reuse. While the beater in the Beater Room required very little work from our crew, the one in the sub-basement below the No. 3 and No. 4 paper machines could turn an eight-hour shift into a night of pure hell. Every shift our crew worked, we dreaded being sent to a place that we called the "broke pit."

34

PUSHING BROKE

The Fourdrinier paper machine is the primary technology in a paper mill. It is a complex machine that has gotten larger and faster over time, with enhancements that have improved the paper's quality and strength. The Fourdrinier utilizes the same fundamental operating principles today as when patented in 1806. I recall being overwhelmed by the size of the Hudson River Mill's No. 11 machine when I first viewed it during a 6th-grade tour of the Mill in 1962. The Mill's other machines at the time, Nos. 1, 2, 3, 4, and 10 were only a fraction of No. 11's size. While growing up, I would hear my Father, Uncle Freddy, and other men in Corinth refer to No. 11 in near-transcendent terms. I became accustomed to its massive scale during my five summers at the Mill, yet I never tired of watching it make paper. As a historian of the Hudson River Mill, it was fitting that I was on hand to see No. 11 produce its final roll of paper on November 1, 2002.

The mood was gloomy on No. 11's final day. I took some video footage that shows a hundred or more of the Mill's somber-looking employees gathered at the dry end of the machine to witness the event. The last roll remained in motion long after the sheet had been broken off, spinning ever-so-slowly to a complete stop. Several people approached the roll and peeled off a sheet as a souvenir. Although a relatively modest-size Four-drinier machine compared to modern 2002 Fourdrinier machines, at over 600 feet long, the No. 11 was a monumental piece of technology. The machine made the manufacture of paper appear magical. During its 44 years of operation, No. 11 manufactured approximately 1,000,000 miles of paper, enough to reach the Moon and back twice.

Few people outside the paper industry have seen a Fourdrinier in operation. The machine has a head box at the "wet end" containing wood pulp piped into it from a beater room. Pulp from the head box is sprayed evenly onto the paper machine's continuously moving, fine mesh screen called the "breast roll." The wet pulp becomes embedded in the screen as it moves, and suction boxes underneath the wire remove excess water. The pulp-laden wire quickly reaches the "couch roll," which facilitates the transfer of the forming paper sheet to a pickup roller on the press section of the machine. There, the paper sheet is pressed between two steel rolls, allowing a fiber bond to form. The formed paper sheet, which on most modern machines can be over thirty feet wide, continues to the dryer section, where the sheet passes over a continuous piece of felt. The dried sheet goes from the moving felt through a "calendar section" consisting of stacked and heated steel rolls that dry the paper. From there, the sheet leaves the machine to form a finished roll.

While the paper machines represented the central production technology at the Hudson River, Nos. 3 and 4 paper machines at the Mill were the bane of our work as beater helpers. The most demanding part of our work in the Beater Room came during those shifts when we were sent to the "broke pit," the name we gave to the basement directly beneath the Nos. 3 and 4 machines where a broke beater was located. The beater was used to process and recycle paper that came directly from the overhead paper machines whenever there was a break during the production of a paper roll. Whenever this occurred, thirteen-foot wide sheets of paper would fall through a wide slot in the ceiling above at a rate of up to 1300 feet per minute. Rarely did both Nos. 3 and 4 break simultaneously, but the Beater Room Boys could be in the basement filling the beater for hours, even if just one did.

A break can pose a severe problem, for the principal feature of a Fourdrinier machine is the production of a continuous sheet of paper. When the sheet on a machine breaks naturally, the paper quickly piles up on the floor between the machine's rolls where the break occurred, requiring the machine's crew to go inside the paper machine to remove the fast-piling paper. Another of the machine's crew then goes to the location where the floor opening is located. He purposely breaks the sheet at that point so the paper falls through the floor to the basement and below. Some breaks were created intentionally by the paper machine's crew. This was done to stop the paper production after an imperfection in the sheet had been found. In this instance, a break is made in the sheet at a designated place in the machine where the paper – still being produced at full speed - can be pushed down through the slot in the floor towards the broke beater. Once in the slot, the paper passes through unassisted aided by gravity. Regardless of what caused the break, the paper machine runs at a speed of 1200-1300 feet per minute, or about a mile of paper every four minutes.

Depending on how long it lasts, a machine break can be costly. In instances when a break is due to a faulty wire at the "wet end," the whole machine must be shut down so that a new wire can be installed. The crew that changed paper machine wires was called the "bull gang." These guys, who did all the heaviest work at the mill, were a specialized group within the Hudson River Mill's Repairs Department. My uncle Freddy, my Mother's brother, was on the bull gang at the Mill, so I often heard about his work. He made a great hourly wage, but the labor union agreement he worked under required that he come to the mill whenever called to complete necessary paper machine repairs at all hours. While he often had to get out of bed and come to work in the middle of the night, Uncle Freddy was given a guaranteed number of hours of pay regardless of how long it took to get the job done. In those days, the wires that the bull gang changed were brass, while most modern ones are plastic. While the pay was good, my Uncle hated being called in for a wire because changing one required that parts of the wet end of the paper machine had to be taken apart and reassembled. It was heavy, dirty, and exhausting work.

I recall the first time our foreman, Ken, brought us to the broke pit after a break in the No. 3 machine. The basement area was well-lit, and overhead, all manner of pipes and conduits ran through the ceiling's steel framing that was part of the electrical and plumbing systems for the paper machines. The walls and ceiling were painted grey except for the occasional splash of industrial green. It was quieter than the machine room overhead, but the decibel level was still high. Vibrations from the powerful machines overhead could be felt through the concrete floor. I don't recall that we were ever given ear protection, or eye protection for that matter. And the broke pit was hot!

Ken directed us to take one of the several long poles that rested against a wall. Each ten-foot long, ash wood pole was thicker than a typical house broom, closer to the width of a shovel or rake handle. A small piece of plywood shaped like a square head broom was attached with screws to one end of the pole. The handles were worn smooth from years of use. Our job was to use the poles – or rakes - to gather the broke that was falling from the ceiling and push it into the beater where its steel blades and water would beat it back into pulp. It seemed simple enough.

I was stunned by the sheer amount of paper accumulated the first time we went to the broke pit. We looked at a mile or two of paper piled on the floor. The pile reached up to the ceiling and spread out in all directions. Its scale was overwhelming and still cascaded down from the ceiling. The five of us on our crew looked at each other momentarily but began to work feverishly to push the pile into the beater. It took us only a short time to figure out why our poles were so long. There were no protective barriers between us and the opening at the edge of the floor where the beater was. We first created individual broke piles but then discovered that two or three of us working together could create one large pile to push into the pit. This made our work go more quickly. Fortunately, our first machine break lasted only about 30 minutes, yet we probably spent over an hour cleaning broke from the floor.

A week or so later, we were not so lucky. One night, Ken sent us directly to the broke pit when we arrived at 10:30 PM. Once there, we found the crew we were to relieve battling a huge paper pile created by the No. 4 machine. We took over for them and began wielding our ten-foot rakes. The paper kept falling through the ceiling above—first one hour, then another hour, and then another. The paper never stopped raining down. We wondered what the hell the No. 4 machine crew overhead was doing. Why couldn't they get a good sheet going? At some point, one among our crew returned to the Beater Room to retrieve our lunch boxes because we knew we would be in the pit for a while. Finally, around 3:00 AM, the sheet on No. 4 was restored, and we had a chance to rest and eat. We wanted to get out of there for a while, yet given the machine's poor performance that night, we decided not to venture very far. So we looked around until we found a quiet place nearby.

Our retreat was the room where the mill's Repair Gang stored their tools and gear. The room was an authentic man cave. It was not the type you would find today in a home basement or garage, furnished with a wide-screen TV, foose-ball table, beer-filled refrigerator, and Bud-light clock. The men who used this room equipped it with the tools essential to their trade: large wrenches, ropes and chains, heavy-duty block-and-tackle setups, and a bench vise the size of a shoe box. There were several chest-high mechanic toolboxes, grey metal ones on large caster wheels. The tools in this room were used to maintain the Mill's thousands of motors, pumps, and valves through which water, wood pulp, and mill waste flowed, all critical mill functions. Dickie's work pants and shirts hung in open steel lockers, and one-piece dark-blue jumpsuits and light-blue striped coveralls were draped over metal hooks. A few locker doors were decorated with *Playboy* centerfolds. The whole room smelled of grease, oil, and sweat. This was a room for men who performed manual labor for a living.

Our break lasted only 20 minutes before we had to return to the broke pit. First, it was a break on the No. 3 machine, then a break on No. 4. One machine, then the other. On it went. We were there for all eight hours of our shift. I don't recall if the break had been resolved by the time the 7 AM shift arrived, but I am sure no one on our crew would have been willing to work a "sixteen" if our relief failed to show up for work. My arms and back ached from pushing so much broke, and my tee shirt was soaked with sweat. I recall returning home around 6:45 AM and skipping breakfast, which my Mother often cooked for me when I worked the night shift. Instead, I went straight to bed and slept until mid-afternoon. The next day, I calculated that our crew had pushed over 500,000 feet of broke that night, nearly 90 miles of paper.

Not many days later, during the same 11-7 AM tour, Terry showed up to work drunk. I mean, he was plastered! When we saw him come into the Beater Room, we could not imagine how he had ever made his way there in his condition. Fortunately, our foreman, Ken, was not around when he arrived. So that Terry wouldn't get fired, we brought him down to the broke pit and hid him until he sobered up. We knew it was unlikely anyone would find him there. We maneuvered him into a small space shielded from easy view by a cement block wall. We found some random pieces of broke that had not been pushed into the beater and fashioned a bed, covering Terry with a bed-sheet-size piece of broke. We left Terry there and returned to the Beater Room, although we took turns going back to check on him. We made an excuse for his temporary absence whenever Ken asked where Terry was. This continued until about 4 AM, when Terry finally woke up, sober enough to rejoin our crew. He thanked us profusely for covering for him.

When it was time to leave the Mill at the end of our shift at 6:30 AM, Terry asked if I would help him find his car. We clocked out and wandered around the parking lot until we found his ride. Well, it wasn't a car but a used Freihofer bread truck that he had just purchased, similar in shape and size to the vehicles used today by UPS. The words "Friehofer" and "Bread and Cakes" in faded gold lettering were still visible on the side of the dark red van. The front bumper was smashed against a tree, the only one standing in the lot. The collision had broken the windshield on the passenger's side, so glass and wood bark were all over the floor. Beneath the steering wheel was an empty bottle of Puerto Rican rum, which helped to explain Terry's condition the night before. As I waited outside on the passenger side, Terry climbed into the driver's seat, got the van started, and sputtered off, blue-black smoke spewing from his exhaust as he waved goodbye.

Terry was a very likable guy. His humor was dry, rarely satiric or ironic. He could say the funniest things and keep a straight face. Terry, by no means, pretended to be innovative. Instead of wearing a sweatshirt that said "College" as John Belushi did in *Animal House*, Terry's shirt would read "Factory." I never understood where Terry's irreverence originated, but it probably came from his family situation. His older brother, Tom, a naturally gifted basketball player, seemed more rebellious and had a more biting sense of humor. Although we were in the same class at Corinth, Terry and I were never in the same classroom together, except for gym. Until the summer of 1969, I had only a few encounters with him, so most of what I know about Terry I learned during the summer we worked together in the Beater Room. I think I saw him once more after the summer of 1969. Terry Ide, also known as Emmet, died in a car accident in Florida in 1999.

35

EVERYONE'S GONE TO THE MOON

The Moon Landing was the most anticipated event of 1969. It represented the culmination of the NASA Space Program that permeated American life throughout the 1960s. Nearly everyone had been following the flight of Apollo 11 since it blasted off from Cape Kennedy on July 16. News of it was inescapable, with America's three national television networks covering the mission throughout the two weeks before the launch. The local *Glens Falls Times* carried a headline on July 16 that stretched across its front page: "ASTRONAUTS OFF TO THE MOON." After weeks of anticipation and media build-up, Apollo 11 finally touched down on the Moon on July 20. Neil Armstrong's first step onto its surface was scheduled for the same day.

The Beater Room Boys shared a determination to witness the historic event. Yet our crew was at risk of missing some or all of the landing and Moon walk because we were scheduled to work the 11 PM-7 AM shift on July 20. We were each invested in the Moon mission, having grown up during the Mercury, Gemini, and Apollo programs while viewing most of the twenty manned space shots that preceded Apollo 11. The Beater Room Boys were determined to be among the estimated 650 million people who would witness the moon landing and the moonwalk that night. Each of us intended to watch Neil Armstrong step onto the Moon's surface at home if it occurred before the start of our shift, but if not, we planned to listen to the event together on a radio at work. Everyone agreed to bring a transistor radio to the mill the night of July 20 if Armstrong had not left the Eagle by the time our shift began.

Our entire crew were children of the space race, products of a campaign by the Federal Government to get Americans to fall in line behind the nation's Cold War battle against the Soviet Union in all of its forms. By the time the Class of 1969 members had left the 6th grade, we had already viewed no fewer than six NASA launches in the elementary school cafeteria. The race into space against the Soviets was part of the Cold War. Like other similar classrooms nationwide, Corinth's elementary school children were on the front lines of that war.

Watching the Mercury rockets blast off, however, was not the only time that elementary-age kids in Corinth had been subjected to American Cold War propaganda. Children began to figure prominently in the nation's nuclear preparedness campaign soon after the Soviet Union detonated its first atomic bomb in 1949. The best-known example may have been the cartoon character Bert the Turtle, who served as a spokesman for the government's nuclear defense initiative that featured "duck and cover" as a personal strategy to escape the immediate impacts of a nuclear bomb. A widely shown, nine-minute, black-and-white instructional film released in 1951 consisted of Bert cartoon sequences interspersed with narrative scenes that featured child and adult actors.

As a cartoon character, Bert became the most recognizable symbol of a national campaign that sought to downplay the carnage that would result from an atomic bomb dropped on the United States. In one cartoon sequence, Bert is shown retreating into his shell as a nuclear blast levels a nearby tree and wrecks a house. Following Bert's example, the children who appear in the film dive under their classroom desks or curl up next to an interior school wall. In the same film, a boy rides his bike on a sidewalk near a park. An authoritative voiceover tells him that if he sees the flash of an atomic bomb, he can find safety by hiding under something and covering his head. The subtle narration implies that such maneuvers will allow an escape from burns and flying debris. A jarring camera movement and the sound of an explosion simulate a nuclear blast in the film, and the boy quickly ditches his bike to dive under a nearby brick bench. The government film, however, failed to show if the boy survived.

Corinth offered an equivalent fantasy about the bomb in the air raid drills we practiced in elementary school. When the air raid siren went off, our practice drill required the girls to leave the classroom first, enter the hallway, and then get on their knees and face its gray-glazed cement block walls. They were to bend forward as far as they could, heads down. Boys were to follow the girls into the hall, select one of them, and get down on their knees behind her. We were told to stretch our arms over the girl in front of us, touching the wall with the palms of our hands to create a "protective shield" over her. While our school's air raid drill created the illusion that the girls in our class would be saved from the bomb by the boys, we never learned who would save us.

Drills like the one we practiced in school could not save children from a direct nuclear hit. While the Federal Government knew this, the truth was not exposed broadly until 1982 with the release of the documentary film *The Atomic Café*. The film's genius was in using archival government films – without any editorial narrative – to juxtapose what government officials knew about nuclear bombs and radioactivity against what they told the public. Our Government understood that a nuclear strike would inciner- ate millions of Americans – just as the Japanese had been incinerated at

Hiroshima and Nagasaki – yet it sought to perpetrate the lie that simple protective measures would save you.

What we practiced in elementary school following an air raid siren prompt represented propaganda. It served as purposeful disinformation designed to make the American public – children, in this case – believe that Washington had things under control. But, of course, it didn't. Our government was in uncharted territory. Corinth teachers surely knew better than to believe that the 70-pound body of a 4th-grade boy could protect a small girl from a nuclear blast, yet in conducting the drill, they were complicit in producing atomic theater in their classrooms.

America's Cold War domestic politics required the engagement of the nation's school systems. The *Weekly Reader,* distributed in Corinth's elementary school classrooms in the 1950s and early 1960s, regularly included articles on the Soviet Union and China, often describing life there as uninviting. During the years of the Korean War, the *Weekly Reader* noted that the United States was concerned for the future of Southeast Asia, comparing the region to a child's toy. Using a variation of the "domino theory" metaphor later used to justify American involvement in Vietnam, one article told its readers that "Communism is somewhat like a giant jack-in-the-box with dozens of lids. As soon as you close one lid, another may spring open." The *Weekly Reader,* which was a staple in our elementary school classrooms, was engaged in creating an early justification for a war in Southeast Asia where many of its young readers would one day fight and die.

Articles on Communism often appeared in our *Weekly Reader*, with the construction of the Berlin Wall and the division of East and West Berlin as popular topics. It could be challenging to teach ten-year-olds lessons in Cold War ideology or that the Soviets were evil, yet we could understand its practical effects. I recall my 6th-grade teacher, Mrs McKnight, using my shoulders to illustrate the width of a hand-dug, twenty-inch-wide tunnel through which some families escaped from East to West Berlin, from communism to freedom. She stood behind me one day in class, discussing the article we had just read, her hands placed on the outside of my shoulders to illustrate how narrow the tunnels were and, implicitly, how badly Germans wanted to be free from Communism. Mrs. McKnight's illustration impacted me, for I clearly remember that day in class 60 years later.

Elementary school readers of the *Weekly Reader* were exposed to what was happening in the United States and worldwide, even if its articles were biased. Exposure to world and national events was possible once in high school. *World Week*, a weekly news magazine published by Scholastic Magazines, was distributed in our 9th-grade social studies class at Corinth High in 1965. 1965 was the year when the United States first sent combat troops to Vietnam, and by year's end, nearly 200,000 men had been depl oyed. *World Week* first addressed Vietnam in its November 18, 1965 issue when it published an impressive 14-page article on the War that quoted several dissenting voices, which were rare early in the conflict. I am unsure if we were required to study the article for class or if I read it on my own, but the issue still in my possession reveals that I attempted to complete the crossword puzzle quiz at the end.

World Week did not follow us when we became sophomores in the Fall of 1966. We were no longer regularly exposed to the world and national news – urban riots, air and water pollution, poverty, the Cold War, Vietnam - that appeared in its pages between 1965 and 1969. These events were not ignored in the national educational press intended for grade school children and high school students, but news of them was scarce in Corinth's High School classrooms beyond the 9th grade. Teaching restrictions on controversial topics, particularly Vietnam, forced at least one of my teachers to create a covert method for teaching his students about the War.

The Space Race, as a product of the American Cold War engagement with the Soviet Union, also had a prominent place in our elementary school classrooms. The *Weekly Reader* was its leading purveyor. While the political bias of its articles would have escaped the notice of a 4th grader, reading them today, you will find, for example, that the successful launch of Sputnik in 1957 was credited to "man" rather than the Soviet Union. There was periodic mention of the Soviet space program in the *Reader*, but NASA launches gained more expansive coverage.

Attention to the Space Race increased in Corinth sometime around 1960 when elementary school classrooms were upended on the days of a Mercury space launch. Each teacher ushered their class into the gym, where we sat in neat rows before two large, elevated televisions to watch Americans blast into space. We were too young then to understand that our compulsory viewing of rockets blasting off from Cape Canaveral every few months, while certainly possessing educational value, was part of an effort to instill into our impressionable young minds nationalistic confidence in the American Space Program.

The political purpose of the space program was papered over by the idea that it was an extension of the myth of the American frontier. President Kennedy purposefully tied the space program to America's Western experience in his famous speech at Rice University in 1962. The transformation of NASA astronauts into Western-type heroes had a cultural parallel in the character Major T.J. "King" Kong in Stanley Kubrick's film *Dr. Strangelove* (1964). In the movie, Major Kong becomes a veritable astronaut cowboy when he dons a western hat and rides a hydrogen bomb toward his Soviet Union target.

There also were efforts to convince Americans they benefitted from the space program. Astronaut John Glenn's use of Tang - a preexisting powdered orange drink – when he became the first American to orbit the Earth in 1962 generated the myth that Tang was created expressly for the space program. Glenn's use of Tang became a public relations bonanza for General Foods and NASA, which allowed the agency to suggest that the tremendously expensive space program had practical advantages for America's moms.

The justification for the expense of the American space program became less problematic after 1963 when it was transformed into a mission to honor a fallen President. JFK had pledged to get a man to the moon and back by the decade's end. Regardless, the NASA enterprise after JFK seemed so abstract and remote to our Corinth experience that, at times, it didn't seem real. This could be due to our limited working-class vision of our future selves. Now that I think about it, I do not recall that a single boy in my class ever professed to want to be an astronaut when he grew up. The concept of space itself was so far beyond our imagination.

Even the most jaded American could not escape Apollo 11 in 1969. I sat with my parents on July 20, watching the landing on TV, anxious to see Neil Armstrong's descent from the Eagle to the Moon's surface. It was just after 4:00 PM when the Eagle touched down. However, news coverage indicated that Armstrong would not emerge from the lunar capsule until later. I knew then my only chance to witness Armstrong's Moon walk might be at work. He was still inside the capsule when I prepared to leave the house for the Mill at 10:15 PM. I kept my car radio on during the short drive and then switched to my transistor radio once I parked and set out on foot. Armstrong still had not left the Eagle when I lost the radio signal as I entered the first building on my route to work.

When I arrived at the Beater Room, crew members had already tried to tune into several area radio stations. All they got was static. We figured the Beater's Room's electric motors and its exposed steel roof girders overhead were creating interference. With no cull rolls to manage and with the permission of our foreman, we headed for the loading dock in the hopes of getting radio reception there. We walked through the Mill to the finishing room, past the storage building where the paper rolls and forklifts were kept, and then to the dock. We realized the only thing that could derail our plans to hear Armstrong set foot on the Moon was a break on the No. 3 or 4 paper machine that would force us into the broke pit.

Our radios picked up several stations once we reached a small storage room adjacent to the loading dock. Rolls of paper ready for shipment, wrapped in heavy brown paper made by the No. 10 machine, were stacked on their ends on two sides of the room. The radio with the clearest broadcast was left on. Although we picked up a radio station from Glens Falls, the broadcast we heard originated from a national network, CBS and Walter Cronkite, which had the nation's best news coverage in those days. We arranged ourselves among the rolls of paper. Bruce, Paul, and I jumped and sat on the butt ends of the wrapped rolls. Terry and Pierre sat on the cement floor, their backs against two adjacent rolls. We had only been set up for ten minutes before we heard Neil Armstrong's voice. It was a bit garbled, yet we heard him describe his descent from the Eagle, placing his foot on the Moon, and then utter his unscripted words memorializing the event. After nearly a decade of anticipation, the Moon landing was over.

We remained at the loading dock for a while, listing to post-landing transmissions from the Eagle, CBS reporter commentary, and that infernal beeping of NASA's radio transmitters. I don't recall that we celebrated what we had just witnessed. I'm sure it would have impacted us more if we had been able to view the event live on TV as some 650 million other people had. Nonetheless, the landing seemed rather anticlimactic. Perhaps it was because we had been primed for a Moon landing since 1961 and that NASA's consistent successes – except for the tragedy of Apollo 1 – made for little doubt the mission would be a success. We were, after all, children of the space race and true believers.

36

— · —

LONG AND WINDING ROAD

The Moon landing in July 1969 was only one of several notable events that occurred that summer. Perhaps the most notorious occurred over two nights in early August when the "Manson Family" killed seven people in Los Angeles, including the actress Sharon Tate, who was 8 1/2 months pregnant. Charles Manson created a cult-like following during the late 1960s consisting of over 100 people who believed he was a manifestation of Jesus Christ. The group lived together communally in Southern California, used psychoactive drugs and hallucinogens, and generally embodied the Hippie culture that had become a prominent component of America's counter-culture.

Manson directed a small group of his followers, including three young women, to commit the series of gruesome acts that came to be known as the Tate-LaBianca murders. The killing of seven people in what appeared to be a ritualistic fashion shocked the nation. The public perception of the murders was fostered by sensationalist reporting in newspapers like the *Sunday News,* which ran a headline across its front page after Sharon Tate's body was found, "ACTRESS AND 4 SLAIN IN RITUAL," and the *Los Angeles Times,* which ran a headline after the LaBiancas were murdered in their home the next day: "SECOND RITUAL KILLINGS HERE."

The gruesome nature of the Tate-LaBianca murders shocked the nation, leading many Americans to interpret the acts of Manson and his followers as the worst possible manifestation of drug-infused American youth culture. The murders became part of the public consciousness in the late summer of 1969, even before members of the Manson Family were arrested weeks later.

About the time of the Manson killings, the Beater Room boys began to realize that summer was drawing to a close, and our crew would gradually disband. Three of us would soon leave for college, while the other two planned to work until IP no longer needed temporary workers. At the end of a 3-11 PM shift one night, a few of us decided to go out after work for something to eat. A few bars in Corinth remained open after 11 PM, yet we knew, at best, we would find only a packaged ham and cheese sandwich heated up in a Stewart's brand, In-Fra-Red oven that most bars kept on the back counter.

One of these ovens used to be in the Belvedere, a bar located at the southeast corner of Main Street and Sherman Avenue that a high school classmate's father once owned and operated. In 2024, the bar's former location remains an empty lot 16 years after a fire leveled the block where it stood. Stewart's pre-made sandwiches at the Belvedere were enclosed in a sealed plastic bag, tossed into the oven, and heated miraculously without burning the wrapper. Its use permitted the Belvedere and other bars to skirt New York State laws that required that food be sold with alcohol. But instead of feasting on late-night Corinth cuisine, we decided to drive to Glens Falls, where we knew at least one restaurant was open all night: the New Way Lunch on South Street.

The Beater Room Boys met at Eddie Madison's service station around 11 PM. There, we packed into my Corvair for the trip to Glens Falls. It was a weekday night, so our downtown was pretty quiet. Once across the

Hudson River bridge and past Bus and Ret's Store on East River Drive, we turned right onto Call Street to head over "Hogsback." The road between Corinth and Glens Falls was the scene of many serious accidents. One of the earliest occurred in the winter of 1919 near Hartman Hill when a horse-driven wagon load of lumber driven by William Bailey plunged over a steep embankment. Bailey and his horses were severely injured, and the wagon was a complete loss.

My Mother was involved in a Call Street accident on a foggy Saturday morning in October 1962. It was on the flat stretch above the street's intersection with East River Drive. The road at that point bisects the fields of the old Winslow farm before it becomes winding and mountainous until it descends Hartman Hill to run parallel to the Hudson River. She drove our new, yellow, 1962 Chevy Impala for a half-day at Clark Brothers glove factory on Elm Street.

With visibility severely limited by the fog, my Mother was side-swiped by a car traveling in the opposite direction. After she and the other driver stopped and stood together in front of the Impala to examine the damage, my Mother was hit by her car and thrown into the adjacent field when a third car rear-ended our Chevy. She was severely injured and remained in the hospital for three weeks. Somehow, either the chrome bumper of the Chevy or the barbed wire fence at the edge of the adjacent field tore a hole in her ankle the size of a tennis ball. The wound was so severe the surgeon had to use wire to close it.

That morning, hours before I learned of the accident from my Father, I was hanging out at the athletic field on Main Street. Boys of all ages would often gather there to play pick-up baseball in the summer and tag football in the fall. I was 11 years old at the time. I looked over and saw a few older boys huddled in conversation before one of them emerged, the kid who arguably became the best all-around athlete in Corinth's history. Jimmy

Hopkins called out to me and passed a football in my direction, engaging me in a game of catch. He never said anything but just kept throwing the ball back to me. I felt pretty special playing catch with him, as this was something that the older boys rarely did. Only years later did I suspect that one of the other boys had learned of my Mother's accident and told Jimmy, which seemed to make him empathize with a 6th grader he didn't know. I have never forgotten his kind gesture.

Some forty years later, I found photographs of my Mother's accident. I came across several made by George Holland, the editor of the *EMBA News*, who had taken them that morning on Call Street. George often took photographs of local car accidents and sometimes their victims, probably for insurance purposes. The fact is that George Holland took photographs of nearly every car wreck that ever occurred in the Corinth area since around 1950, images whose contents suggest he often arrived on the scene before the police or the Emergency Squad.

But on this occasion, the photographs of the accident were taken after the ambulance had already taken my Mother to Glens Falls Hospital and before the wrecker from Pikes Garage had arrived. Holland's photographs show our totaled Chevy, the car that side-swiped her, and the field beyond where she was thrown. No fog was left on the highway when the photos were taken. Yet in one image, the morning sun reflects off the thin blanket of fog that remained over the field beyond the barbed wire fence where my Mother's body had lain. These were jarring images to see for the first time, even as an adult.

Call Street was also the scene of an attempted triple-murder in the 1890s. Edward Whitmore and his wife, Melissa, lived with their 15-year-old daughter, Dora, on a small farm near the western entry to the Hartman Loop. Mrs. Whitmore's 55-year-old nephew, Leonard Blodgett, lived with them. Blodgett, who was believed to be obsessed with Dora, tried to kill both of her parents with a 22-caliber revolver, presumably to remove them as a barrier to his intentions. After shooting Melissa and beating Edward unconscious after he tried to intervene, Blodgett attempted to rape Dora after her mother fled through the door and into the night. Dora, who cleverly asked to go into the bedroom to change, fled through an open window. Unable to find either one of them in the darkness, Blodgett ran off. Five days later, his body was found floating in the Hudson River by a fisherman; his death was ruled a suicide.

None of the Beater Room Boys knew of the Whitmore attacks the night we drove over the Hogsback and past the Hartman Loop. Just past the Loop, where Hartman Hill descends to the Hudson River, Call Street becomes Corinth Road. In the daylight, remnants of an earlier road can be seen on the left. That night, the River was visible under a full moon. After the River left our view, we passed the farm stand near the junction of Corinth Road and West Mountain Road, where my parents would buy fresh corn for 75 cents a dozen. There, Corinth Road curves sharply to the right.

We continued on the straight stretch of road that begins just past the curve. I recalled traveling that section with my parents one morning after a tornado hit the Glens Falls area around 1960, extensively damaging several properties. We passed a mobile home that was torn apart by the tornado the night before. The homeowners must have kept chickens, for several of them had been blown into the side of the trailer and were still lodged between its storm-exposed framing and insulation, their feathers scattered all over the grass.

Corinth Road veers sharply east before reaching West Glens Falls, a quiet residential area with only a few businesses. A small aquarium had been a fixture there for as long as I could remember. Closer to our South Street destination, Corinth Road splits into Broad Street and Hudson Avenue.

Hart's Café was then located on Hudson, where The Talk of the Town restaurant currently operates. Sometime after I received my driver's license, my Uncle John would pay me to drive to Harts from Corinth to pick up cheese pizzas for him, often four or five at a time. I seem to recall they were only $1.00 each.

After completing my mission to Hart's and returning to my grandparents' house, where my Uncle lived, I would stack the pizzas on the kitchen table. My Uncle John would open the top box and take a slice for each of us. I would usually leave after eating just one piece, but he would devour the rest of the pizza that night and the remainder of the pizzas during the week. I remember the wonderful taste of Hart's pizza when I passed the Café that night, and if it had not been closed at that late hour, I might have persuaded my companions to eat there. Instead, we continued to South Street, parking the car in front of the New Way Lunch.

37

SUMMER IN THE CITY

Glens Falls, New York, home of the New Way Lunch, was then a small city with a population of around 17,000. Compared to Corinth, Glens Falls had many exciting things missing in our hometown. I was always excited to go there as a boy. There was a W.T. Grants, a Woolworth's, and a Kresge's, all on Glen Street. There were two movie theaters and a bookstore. And there was City Park, the heart of Glens Falls, where you could sit on benches and feed popcorn to the pigeons. A remarkable postcard made of downtown Glens Falls during the 1950s vividly depicts how vibrant the city used to be. Whenever my Mother took me to Glens Falls for clothes shopping, we would eat at Woolworth's lunch counter.

Afterward, I would wander off to the pet department at the rear of the store and watch the parakeets and canaries fly around in their cages and peer into the aquariums that held several varieties of colorful fish. When we were ready to leave, I would pass down one of the long aisles with wide horizontal bins full of merchandise on both sides. My feet would slip into the wooden floorboards worn down by decades of traffic. Corinth had a five-and-dime store, but it could not compare to Woolworth's.

We once bought a parakeet at Woolworths that my mother taught to speak. The bird had about a 20-word vocabulary. My mother was so fond of our parakeet that every Saturday, she let it out of its cage to fly around our TV room, shutting it out of the rest of the house by closing its sliding door. Once, when we went to Canada to visit my Aunt Edith's family, we left the parakeet with my grandmother. She set up the cage and its stand next to her living chair where she watched TV. When we returned to Corinth after a few days, my grandmother was notably upset, claiming the parakeet told her he was going to kill her. While the bird must have learned the words from the television and was probably joking, my grandmother's East European "old country" superstitions led her to believe our parakeet was inoculated with evil.

Most of the Glens Falls streetscape my Mother and her sisters walked in the 1930s and 1940s was still in place in 1969. Yet the winds of progress had already hit Glens Falls in full force. The era generated a craving in the city for things shiny and new to signal it had a progressive, contemporary spirit. The wrecking ball had become a common element of the 1960s Glens Falls landscape. The historic Crandall Block that had taken up the corner of Glen and South Streets had been purchased by Glens Falls National Bank and demolished in 1963. The city's urban renewal mania would soon level every building in the downtown block bordered by Glen and Warren Street. Lost was Boxer's Drug Store, my Mother's favorite retail store, and the original location of the Outlet, a clothing store where we went to buy my pants and shirts. The demolition of the block left a massive hole in downtown Glens Falls, with nothing planned to replace it. It was ten more years before the corner was rebuilt. Conclusive evidence that the city's civic and business leaders had lost all regard for the historic architecture of Glens Falls came a few years later with the demolition of the Glens Falls Insurance Company building. After losing the structure and numerous others, the city shifted its redevelopment strategy from "demo-and-build" to "preservation-and-reuse."

Glens Falls in 1969 was more than three times the size of Corinth. Although a much larger class A high school, Glens Falls played against Corinth as a member of the old Northern Conference athletic league, which included Class A, B, and C schools. Small schools playing in the same league as schools like Glens Falls and Hudson Falls, which had more boys to play sports, resulted in some lopsided sports scores. Not only did Glens Falls have more kids, but they also seemed more sophisticated and knowledgeable than Corinth kids. This fact became evident during a match against Glens Falls that I played as a member of Corinth's varsity golf team in the Spring of 1968 at their home course, the Glens Falls Country Club. It was then that I also learned first-hand that small-town and city kids were different, the latter more affluent and entitled.

The Glens Falls County Club, which dated to 1912 and featured a Donald Ross-designed course, offered those of us who had grown up playing the relatively pedestrian Bend of the River or Brookhaven course our first glimpse of a golf club built for the well-to-do. To enter the course, you had to go through an entry gate made of tall stone pillars and drive down a long road before reaching a substantial clubhouse not unlike a large estate I might have seen on TV. The team entered a different world when we arrived.

Our match that day was memorable for two reasons. The first was that our coach, Dick Stein, drove us to Glens Falls in his brand-new Ford Thunderbird. Mr. Stein, a full-time English teacher, was our "coach" whose only qualifications seemed to be having a driver's license and owning a set of golf clubs. Mr. Stein might have been an excellent golfer, but I never saw him play. Nor had I ever been in a car as nice as his Thunderbird or a vehicle with power windows. I was fascinated watching the T-Bird's window on the rear passenger door go up and down with a finger flick. It rained hard on our way over and continued after we arrived, so we sat in the Thunderbird, talking until it stopped. It was the first time that I had ever been in a conventional conversation with a teacher. Mr. Stein was funny, sarcastic, and entertaining, so it made for a good time.

The other memorable event that day occurred after the rain stopped and the match got underway. My foursome reached the third hole and was preparing to tee off. Before the first ball was hit, one of the Glens Falls golfers opened his bag and pulled out a six-pack of beer. Yes, a six-pack! He handed a beer to his teammate before opening one for himself. These guys didn't even look around to determine if anyone could see them before taking gulps from their cans. My teammate and I were offered beers, but we declined. I was stunned to see the two Glens Falls kids drinking beer while playing in a varsity match. Who did that? Not any athlete from Corinth that I knew. My teammate and I felt pretty "square," a common self-deprecating expression at the time when we refused to drink. I realized that day our Glens Falls opponents, who were city kids to us, came from more privileged backgrounds than we did, where rules did not apply to them. Remaining sober didn't do us much good, for we still lost the match.

The golf team lost so many matches during the four years I played that I have retained only one other golf team-related memory. We had a match one day at Brookhaven in South Corinth. Two team members, Charlie and Wesley, lived in that part of Corinth. Wesley was very excited when we got into our coach's car to make the five-mile drive to the course, for his mother was to have gone out that day to buy him a new set of golf clubs. She would leave them at Charlie's house on Chapman Street, a convenient pick-up location off Route 9N. We stopped at the house, got the clubs, and threw them into the car's trunk. We got to the course a few minutes later. We carried our bags to the first tee to meet the opposing team, who had already arrived. As each of us took out a club to take practice swings, Wesley reached into his bag of new clubs, pulled out his driver, and removed the head cover. He took his stance and gripped the club but stopped suddenly in mid-swing. Looking perplexed, he put the club head on the grass, realizing his mother had purchased him a set of left-handed golf clubs. I can't recall how the situation was resolved that day, but it undoubtedly boosted our opponent's confidence.

Hot dogs rather than golf was on my mind that night in Glens Falls when I turned off Broad Street onto South Street with the Beater Room Boys. Our destination was located arguably in the most run-down part of Glens Falls. South Street was the City's ghetto. While Glens Falls had old money from its heyday as a thriving upstate manufacturing and commercial center, it also had a considerable working-class population. The city's late 19th and early 20th-century wealth is reflected in the large, gracious homes built on Lower Glen Street. After *LOOK* magazine featured Glens Falls in a 1944 issue, calling it "Hometown, USA," the city's municipal leaders became even more self-aware, newly determined to offer Glens Falls as an example for other small municipalities. But just as the city's civic leaders launched a long-term urban renewal and commercial development project, the construction of Interstate 87 and America's growing obsession with shopping malls and fast-food restaurants quickly shifted commercial development north to Queensbury. Glens Falls would never be the same.

Glens Falls had been independent of the Town of Queensbury since early in the 20th century, so all its civic and business leaders could do was sit by and watch Queensbury grow. This included the construction of the Northway Plaza and the opening of the area's first McDonald's restaurant, both in 1964. Several prominent downtown Glens Falls businesses soon closed and relocated to the Plaza. Sometime after receiving my driver's license in 1967, my Father permitted me to use the family car one Sunday afternoon. I was not supposed to leave town with our Oldsmobile. Yet, I made a covert trip to Queensbury with two friends, some 14 miles away, driving over the Hogsback, down Hartman Hill, and then jumping on the Northway at Exit 17 and off at Exit 18 to hit the newly opened McDonald's. There, we ate 15-cent cheeseburgers and drank 25-cent chocolate shakes. The Big Mac was far in the future, and so was the Aviation Mall, yet Queensbury increasingly became the place to go in the late 1960s.

But on this night in August 1969, the Beater Room Boy's destination was Glens Falls. The city's bus station was on South Street, and so were two run-down hotels. A small textile factory anchored the west end of the street, and there were at least four or five bars and small diners along a short stretch opposite the bus station and near the hotels. Sandy's Clam Bar was the most notorious establishment on South Street, where fist fights that started inside often spilled out onto the sidewalk late into the night. Down the alley next to the bus station was the legendary Empire Billiards, a dark and smoky basement pool hall. It was located in the building constructed in 1898 to house the Empire Theater with seating for 1200. When my Father brought me to the billiards hall for the first time to buy a leather pocket for our old pool table at home, I felt like I had entered a crypt that had not been opened since the 1920s. The broadsides pasted to the walls told of legendary pool matches that were held there. I fully expected to see Minnesota Fats and Fast Eddie Felson emerge from the room's dark corners - in a *Field of Dreams* fashion - and start playing a game of straight. I knew the South Street area well; the Clark Brothers glove factory, where my Mother had worked for over thirty years, was just a block away. I had been eating New Way hot dogs since I was ten.

The New Way Diner's distinctive aroma swept over us as soon as we walked through the door. It was the melding of the stale smell of body order and spilled beer with the savory fragrance of the diner's secret meat sauce. Hot dogs lay warming on the grill, steam escaping from the stainless steel bin that warmed the hot dog rolls. A few pieces of cake and pie were on the counter. The diner was empty except for a lone counter person, a thin young man with dark curly hair and tattoos on both shoulders, made visible by the rolled-up sleeves of his white t-shirt. He seemed bothered he had to serve us. We sat in a booth and ordered a dozen dogs with the works and Cokes. The Beater Room crew who went to South Street that night did not have enough history together to reflect wistfully on our summer together as my Class of 1969 classmates and I had done two months earlier. Although we did discuss one or two memorable events like the night Terry came to work intoxicated and our effort to experience Armstrong's walk on the Moon, our trip to the New Way that August night was more practical and purposeful. We were hungry and wanted something to eat.

Before long, several regulars came in and sat in the back. I could tell they were from the neighborhood because they behaved like they owned the place, and no matter how much of a disturbance they made, the counter person remained stoic, sitting on an aluminum chest cooler, engaged in a paperback. I began to consider that the people I observed at the New Way differed from those who lived in Corinth. At least, I thought so. Some were recognizably working class like many Corinth families. However, others were likely the minimum wage working poor, the unemployed, the retired, and those who lived at the margins of Glens Falls' social and economic life. Diane Arbus would have found the New Way of interest and might have photographed its most frequent customers.

The diner's menu, low prices, and worn décor ensured Glens Falls' finest citizens went elsewhere. The New Way had regulars from the neighborhoods around South Street, often disheveled and sometimes loud, ragged souls who always occupied the back booths. Management tolerated them, understanding the diner was their refuge. I thought about social class whenever I went to the New Way. It seemed easier to contemplate and attempt to reconcile the perceptible social and economic disadvantages among people in a town other than my own. I had yet to take a sociology class, so my awareness lacked an academic perspective, an analytical means to interpret what I observed. Yet, my perception was the regulars at the New Way seemed to have less than I did, even though I came from a working-class family of limited means. At the time, I lacked a frame of reference to understand where I came from, what those of us who grew up in Corinth had, and what we didn't have. That insight would come years later.

38

THE WEEK AFTER WOODSTOCK

It was Monday, August 19. The Woodstock Festival held downstate over the weekend had made the national news. The enormous size of the attending crowd, estimated to have been as large as 500,000, shocked its organizers and the press, who considered that Woodstock would be just another rock festival. Billed as "3 Days of Peace and Music," Woodstock reflected the Zeitgeist of the 1960s and became the defining event of the era's counter-culture. I knew our co-worker, Bruce, was planning to attend, so I was anxious to hear what he had to say when he returned to work. Yet, like thousands of other kids prevented from reaching the festival due to traffic jams and road closures, Bruce had no stories to tell, only one about his aborted effort to get there.

By the time of the Woodstock Festival, I had learned much about the culture of the Hudson River Mill. One was work expectations, which became elastic in the evenings and overnight. Most of the mill's salaried personnel had left for home by 5 PM, except for men who had supervisory responsibility for the paper machines. Because many of the bosses were gone, it was not uncommon for some paper workers to get a few hours of sleep during the night shift, depending on the nature of their job and its location inside the plant. Plenty of places existed in the Mill where a paper worker might nap and where they would not be seen or easily found. I never observed anyone sleeping, but I know that it was done. The night our beater room crew hid Terry from our foreman until he sobered up from a night of heavy drinking is an example of how a paper worker could get away with being off the job for several hours. Any crew member could have left the Mill after clocking in to revel the night away elsewhere, returning in the early morning hours to clock out, provided that he had the cover of his co-workers. None of us contemplated such a thing, nor did I hear anyone ever stepping out, but it was indeed possible.

Our Beater Room crew sometimes exploited the mill's loose work culture. The most benign instance was when we used to "play golf" in an alley-like area outside the west end of the Beater Room. Our crew often hung out outside the No. 10 machine room when work was slack. The space was open to the sky above and was just far enough beyond the Mills' walls to reduce the paper machines' noise to a dull hum. One day, when we were sitting on some outside benches, we began discussing golf. Bruce, the most enthusiastic among us, said he wanted to learn to play. I had been playing golf since I was eight or nine years old and knew enough about the game to give him a lesson. So, we scrounged around and found a stick about three feet long to serve as a golf club. I found some broke and rolled it up tightly to serve as a ball. I showed Bruce the correct stance, how to hold and swing his club, and then how to contact the ball. Bruce got into it, smacking the broke-balls that traveled only five or six feet. We did this for maybe half an hour. I don't remember whether anyone else played or if we even returned another day for Bruce's second lesson. Still, I recall the camaraderie we enjoyed in our effort to enjoy a brief respite from our Beater Room work.

The alley location was near the wet end of the No. 10 paper machine that manufactured the heavy brown paper used to make cores for shipped paper and for wrapping finished paper. The wrapper protected the rolls during shipment and provided a place for large labels to be fastened that identified the product and its destination. The No.10 was a slow and narrow machine compared to others in the mill, so its crew was paid less than other paper makers. Because the machine moved so slowly, its crew moved slowly. During afternoon and night shifts, the men working on No. 10 often had a large crockpot on hand to cook their dinner. A small kitchen-like area had been arranged near the dry end of the machine. When kielbasa and sauerkraut were on the menu, you could savor its pungent smell over the Mill's often noxious chemical odors. The machine's crew made enough food on most nights that the surplus was sold to men working elsewhere in the mill for $1.00 a plate. I often saw two or three men near the dry end of the machine waiting to get a serving, but I never stood in line with them. Many years later, when I bought kielbasa and sauerkraut to cook at home, I recalled the meals prepared by the No. 10 machine crew.

Perhaps the most memorable instance of exploiting the mill elastic work culture occurred one day towards the end of a 3 -11 PM shift. One of our duties as beater helpers required that we go to an area of the mill where the rewinders were located. There, paper manufactured on the No. 3, 4, or 11 paper machines was placed on rewinders where the "parent roll" was unwound and cut into "daughter rolls" in widths specified by a customer. Sometimes, one of the daughter rolls would be damaged, or there was a small roll left over from the parent roll after the daughter rolls were cut out. In these instances, the leftover portion would be considered a "cull roll" or "broke roll" and would have to be transported to the Beater Room, cut down by the roll splitter and processed back into pulp. We usually had to retrieve these rolls at least once each shift.

One night, we went to look for some cull rolls but found none. We wandered around a bit, eventually finding our way into the mill's Finishing

Room, where the paper was cut into sheets for special orders and pack-aged for shipment. The Finishing Room was clean, quiet, and brightly lit, and since it only operated during the day shift, there was no one around after 4 PM. The room was a pleasant reprieve from the noisy production sections of the mill. The other end of the finishing room opened to a large storage area adjacent to the mill's railroad loading dock. We listened to Neil Armstrong describe his first steps onto the Moon just outside this room. Large rolls of paper wrapped in brown shipping paper with labels attached sat stacked end-on-end. Six-foot wide pathways made of heavy gauge, corrugated steel flooring, their surfaces polished bright from heavy use, intersected several large groupings of stacked rolls, three or four high. We spotted several orange, battery-powered forklifts on the far end of the room that were used to move the rolls around the room and place them in the railroad cars for shipment. Each was plugged into the wall and fully charged.

Terry was the first to unplug and drive a forklift around the room. Soon, each of us had taken one from its charging station. After figuring out the forklift's controls, we started to zoom around the steel pathways, sometimes coming close to a roll of paper, other times another crew member, close encounters that forced one driver to back up and get out of the way. We raced around the room, taking turns returning to the Beater Room to see if we were needed in the broke pit under No. 3 and 4. The forklifts had a low top speed, but we went round and round nonetheless, eventually following the same counter-clockwise route that prevented us from banging into each other. We tried to vary our routes, but we always encountered someone coming around the corner of a stack of rolls.

Terry was the predictably most reckless driver among the crew. The forklifts had a steel cage covering the seat to protect the driver from a falling roll of paper, but they did not have seat belts, so getting T-boned by another forklift could have sent one of us crashing to the floor. Forklift racing continued for 30-40 minutes. We called it quits only when we were near the end of our shift, returning the forklifts to their parking spaces and reconnecting the charging cables. Off we went, back to the Beater Room. Racing forklifts like amusement area bumper cars during a 3-11 PM shift in a largely deserted part of the Mill represented our most extreme testing of the Mill's elastic work culture.

We had a good time at work that night, so a few of us decided to meet up after our shift. We convened again at Eddie Madison's Garage, debating between going to Saratoga Springs or Lake George. In the 1960s, Saratoga Springs, unlike today, offered only a few good places for young people to hang out. There was Café Lena on Phila Street for folk music, or the Tin-and-Lint, a quintessential dive bar on Caroline Street where it is alleged that Don McLean penned the song "American Pie." (The singer has denied it) For a short period in the 1970s, the Tin-and-Lint became a site for illegal substance transactions that resulted in the arrest of a number of its patrons. There were a few other destinations in and around the city where young people might congregate, but Saratoga was a sleepy place compared to today.

Saratoga Springs was then in the initial stages of its renaissance, which began with the opening of the Saratoga Performing Arts Center (SPAC) in 1966. Intended originally as the summer home of the Philadelphia Orchestra and the New York City Ballet, SPAC gradually began to host non-classical performers. By the 1968 summer season, SPAC featured Judy Collins, Arlo Guthrie, Simon and Garfunkel, the Doors, and other groups popular with teenagers. The WHO and Janis Joplin would soon follow. However, the concerts did not immediately change the culture in Saratoga Springs. The city was dead most of the year except for when the Saratoga Race Course was running, which, during the 1960s, was for only four weeks in August. Saratoga seemed to be a place for older, well-to-do people in July and August, not a prime destination for teens and 20-somethings.

We decided instead to go to Lake George, which college-age kids ruled in the late 1960s. New York's 18-year drinking age contributed to the town's party atmosphere. Several bars were downtown on Canada Street, interspersed with souvenir shops and restaurants. Mother's and The Garrison were the most popular bars on the eastern end of Beach Road. Mothers often had live music and sold draft beer for 50 cents. Both bars exploded with college-age students in 1969 and could get quite rowdy. A popular hangout on Beach Road in the former Lake George train station, called The Station, also featured live music. A section of the bar that faced the Lake was open to the street, allowing the Station's atmosphere to flood onto the sidewalk. Other popular Lake George destinations for college-aged kids were Towers Hall at the Lake George Inn and the Airport Inn.

After we arrived in Lake George that night, we found a place to park near Ft. William Henry. We went to a popular pizza shop at the corner of Canada and Beach that remained open late into the night, ordering slices through its small window. We walked along Beach Road to find an empty bench. Lights along both shores of the Lake were visible in the distance as the three of us sat in the semi-darkness, eating pizza. Listening to the Lake's waves lap against the rocks in front of us, the heroic effort of Diane Struble, who successfully swam the entire 32-mile length of Lake George in 1958, came to mind. I was only seven then, but her feat was a big deal. Struble's 35-hour swim made the national news, landing her on the NBC Today Show a few days later. Sitting there that night in 1969, I tried to imagine what it was like for Diane Struble. 25-year-old single mother, to swim in the darkness like I saw before me, with the lights from cottages and boat docks reflecting off the Lake in the distance. When I was a kid,

Diane Struble was a heroic figure in an era when it was uncommon for a female athlete to garner national attention.

Whenever I am in Lake George today, I make a purposeful stop at the Adirondack Pub and Brewery on Route 9. Behind the bar is a remarkable black-and-white panoramic photograph of the Lake George Swim Club in the 1920s. Perhaps six feet long and two feet high, it depicts about 50 young people in their teens and twenties, each wearing fashionable yet modest swimming attire of the time. Assembled in two rows, most men wear tank tops while the women sit on the grass wearing one-piece suits that fully cover their hips. The young people in the photograph plied the waters of Lake George 100 years ago, yet the image has frozen their youth in time. Life's promise was still ahead of them: careers, marriage, and family. But so, too, was the Great Depression and World War II. All of them are gone now, but some of their descendants likely swim in Lake George today. I have often sat at that bar and looked into their faces, full of enthusiasm and possibility, wondering what their lives were like in the years after the photograph was taken. What became of them?

Our trip to Lake George the week following the Woodstock Festival occurred close to the day when the Beater Room Boys worked their final shift together. I don't recall that we made a big deal about it. I never saw Bruce or Pierre again. I ran into Paul and Terry only once or twice in Corinth, then just in passing. Only in my final summer at the Hudson River Mill several years later did I realize how much I valued being one of the Beater Rooms Boys. It was that summer I came of age as a young man.

My summer at the Mill had been eventful, but so had the world beyond Corinth. In just the three months between my 18th birthday in May 1969 and when I left work on my final day at the Hudson River Mill, the movie *Midnight Cowboy* had been released; John Lennon and Yoko One had conducted their famous "bed-in"; the 28th American airliner of 1969 had been hijacked to Cuba; the Stonewall Riots occurred in Greenwich Village; Mary Jo Kopechne was killed at a Martha's Vineyard bridge in a car driven by Sen. Edward Kennedy, an event that doomed his chances of ever becoming president; Neil Armstrong walked on the Moon; Charles Manson and his followers murdered seven people in California; the Woodstock Festival was held in upstate New York; Lieutenant Willam Calley was charged with murder for his role in the My Lai Massacre, and the withdrawal of United States troops from Vietnam had begun. The summer of 1969 proved to be memorable for many reasons.

39

HOMEWARD BOUND

I left Corinth in September 1969 and lived in the Midwest for nine years, attending college and finishing graduate school. I returned to Corinth each May during those years, with four additional summers between 1970 and 1976 spent working at the Hudson River Mill. I didn't work at the Mill during the summer of 1977 or elsewhere, but I began researching the 1921 Paper Strike in Corinth, which became the basis for my doctoral dissertation. My high school friends followed paths different from and farther away than my own, so I saw less of them as the years passed.

My primary friendships shifted to the Midwest in the 1970s. However, I never felt at home in the region's flat landscape nor embraced its conservative culture, which was heavily influenced by its agricultural history and economy. And the State of Indiana, in particular, was prone to periodic mass hysteria over sports, particularly basketball, that bordered on sheer lunacy. While Midwesterners were remarkably friendly, I couldn't wait to leave the region. I increasingly valued where I came from, vowing to return East after completing my graduate work. While in the Midwest, I was fortunate to have found academic mentors whose progressive spirits fostered my creative and intellectual growth and to whom I will always remain indebted.

I earned a Ph.D. in American history in 1978 and received my first undergraduate teaching position at a New Hampshire college that Fall. I taught undergraduate American history and American studies at several institutions over the next 40 years, retiring from full-time teaching in 2016. I did very little research and writing during my four-decade career because the institutions where I worked considered themselves "teaching colleges" where faculty were discouraged from doing much of anything else. I returned to Corinth frequently to visit my parents, but my life was firmly centered in New England from 1978 until 2002. The closure of the Hudson River Mill changed this.

I spent more time in Corinth after 1996 to help my widowed Mother. She could do much on her own, which included daily four-mile walks through the village streets, but I returned to town perhaps twice a month to take care of the yard and complete essential home maintenance. I was on sabbatical leave in the Fall of 2002 when IP announced that production would end at the Hudson River Mill on November 1 of that year. On one trip to Corinth, I contacted the Mill's manager, offering to advise him on cataloging and preserving the Mill's historic materials. This led to my effort to document the Mill while it was still operating and resulted in an invitation to be on hand to witness the production of the Mill's final roll of paper. I had no idea at the time I would remain directly and regularly engaged with my hometown and some of its citizens for the next twenty years.

The closure of the Hudson River Mill in 2002 incited a strong personal interest in its history. I knew something of the Mill during the IP era, especially surrounding the 1910 and 1921 Paper Strikes. Still, when I began to look for information about IP's predecessor, the Hudson River Pulp and Paper Company (HRPP), which operated at Palmer Falls from 1869 to 1898, I was struck by how little was known and written. After beginning my research, I quickly learned that HRPP was an innovative 19th-century company, and its Palmer Mill was widely considered the largest pulp and paper mill in the United States. Yet its history lay buried.

Like many small companies that pioneered the use of wood pulp in the manufacture of paper during the late 19th century and later became part of a large corporation like IP, the history of HRPP was ignored by the company that purchased it. Evidence of this fact appears in the front of IP's former administration building on Pine Street in Corinth – the Time Office – in the historical marker placed there many years ago by the Company to celebrate its 1898 founding. A more appropriate marker would acknowledge the beginnings of the Hudson River Pulp Company thirty years earlier, in 1869. That event was more historically significant.

International Paper's announcement in June 2002 that it would close the Hudson River Mill shocked Corinthians, but it did not come as a surprise. The storied Mill had been shedding jobs consistently since the mid-1960s as shifting paper markets, IP's changing business priorities, and the Mill's aging production technology left it increasingly unable to compete. With a peak payroll of over 1500 workers in the mid-1960s, mill employment shrunk to 1000 in 1970, 600 by 1998, and 500 in 2001, just before one of its two remaining paper machines was permanently shut down. There were just 290 workers left in 2002. None of the desperate efforts to keep the plant running had a chance of succeeding when the Mill's most modern paper machine, No. 11, was nearly fifty years old with a production capacity one-quarter of a modern Fourdrinier machine.

I was on hand for the No. 11 machine's final day. Peter Connery, the Mill Manager, tried to make the event festive by serving refreshments and inviting a retired machine tender, Arnold Dalaba, to handle No. 11's controls. Yet the effort seemed ineffective. The paper workers on hand to view the shutdown were visibly sullen. There were but a few smiles. Their jobs were gone, and so was the Mill they had long known. It was clear the closure of the Mill would mark the end of an era in Corinth, so I set aside the sabbatical leave project I had planned for that Fall to begin researching the Hudson River Mill's history instead.

The idea that the IP building on Pine Street might serve as a pulp and paper industry museum emerged soon after the Mill's closure. The concept eventually found expression in the organization of the Hudson River Mill Historical Society in 2004. Its founding members included several of Corinth's most prominent civic and business leaders. The painstaking process of securing the necessary State and Federal certifications and the difficulty in finding a local community member to manage the application process led me to organize the Hudson River Mill Project, a parallel organization. The Project was intended as a short-term effort whose mission was to collect, assemble, and disseminate the history of the Mill until the Society could be formally organized as a non-profit.

The Project sounded like a formal operation, which was the point, yet I managed it independently, often in partnership with the Town of Corinth. The Town served as the non-profit government body through which several grants were obtained. Project funding resulted in an exhibit at the Corinth Free Library and the creation of a Hudson River Mill Project website where all that was then known of the Hudson River Mill's history was posted. The Glens Falls *Post-Star* ran an article about the website on its front page in early 2005 that got the attention of someone at IP. A few months later, I was invited to a meeting with Company officials at the Virginia offices of the History Factory, which had published IP's *Centennial History* in 1998. Historical materials from the Hudson River Mill had been relocated and stored at their facility earlier that year.

The Virginia meeting included the International Paper Company Foundation Director and an IP attorney. I was asked about the Historical Society and the Hudson River Mill Project and my vision for a potential museum in Corinth, which the *Post-Star* article had mentioned. It became apparent during the meeting that IP officials wanted to know I was committed to the Project and the Museum idea and would remain personally involved in both going forward. The meeting concluded with the Foundation's Director promising $50,000 in funding towards a museum and the Company's lawyer suggesting the title for the IP building could be transferred to the Town of Corinth within 90 days, with the intention that it would be conveyed to the Historical Society once all of its approvals were in place. The IP officials at the Virginia meeting did not know that at the same time, another part of the Company was selling the 380-acre Hudson River Mill site, including the Building to be gifted.

In September 2005, IP announced that it had sold the Hudson River Mill to Philmet Capital, the real estate arm of New York City-based Phillips International. The sale, which included the IP Building on Pine Street, seemed to eliminate the structure as a site for a museum. The Hudson River Mill Historical Society dissolved soon after the sale. I continued work on the Hudson River Mill Project because I remained convinced that the Mill's history should be assembled and shared, if not in a museum, then in publications and online forums. If IP had separated the Pine Street building from the larger property, which it could have done, and transferred its title to the Town of Corinth in 2005 before it sold to Philmet, a museum might be open today. That was 19 years ago.

The period from 2004-2008, when the Hudson River Mill Project sought to gain traction toward realizing its mission, was an explosive period for Corinth. The June 2002 announcement of the Mill's imminent closure precipitated interest in community renewal that led to the adoption of a comprehensive plan by the Village Board. The Board contracted a regional planning firm to conduct a market study and create a strategic plan for community revitalization. However, the Trustees received immediate blowback, particularly from community members who opposed anticipated zoning regulations. There soon was a replay of the 1994 community debate over zoning, whose opposition had been led by a former Corinth Town official who lived outside the village yet believed zoning would impact his farm. A local business owner who had supported the Village's 1994 plan spoke at a public hearing, arguing that residents needed to start welcoming new people and new ideas into the community, suggesting that Corinth's provincial view of outsiders had to change. What became clear is that the closure of the Hudson River Mill in 2002 prompted a debate over Corinth's future that would likely not have occurred if the Mill had remained operational.

Indignation towards IP for shutting down the Hudson River Mill remained palpable in Corinth. Philmet's early attempts to develop the mill property exposed and deepened community divisions. Some Corinthians wanted jobs at any cost, others wanted to see industry without environmental impacts, and newcomers to town wanted no industry at all. Most citizens appeared to look to an industrial future for Corinth, while the consultants hired by the Village recommended an alternate direction. The Report of Village and Town of Corinth Joint Economic Development Committee issued in April 2003 contained a narrative that, in part, urged the community to embrace its strategic location in the southern Adirondacks along the Hudson River to exploit the growing interest in tourism and recreation.

The Report's ambitious development plan had barely been started when a fire leveled five downtown Corinth buildings in February 2008. An accidental cause for the blaze was quickly suspected, yet news reports suggested that properly outfitted sprinkler systems in the buildings could have saved the historic structures. Such reports fit into a pattern of news accounts that dated to the 1800s, whose content subtly implied Corinth was a backward community. Sprinklers or no sprinklers, the buildings on the block had burned at least five times previously. The largest among them, known as the Proller Building in 2008, had been the site of an earlier building owned by R.S. Mallery that burned for the first of three times in 1897. The restored structure, known as the McDonald Building, avoided a fire. Not long after it was sold to Harry Shorey, the McDonald building burned in 1922. Another fire hit the block in 1950, resulting in a complete loss for Proller's Clothing Store and Billings Five and Ten Cent Stores, causing smoke and water damage to the adjacent Meyer's Department Store. While the buildings damaged by earlier fires were either rebuilt or repaired, the downtown lots where five buildings were destroyed in 2008 remain vacant in 2024.

The urgency of community redevelopment loomed ever greater after the 2008 fire. By late 2008, it became clear that Philmet would not solve Corinth's need for economic redevelopment. The American economy had gone into recession, creating a tight credit market. Philmet complained that industrial wastes and toxic materials on the Mill property would require a $50 million clean-up effort. The numerous articles in the local press on Philmet's contentious relationship with Corinth Village and the vitriol, name-calling, and accusations that citizens leveled at public officials turned Corinth into a regional curiosity. Neighboring towns looked on and saw a community that appeared to have hit rock bottom. It was remarkable that Corinth's civic leaders and local citizens remained optimistic for the community's future after the setbacks between 2002 and 2008.

I came to believe the use of the IP Building at 17 Pine for a potential museum was lost under Philmet's ownership. I continued researching the

Hudson River Mill's history by collecting historical materials I found for sale online, in antique shops, and in the public domain. I began offering local lectures, making regional and national history conference presentations, and publishing articles on the new knowledge emerging from my research. Humanities NY provided a second grant to the Hudson River Mill Project in 2010 to support the publication of a new website, *The Corinth Social History Project,* based on the photographs of George Holland. Multiple attempts to contact Philmet in these years to secure historical materials I knew remained in the Mill proved fruitless.

Philmet's Corinth Mills Industrial Park project proved to be a colossal failure. The Hudson River Mill property came back under IP control in May 2009, but not until Philmet reportedly salvaged the Mill's most valuable metals, prompting a lawsuit by IP. Hopes were raised that the Mill property, now out of Philmet's control, might be redeveloped to provide jobs for the community when the Saratoga County Economic Development Corporation (SEDC) presented an ambitious three-part development strategy for the property in 2010. While this was good news for the community, one press account seemed doubtful, implying that the SEDC plan offered an overly optimistic vision of Corinth's future. The SEDC plan included a cryptic caveat when it suggested: "The town's fate rests with businesses themselves and whether or not they want to locate there." The subtext of this qualifying statement was all too obvious.

IPs' regained control of the Mill property resulted in two disparate results. The IP Building was back on the table for use as a Museum when the Company announced it would convey ownership of the structure to the Town of Corinth. The transfer, announced in a gifting ceremony held in the building in the Fall of 2011, was completed in 2012, Yet IP also announced the unthinkable: it planned to demolish the Hudson River Mill. By then, no one harbored any hope the mill would ever again manufacture paper, especially after IP welders used acetylene torches to burn holes through the dryer rolls on the No. 11 paper machine in 2005, rendering it unusable and unsaleable, save for salvage. Yet it seemed inconceivable to me, as it did to others, that the building of the Hudson River Mill would ever fall.

The Company, however, could not be deterred. I tried to use what connections I had to remove items from the mill that might be usable in a future museum, like the ornate 19th-century paper machine parts I had discovered in a storage area. The red brick building along the Hudson River that served as the Mill's Core Plant would have served as a beautiful performance venue for the Corinth Theatre Guild, yet the official I spoke with about preserving the structure for the community made it clear IP's demolition plans, intended to reduce the Company's tax burden, were irreversible. The Town of Corinth received permission to collect the Mill's extraordinary collection of engineering records just as contractors were removing its roof overhead.

NorthStar Demolition USA finished leveling the Hudson River Mill in 2012. Some 50 structures were torn down, including several 19th-century brick buildings like the Beater Room, where I had worked, several modern steel structures, and a 1,500,000-gallon oil tank. The demolition took much longer than planned after Northstar discovered the Mill to be full of toxic materials. The Company reported removing 400,000 square feet of asbestos roofing, transformers containing PCBs, and mercury waste. The Mill's buildings were eventually torn down and processed into 70,000 tons of concrete and brick to backfill the site. Over 16,000 tons of steel and 350 tons of non-ferrous materials were removed, processed, and recycled. Northstar finished their work by pouring a concrete pad eight football fields long over the site that had once been the Hudson River Mill. I recall with horror my first viewing of the leveled Mill in 2014. I don't think anyone who worked at the Hudson River Mill or grew up in Corinth while it was still operating could remain unemotional upon viewing the veritable sea of concrete where the Mill once proudly stood.

40

— · —

THIS TOWN

The prospect for a pulp and paper museum to be developed in the Pine Street building was rekindled when the Hudson River Mill came back under IP's control. Initial community interest in a museum had waned considerably by 2012 when IP turned the building over to the Town as ten years had elapsed since the Mill closure. The passage of time and the changes Corinth had undergone since the Mill's closure in 2002 had left much of the community in an inert state.

In 2016, the Corinth Town Board finally retained me to develop a museum in the building. I was under a part-time contract, yet I became fully engaged in the project, retiring from my full-time academic position several years earlier than I had planned. I was so committed that I left tens of thousands of dollars in salary and pension benefits on the table to assume responsibility for the project. Initial Museum development occurred between 2016 and 2018. New York State chartered the Hudson River Mill Museum, and it then received tax-exempt status from the Internal Revenue Service. Finally, the IP Building became the first and only building in the Town of Corinth to be listed on the National Register of Historic Places. With all necessary approvals, the Museum was prepared to move forward at the beginning of 2018, just as Corinth's Bicentennial celebration was planned.

I expected it would take up to ten years to complete the Museum due to the anticipated costs of the IP building restoration and its concurrent repurposing as a museum. Knowledgeable professionals indicated that building restoration projects in small Adirondack towns like Corinth typically occurs in stages due to funding challenges, lasting a decade or longer. A preservation architect estimated that the restoration of the IP Building alone might run between $750,000 and $1,000,000, including a new ground floor, ADA-compliant entrance. After reviewing the costs of museum development in a restored rail station in a Florida town about the size of Corinth, I calculated that museum exhibits, if built to contemporary standards in a building of the size of the IP building, would require an additional $750,000. Accounting for inflation over ten years, I calculated a total price tag of $2,000,000, the approximate cost of the new Corinth firehouse built in 2005.

I soon became reluctant to recite the estimated costs for the Museum while in Corinth. I heard nothing but disbelief the first time I did: "Are you crazy? Corinth does not have the money to do something like that!" And this was the reaction of a member of the Museum's Board who lived in town. They seemed to think the community would be asked to underwrite Museum costs. While the idea that Corinth would someday be home to a museum of the pulp and paper industry might have seemed implausible to some residents, the adverse reaction to its projected costs was understandable, given the town's deteriorating economic condition. The context for the responses I heard to the Museum's projected price tag was provided in an Albany *Times-Union* article published in 2018. The piece was ostensibly an acknowledgment of the Town's Bicentennial

Celebration. However, what should have been a "fluff piece" celebrating local history became an indictment of the community's shortcomings.

The article suggested that poverty in Corinth had been growing much higher than communities "similar in character and location." The *Times-Union* reported the percentage of Corinth students eligible for a free or reduced-price lunch – a key measure of poverty - had grown by 100% between 1996 and 2016, from 22.6% to 50.0%. The article also noted the Village of Corinth had fared worse economically than the outlying Town of Corinth. According to the *Times-Union*, the Village's median household income declined by 14% between 2010 and 2016, while the Town's median increased by 6%. Other data in the article suggested Town residents were doing better than Village residents. Between 2010 and 2016, the poverty rate for the Town declined by around 5%, from 16.2% to 11.5%, while the Village poverty rate increased, from 14.1% to 20.0%, a level the newspaper claimed was "significantly higher than other Saratoga County towns." That Corinth was home to two "dollar stores" and three convenience stores was seen as an anecdotal marker of the community's economic decline following the closure of the Hudson River Mill.

The *Times-Union* appeared to cite State and Federal data correctly. Yet, its implication the closure of the Hudson River Mill in 2002 was the single causal factor responsible for increased poverty in Corinth Village was overly simplistic. If IP's departure from Corinth in 2002 resulted in growing poverty in the Village, why had the economic status of Town residents improved? The fact the data suggested Town residents were economically better off than those residing in the Village required a more complex and nuanced explanation than the *Times-Union* writer could provide. Nonetheless, the article gave voice to what Corinth residents already knew: the local economy had gone from bad to worse since the Mill closed. How could the community imagine and support a $2 million museum?

Even before the Museum had its organizing permissions in place, I had begun to see indications that creating a museum in Corinth would pose a formidable challenge. The first insight came in 2017 when a citizen group sought to save the Main Street School from demolition. The School Board wanted to demolish the structure to increase parking for football games and offer other public amenities. When I came to Corinth to attend the initial School Board meeting that opened the topic for discussion, I observed two groups of people living in the same community – the School Board and the Save the School Committee - that possessed radically different visions of the public interest. School Board members appeared not to appreciate the historic preservation values offered by the Committee or understand the emotional pull of the Main Street School in a community that had lost so many historic structures. One member of the Board was quoted in meeting minutes posted online, equating historic preservation goals with "living in the past." The Board appeared that night determined to level the structure and repurpose the site to support athletic events held at the Main Street field. Discouraged by what I observed, I left the meeting convinced the building was doomed. What chance was there to gain support for preserving the IP Building in such an environment?

Corinth's 2018 Bicentennial Celebration further demonstrated that museum development would be challenging. The Hudson River Mill Museum was not invited to participate in Corinth's Bicentennial in any meaningful way, save for the offer to set up an information table in Pagenstecher Park. The Museum's exclusion from the Bicentennial was astonishing, given the pulp and paper industry's determinative role in Corinth's history and the amount of new historical information I had presented in public programs during the previous few years. While it was easy to interpret the Museum's snub as personal, I came to believe the exclusion of Hudson River Mill history from the Bicentennial – save for artifacts contained in an exhibit at the Corinth Free Library - was purposeful, in part because of the hard feelings towards IP that lingered in the community. Political and personal factors also played a role in determining that the Museum would not have a formal role in the celebration.

The Bicentennial Committee was nonetheless willing to use a symbol of the Hudson River Mill's history to raise money to pay for its celebration. Newly listed on the National Register of Historic Places and the last remaining symbol of Corinth's long paper-making history, the IP Building on Pine Street could easily have been included as a venue during the Bicentennial, as the site for a program or for small group tours of the structure. Ironically, the only formal role the building played in the celebration's scripted activities – as far as I know - was its appearance in a primitive-style painting, with print copies of the artwork sold to help pay for the Town's birthday party. It was astounding that Bicentennial planners would appropriate a romanticized image of the IP Building to help underwrite the cost of the Bicentennial yet ignore the building itself. This fact was particularly vexing given that IP reportedly donated $10,000 towards the celebration.

Further evidence that Museum development in Corinth would be problematic appeared in 2019. The idea that the non-profit Museum would lease the IP Building from the town had been the informal operational plan since 2012. Yet when the Town Board presented the Museum with a proposed lease in 2019, it contained several stipulations that would have crippled the non-profit. The most objectionable condition gave the Museum 90 days to vacate the structure should a new building owner refuse to honor the existing agreement. This stipulation implied the Town was prepared to sell the building instead of committing its use for historic purposes. The potential for eviction and the short five-year term of the lease had the Museum Board agreed to the Town's terms would have made it impossible for the organization to raise money to support its development.

The overall situation soon became more difficult. In July 2019, the Preservation League of New York awarded the Town of Corinth a grant, whose application I had written and submitted, that would have contributed $10,000 towards the cost of an IP Building condition study by a preservation architect, the necessary first step towards the building's restoration. Yet the Town of Corinth, which had a budget of several million dollars in 2019, defaulted on the Preservation League Grant when it failed to submit the required $4000 in matching funds. While shifting economic and political forces within the Town and on the Board had affected its willingness to spend more money on the Museum project, the Museum Board was powerless to avoid the outcome. It would be a full year before another grant application could be submitted.

The Town's proposed lease terms and the forfeiture of the Preservation League grant represented considerable impediments to the project. Yet the Museum had its own discouraging experiences. Growing evidence showed that public interest in the Museum project was tepid at best. Over 1000 members of the greater Corinth community showed enthusiasm for the Museum idea by following its Facebook page. Yet, analytics I collected showed that only 10-20% of the Facebook audience followed the links from the page to the Museum's website, where most of the substantive historical content was posted. Facebook posts received very little attention unless a photograph or an image was posted along with textual history.

Another disheartening development occurred in 2019 with the Museum's effort to sell commemorative bricks to raise needed operational funds. The effort was a monumental failure. People were invited to purchase a brick for $100 that featured the inscribed name of a former Hudson River Mill worker: a mother, a father, a grandfather, or anyone to be used in constructing a commemorative walkway. The set price was far less than recommended by the brick fabricator and dramatically less than the $500 donation requested by the Slate Valley Museum in Granville to purchase an inscribed "legacy tile." Tens of thousands had worked at the Hudson River Mill during its 133 years of operation, three to four generations in some families, so there had been great confidence the bricks project would succeed. But after six months, only 35 bricks had been purchased. The Museum was forced to cancel the fundraiser and refund all the money that had been donated. The bricks debacle represented a sobering insight into what the Museum was up against in the effort to raise funds from the Corinth community.

The IP Building lease issue, the Town Board's refusal to submit matching funds to the Preservation League, and the fiasco of the brick fundraiser combined to set the Museum project back three years. I continued my research and public presentations after 2019, and the Museum continued lease negotiations with the Town, an effort that brought lawyers for both sides into the mix. As the process continued, the IP Building continued to deteriorate. The brick-and-mortar interior of the ground level was deteriorating due to high moisture levels; there was evidence of roof leakage, and a crack had formed in a rear foundation wall. By late 2020, I had determined that by not heating the IP Building, restoring running water and sewage, or generally maintaining the structure, the Town of Corinth appeared not to comply with New York State's Consolidated Laws affecting the municipal-owned property.

I wrote a letter to the Corinth Town Board in January 2021 that described my concerns, urging it to sell the IP Building to the Museum instead of leasing it. I suggested it was the best way forward for the Town and the Museum. I identified the State laws I believed the Town should be concerned about, indicating that it had also painted itself into a corner by forfeiting the Preservation League grant in 2019, having rendered itself unlikely to receive future funding from the organization. My letter appeared persuasive. By March 2021, negotiations for the purchase of the IP Building had begun, yet the building sale took over a year to complete. The purchase was finalized in April 2022.

41

— · —

MAKE YOUR OWN KIND OF MUSIC

S hortly after the purchase of the IP Building was completed in April 2022, its Museum Board made development decisions that ended my involvement with the project. While the parting proved beneficial to me in ways unanticipated, which included the time necessary to write this memoir, my exclusion from the decision-making process was troubling and unforgivable. Several Board members who had been high school classmates and friends might have apprized me about what was happening and why, but they did not.

I was no longer on the Board and was not then under contract to the Museum, so in real terms, I had no say in the Board's plan to move forward. While the account of my experience arguably belongs in a memoir describing my "coming home" to Corinth after the Mill's closure, I have written about it elsewhere instead. It is not featured here because, in the end, I determined that including it could prejudice the ongoing efforts of the Museum and its Directors, impeding the restoration of the IP Building, which must be preserved at all costs.

***

If not for the five summers I worked at the Mill beginning in 1969, I would not have committed twenty years to studying the history of the Hudson River Mill and laying the groundwork for a museum in the IP Building. My work at the mill, which included at least ten different jobs, was memorable in so many ways. Yet all my Mill experiences often collapse into a single memory. It features my departure from the Mill in the morning following an 11 PM – 7 AM shift. After crossing the enclosed bridge that emptied into the mill yard near the clay shed, I walk up the hill towards the Time Office just after 6:30 AM, through the center of the mill yard, as scores of paper workers file past me to start their day. The yard's steep slope forces me to look up at them as they pass, an apt visual metaphor for the reverence I had come to feel for many of these men.

Wearing Dickie's work trousers, blue work shirts, or fresh white tee shirts, they seem happy, almost anxious to begin their day. They are proud. Some carry black metal lunch pails in one hand, and the *Post-Star* or the *Daily News* tucked neatly under their other arm. Others cradle a wicker lunch basket inside their elbow, flexing their forearm to keep it in place. Some hold a pipe in their other hand, drawing from it deliberately. The aroma of Aqua Velva and Sir Walter Raleigh merge into a palpable single fragrance as they brush by me. Some say "hello" or nod, even if they don't know me, to acknowledge their respect for a young man they think might be beginning the same work-life they started decades before.

Many of the men I saw on these mornings had worked shift work at the Mill for 30 or 40 years. They had made a life for themselves. Many never graduated from high school, yet they gave their families a good home and, some, the chance for their children to go to college. Most owned homes, maintained a garden, and fished or hunted with other paper workers on their days off. They rarely went on vacation. The rhythm of their lives was simple, predictable, and without great expectations. These men and the generations of paper workers who preceded them walked up and down the same hill for most of their adult lives, their labor making the Corinth community where I grew up. I did not understand that then, but I do now.

***

The closure of the Hudson River Mill in 2002 was inevitable. The plant had been in a death spiral since the early 1990s, if not earlier. People under 40 years old today who were born in Corinth and those who have moved into town since 2002 never knew the men ingrained in my memory. At best, they might vaguely remember a marginally operating Hudson River Mill that had been on life-support for a decade before its demise.

With each passing year, fewer and fewer people are left to remember the proud industrial community that Corinth once was. Even a written history cannot capture the memories that older Corinthians, now senior citizens, still hold of the Mill: the crisp thud of pulp wood falling from a conveyor onto the wood pile behind Palmer Avenue, adding to the mountain of spruce in the Mill's woodyard that stretched from Third to Fifth Street; the rotten-egg odor from the Mill's sulfite plant that once smothered the Palmer section of town like a smelly blanket; the human energy visible on Pine Street during the afternoon shift change as paper workers entered and exited the Time Office in two steady streams; the whine and clunking sound of a wood truck down-shifting near Pike's Garage so that it could pull its heavy load of spruce wood up Main Street.

Such were the sights and sounds experienced by the people who lived in Corinth when I grew up in the 1950s and 1960s and, in fact, for much of the 20th century. These visceral memories, tangible elements of daily life in a pulp and paper mill town, will be lost when the last person to remember them is gone. There is really nowhere current and future Corinthians can turn to learn about the Hudson River Mill. A narrative history of Corinth's paper industry has never been written, nor has an effort been made to document and preserve the memories of work at the Mill and life in Corinth that remain vivid in the minds of so many. The pulp and paper industry and IP made modern Corinth, saving it from becoming a ghost town when the local agricultural economy declined in the late 1800s. Yet, the Corinth community and its leadership have distanced themselves from this industrial past, seemingly reluctant to embrace the heritage their town's pulp and paper manufacturing history offers.

This memoir was written because I take pride in my working-class background, paper mill work experience, and former union membership. I retain many powerful memories of growing up in Corinth, although my hometown had its limitations. Many of us born and raised there needed more understanding, encouragement, and support than we received. Yet I am fortunate to have lived in Corinth during its "golden age. And I am proud to be among those who can say I once worked at the Hudson River Mill.

AFTERWORD

For more about the history of the Hudson River Mill in Corinth and the pulp and paper industry or information about the author, please go to **www.adirondackmilltown.com**

Made in United States
North Haven, CT
01 July 2024

54274125R10207